2d Edition

WORD/INFORMATION PROCESSING CONCEPTS

Mona J. Casady, Ph.D.

Professor,
Department of Office Administration
and Business Education
Southwest Missouri State University
Springfield, Missouri

Published by

W61   **SOUTH-WESTERN PUBLISHING CO.**

CINCINNATI   WEST CHICAGO, ILL.   DALLAS   PELHAM MANOR, N.Y.   PALO ALTO, CALIF.

PREFACE

What challenging career opportunities await the future office worker! Many office jobs require an understanding and application of word processing, a part of an information processing system. This book will teach you the basic concepts of a word/information processing system.

As you read office magazines, observe the rapidly changing technology of office machines and note office employment trends. Since the first word processor was introduced in 1964, there have been many technological advancements in the industry. With the development of dictation equipment and word processors, there have also evolved certain concepts, without which a machine is only a skeleton. These word processing concepts explain how specialized people, sophisticated machines, and efficient procedures are coordinated within the proper environment to make word processing work.

Most word processing articles or lecturers assume the reader or listener knows something about word processing. For such articles or speeches to make sense, you need a basic background in concepts and machine applications. This book provides that foundation. After studying this text, you will feel comfortable going into the working field of word processing or pursuing advanced studies in word processing management or information processing systems.

Since schools are incorporating word processing concepts into their curricula in various ways, this book is designed for flexibility. For example, the first three units provide a thorough introduction to word/information processing concepts: why word processing came about, how paperwork flows throughout the word processing cycle, and what basic parts form the word processing system. These three units could be covered within office procedures or secretarial practice, general business, office machines, or business communications classes. In addition, some of the projects at the end of each unit are appropriate for an advanced typewriting class. Units 4-8 offer a more complete and detailed study of word processing concepts:

Unit 4   Input methods, including dictation equipment
Unit 5   Output methods, including text-editing equipment
Unit 6   Applications which illustrate how word processing works
Unit 7   Procedures which control and enhance efficiency
Unit 8   Environmental factors which provide the proper setting

Unit 9 gives pertinent information and suggestions on selecting a word processing career. It lists appropriate questions to ask during a job interview and gives pointers on evaluating a word processing employer. Any course that includes a unit on career education could incorporate Unit 9 for both an enthusiastic and realistic approach to career opportunities in word processing.

Unit 10 explains what a total information processing system is and how various small systems can connect to provide efficient processing of information, whether it be in the form of data, text, voice, or image. This unit gives the main function and pieces of equipment of each subsystem, of which word processing is but one.

To review and reinforce the concepts covered in each unit, questions are given at the end of the unit. These review questions are in the form of fill-in-the-blank, short answer, multiple choice, and true or false. Included in the end-of-unit activities is a special project, which enables the student to apply some of the concepts emphasized in the unit. While the projects that involve typing could be performed on a word processor, all can be done on a standard typewriter.

A comprehensive teacher's manual is available and includes: a complete set of transparency masters, discussion questions, points to emphasize, supplementary lecture material for each unit, classroom activities to stimulate interest, and unit tests.

This introduction to word processing will be exciting and interesting to you. Word processing has captured the respect and admiration of office managers and employees everywhere; its impact will affect you directly should your career path include secretarial work or office administration.

CONTENTS

ACKNOWLEDGEMENTS

For permission to reproduce the photographs for the illustrations indicated, acknowledgement is made to the following:

1-5	Photo Courtesy of IBM
2-5	Hendrix Technologies, Inc.
2-6	Courtesy of Xerox
2-8	Courtesy of CPT Corporation
2-9	Western Union Corporation
2-10	EXXON Office Systems Company
2-11	Western Union Corporation
2-12	The "Data Defenders" by Permission of Ring King Visibles, Inc.
2-14	Norelco Dictation Systems (Philips Business Systems, Inc.)
3-1	All-Steel, Inc.
3-3	Photograph Courtesy of Hewlett-Packard Company
3-7	Photo Courtesy of Dictaphone Corporation
3-8	Lanier Business Products, Inc.
3-12	EXXON Office Systems Company
3-16	Courtesy of CPT Corporation
3-18	Courtesy of Steelcase, Inc.
4-4	Photo Courtesy of Dictaphone Corporation
4-6	Photos Courtesy of Dictaphone Corporation
4-7	Photo Courtesy of Dictaphone Corporation
4-8	Doro International
4-9	Photo Courtesy of Dictaphone Corporation
4-13	Courtesy of NEC Information Systems, Inc.
5-1	Royal Typewriter Co.
	Photo Courtesy of NBI, Inc.
5-2a	Photo Courtesy of 3M Company
5-2b	Photo Courtesy of 3M Company
5-4	Photo Courtesy of Wang Laboratories, Inc.
5-5a	Photo Courtesy of NBI, Inc.
5-7a	Photo Courtesy of 3M Company
5-8	Photo Courtesy of 3M Company
5-9	DSG, Inc.
	Courtesy of Xerox
	Courtesy of NEC Information Systems, Inc.
5-11	Photo Courtesy of IBM
7-13	Photo Courtesy of A. B. Dick Company
7-15	ITT Educational Services, Inc.
8-5	All-Steel, Inc.
8-6	Photo Courtesy of Haworth, Inc., Holland, Michigan
8-10	Gates Accoustinet, Inc.
9-2	Photo Courtesy of Haworth, Inc., Holland, Michigan
9-6	Photo Courtesy of Association of Information Systems Professionals
10-2a	Burroughs Corporation
10-2b	Courtesy of NCR Corporation
10-3	Courtesy of NCR Corporation
10-4	Courtesy of Xerox
10-6b	Minolta Corporation
10-7	Courtesy of Wright Line, Inc.
10-10	Photo Courtesy of Wang Laboratories, Inc.

The Origin of Word Processing

During the past twenty years office workers have been able to do a great deal more work without having to work any harder. This is because office workers have learned to use sophisticated office machines and better procedures to do their work. The system that has helped office personnel to work more efficiently is called word processing. It is the first automated office system that directly increased the productivity of secretaries. Word processing is still having a major impact on office productivity. However, today, word processing is becoming a part of a larger system called *information processing*.

What is word processing? How does it relate to the office of the future? to office automation? to information processing? Word processing means getting ideas into words, the words onto paper or another medium, and the words sent to the right person.

There was little change in the way words were processed during the fifty years preceding the late 1960s. Although electric typewriters, dictation equipment, and calculators had come into use, little else was done to automate office work. However, in the 1970s the office scene began to change. Management saw the need to increase the efficiency of the secretary's work with better equipment.

Automated equipment has brought changes in career opportunities, in the ways in which paperwork is handled, and in the work environment. It has also affected many careers that are related to office systems. Should you plan to become a secretary, an office manager, an executive, a sales representative, a teacher, a consultant, a marketing support representative, or any other office-related expert, you need to know the basic concepts of processing words.

METHODS OF PROCESSING WORDS

What's so different about word processing? Haven't we been writing, typing, storing, and sending information for many years? The tools and methods available today have changed. To better appreciate the efficiency of the new technology, let's review the various methods of processing words.

Manual Method

Writing in longhand or taking shorthand notes is a manual method of processing words. Only a pen or pencil is needed. No machine is used. But for people in a hurry, writing is too slow!

You can appreciate the problem as you experience the times in class when your teacher speaks faster than you can take notes. Your fingers move at a snail's pace. In their race to keep up with the thoughts being expressed, the eager fingers often make mistakes that have to be corrected. Soon your hand becomes tired. Although writing shorthand is faster than longhand, even that speed is slower than the rate of speech. And sometimes when you read your own shorthand it can be like trying to read a foreign language. Isn't there a better way?

Illus. 1-1 Longhand is too slow.

Illus. 1-2 Typewriters process words mechanically.

Mechanical Method

There *is* a better way: using a typewriter. With this tool a person can increase the speed of getting thoughts on paper, for one can type two or three times faster than one can write. In addition, the typed words are easier to read.

In Unit 5 you will learn how typewriters have changed from simple manuals to energy-saving electrics. These machines allow the typist to lift off errors and change the appearance of words by changing type styles and by switching from one type size to another.

The mechanical method of processing words has one main problem: it also is too slow. In 1920, office workers were typing 50 to 60 words a minute (wam) on manual typewriters. In 1980 office workers using electric typewriters were still typing only 50 to 60 wam. The increase in productivity was zero! During this time, however, the number of words that had to be processed and the cost of doing so had skyrocketed!

Automated Method

In addition to processing words manually and mechanically, an attempt was made to process them automatically. Why? Have you ever had to type the same letter over and over with the only change being the name and address of the receiver? If not, just imagine typing a 200-word letter twenty times. If only you could type the letter once and have the typewriter play back that letter nineteen times. After all, pianos had been made to automatically play back songs by the use of punched paper rolls.

It was this idea that led to the invention of the automatic typewriter in the 1930s. Typewriters, like pianos, could be programmed or given instructions to type copy automatically. These automated machines were called *automatic paper tape typewriters*. They were programmed by a paper tape similar to either a piano roll or a computer paper tape. Each hole or combination of holes stood for a letter, number, or symbol.

As the operator typed the original copy, it was automatically recorded both on a sheet of paper and on the punched paper tape. Once the original letter was typed and recorded, it could be played back automatically by rerunning the paper tape. When typing a letter, the secretary would type the date and letter address and then the rest of the letter would be typed automatically. The machine could be stopped at any time so that other variable information could be added. Examples of *variables* that change from one form letter to another are model numbers, prices, or dates. These typewriters had the advantages of low cost, fast playback (175 wam), and easy operation.

Words could be processed automatically! Yet this machine had little impact on office systems. Why? (1) When the writer wanted a sentence changed, there was no way to plug up some of the punched holes or to edit copy. Therefore, this machine was used mostly for repetitive form letters. (2) Because the paper tape frayed easily, a recording could be played back only a limited number of times. (3) A paper tape recording could not be erased so that a new recording could be placed on the same tape. For these reasons, the automatic paper tape typewriter had no major effect in changing office systems.

Illus. 1-3   Automatic Paper Tape Typewriter

Electronic Method—The Breakthrough

Surely an automatic typewriter could be designed that would play back repetitive documents and allow for changes to be made easily! And it was. In 1964, International Business Machines Corporation (IBM) introduced the Magnetic Tape Selectric Typewriter (MT/ST). It had features that could not be matched by the automatic paper tape typewriter.

The MT/ST not only produced documents faster than had been possible before, but it also allowed copy to be added and omitted. Instead of recording the document on a paper tape, the MT/ST used a new *medium*—magnetic tape. Unlike paper tape, a magnetic tape can be reused many times. When there is no longer a need to save the recording, it can be erased and new material recorded over it.

You might think of the MT/ST as an "automatic typewriter connected to a tape recorder." You are already familiar with recording your voice on a tape recorder, changing your mind, erasing part of the recording, and retaping. Recording keystrokes on magnetic tape is similar to recording voice on a tape recorder. Corrections are easily made by backspacing and striking over. This allows a new and correct recording to be put on the tape.

Here is how the MT/ST worked: As copy was typed, the strokes were not only printed on the paper but were also recorded on the magnetic tape. Whenever an error was made, the typist could backspace and strike over that position. The paper would show a strikeover, but the magnetic tape had been corrected in the same way you would correct a recording on a tape recorder. A new recording on top of an error would erase the error from the tape and replace it with the correct stroke.

Once a document had been recorded on tape, corrections and revisions could be made without retyping the entire document. Copy

Illus. 1-4   Text editors produce words electronically.

Illus. 1-5 These features of the MT/ST typewriter gave birth to word processing concepts: corrects by backspacing, stores characters on magnetic tape, and automatically plays back typed characters.

could be played back on the MT/ST at 150 wam—nearly three times the average typing speed. During *playback* the machine could be directed to stop so that names, addresses, or prices could be easily added.

The MT/ST and other early models of word processing equipment were called *text-editing typewriters* or magnetic/electronic typewriters. Now they are commonly called **text editors** or **word processors**. Both of these terms will be used in this book.

Since 1964 the world outside the office has been exploding with electronic technologies. In our homes we have electronic games and electronic calculators. With the touch of a few buttons we can deposit and withdraw money from the bank. Television sets and microwave ovens operate electronically. The mystery of electronics is disappearing as people become more comfortable with machines.

As you might think, the electronic method of processing words has become much more sophisticated over the past twenty years. Unlike electric typewriters and automatic paper tape typewriters, electronic machines have very few mechanical (moving) parts to wear out. Instead,

they have tiny electronic circuit panels (or chips) that are less noisy and give more reliable power. Today's word processors are much faster than the earlier models, have a great deal more storage, and enable the operator to change copy much more easily. Some word processors are able to send and receive messages from similar machines and from computers. Some are able to do math functions. Word processors are the link that will tie many office operations together within the next few years as word processing systems mature.

OFFICE PRACTICES THAT JUSTIFY A NEW SYSTEM

Why have businesses been willing to invest thousands of dollars in word processing equipment? Why have managers been willing to reorganize the structure of their offices? In studying office systems in the 1960s, the experts discovered many problems. Not only were these problems very real at that time, but many of them still exist in offices today. Let's look at the office practices and problems that call for a new system.

Illus. 1-6   The traditional methods of processing words cannot keep up with a constantly growing amount of paperwork.

Growth in the Volume of Paperwork

At least half of the employees in the work force are white-collar workers; you are likely to be one of them. Every *white-collar worker* handles information, most of which is typed or printed on paper. One consultant reports that the average office produces 32 pages of computer printout; prints 4 pages of catalogs, reports, and letters; makes 18 photocopies; files 10 pieces of paper; and buys 46 fresh pieces of white paper for each employee every day![1] The number of documents handled by the average office worker is increasing at the rate of 4,000 a year.[2] Why is business experiencing such a large increase in the amount of its paperwork? There are several reasons.

This is an age of information. More information is available today than ever before. The amount of information available to today's profes-sionals and executives doubles every decade.[3] The Commerce Department estimates that about 60 percent of the Gross National Product is involved with the production, storage, transfer, and use of information.[4] Managers must learn to organize and use information wisely if they are to make new products, meet customer demands, be competitive in the market, and earn a fair profit.

As businesses develop, population increases, and government expands, paperwork is created. Even with today's advanced technologies, paper is the major means for handling information. Each day billions of pieces of information must be processed, changed, recorded, stored, and moved by office personnel. As the amount of paperwork grows, the traditional methods of handling written communications collapse under the strain.

---

[1]Paul Gillin, "Office Automation: More Explosion Than Expansion," *Viewpoints in Business Education* (September, 1982), p. 1.

[2]J. Raymond Sutcliffe, "A Major Opportunity for Office Cost Reduction," *The Office* (April, 1981), p. 79.

[3]Bill Lampen, "Network Applications To Improve Productivity Using a Broadband Local Area Network" (Talk delivered to second annual meeting of Office Systems Research Association, Philadelphia, Pa., February 19, 1983).

[4]*The Directory of Information/Word Processing Equipment and Services* (New York: Information Clearing House, Inc., 1982-83), p. 3.

Revisions (or changes) in documents also cause paperwork to increase. Changes often mean that entire documents must be retyped. A one-page letter that might cost $6 to $7 to send may go out the door costing $12 to $15 because of revision costs. For a 20-page report the cost difference is even greater. Of all business documents, only a few are sent in their original form.

In addition, many written communications are routine (or repetitive) in nature. For example, each time a new customer opens an account at a bank, the bank sends a routine letter of welcome and information about its services. The content of each letter is much the same. Should your class visit an insurance company, the person conducting the tour may wish to send each of you a letter inviting you to take out a life insurance policy. This would be a *repetitive letter*, for each person would receive the same letter. Only the names and addresses would change.

Increasing Costs

A second major problem affecting business today is the rising cost of operating the office. This cost is increasing faster than any other part of business operations. Some studies show that office costs increase 12 to 15 percent a year and that they will double within the next six years.[5] When office costs amounted to 20 to 30 percent of a company's costs, they were not considered too important. But today, office costs represent over half of a company's operating costs (up 100 percent since 1955).[6]

Several factors, including increased building and rental costs and rising inflation, cause these higher costs. But the largest single factor is labor (workers). Labor costs represent 75 to 90 percent of office costs.[7] The Labor Department predicts that by 1990 the work force will consist of approximately 128 million people. Of these, approximately 56 million will be working in the office, a 23 percent increase since 1980.[8]

However, only one third of the labor costs can be charged to *clerical workers*—secretaries, typists, and so forth. The major part of these costs is for the managers, executives, and other professional people.

The rising cost of labor is reflected in the increasing cost of sending a business letter. To find the cost of the average business letter, Dartnell Corporation uses these factors: dictator's time, secretarial time, nonproductive labor, (waiting, illness, vacations, etc.), fixed or overhead charges (depreciation, taxes, interest, cost per square foot, maintenance, light, and heat), materials cost (letterheads, envelopes, copy machine sheets, typewriter ribbons), and mailing costs. The annual study conducted by the Dartnell Corporation showed that in 1983 the cost of an average business letter was $7.60.[9] Other word processing experts claim that the cost of a 250-word document varies from $6 to $12 or more.

Illus. 1-7   The cost of a business letter keeps going up.

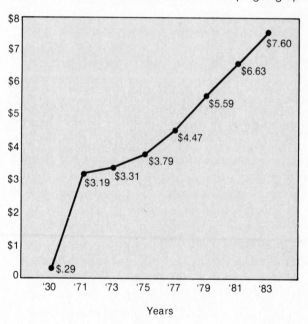

A company cannot control some costs (such as postage). But the cost of performing some steps can be controlled. Four such steps are:

1 How the words originate (longhand, shorthand dictation, or machine dictation)

[5] John J. Connell, "Office of the 80s," *Business Week* (February 16, 1980), p. 19.

[6] *The Directory of Information/Word Processing Equipment and Services*, p. 2.

[7] Connell, *Business Week*, p. 19; Sutcliffe, *The Office*, p. 79.

[8] U.S. Department of Labor, Bureau of Labor Statistics, *Occupational Outlook Handbook*, Bulletin 2200 (April, 1982), pp. 14, 17-18.

[9] Dartnell Corporation, Institute of Business Research, *Cost of a Business Letter* Study, 1983.

2 How the words are transcribed (mechanical or electronic equipment)

3 How secretarial services are organized (typing as one of many secretarial tasks or as a specialized task)

4 How documents are formatted (amount of keystroking and decision making involved)

Labor represents the largest cost factor of a document. The more a document has to be revised, the higher its cost. Word processing consultants report that documents requiring a lot of revision can run as high as $16 a page.

Poor Productivity

Because both the work load and the cost of our work force are constantly increasing, offices are being forced to emphasize productivity. Industry has been able to do this by automating many of its procedures and operations. Can office managers learn from industry's accomplishments? In looking at traditional offices, some interesting comparisons with manufacturing plants can be made.

White-collar workers have not increased productivity at nearly the rate of *blue-collar workers*. One study of a ten-year period showed the increase in office productivity to be only 4 percent while manufacturing productivity increased 84 percent.[10] This finding has been questioned by those who believe that the amount of work produced by a white-collar worker is more difficult to measure than that of a blue-collar worker. Yet, with white-collar workers making up more than half the United States labor force, the problem cannot be ignored.

Another comparison shows that the average factory worker is supported by $25,000 to $50,000 of equipment to automate the job, a farmer by $70,000, and an office worker by only $2,000 to $3,000.[11] But lack of automation is not the only reason for low productivity in the office. Industrial work lends itself to assembly line work in which there is often one task for each person. Office work has many similar tasks that are handled by many people.

At one time managers believed that they could not justify spending much money on the office, since the office was not directly involved in profit making. However, this idea is changing because the number of people working in the office has greatly increased, labor costs are rising, and the office is the least productive part of business operations.

Unproductive Management Time

The productivity of clerical workers is the easiest to study because their tasks can be measured. It is much more difficult to define and measure the productivity of managers. How do you assign a dollar value to creative and intangible activities? Is attending a convention productive? Is accepting speaking engagements productive? By what standards? There are no standards, and management tends to resist the idea of measurement.

Illus. 1-8   Is this manager making good use of her time?

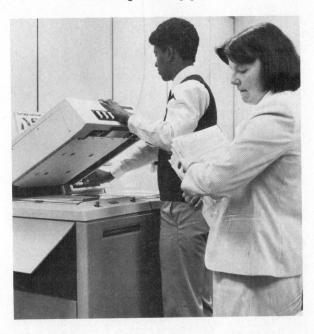

However, a study of over 300 professionals showed that managers and other professionals are spending anywhere from 15 percent to more than 40 percent of their time on unproductive activities.[12] Valuable time is being spent on

[10]Jeffrey E. Long, "Productivity," *Management World* (January, 1981), p. 9.

[11]Sutcliffe, *The Office*, p. 79.

[12]"Time Equals Dollars," *Administrative Management* (August, 1980), p. 11.

routine tasks that can be given to clerical people. If duties such as filing, searching for information, making copies, and arranging meetings are delegated, managers have more time to plan and perform the tasks for which they were hired. A manager earning an annual salary of $36,000 is being paid about $18 an hour for labor. It is easy to see how the misuse of time can be costly.

Approximately one half to two thirds of the total labor costs in the office are associated with managers and professionals rather than with clerical workers. If significant results are to be attained in lowering costs and increasing productivity in the office, new tools and methods must be developed to measure management productivity.

The high cost of management justifies automation. In the past, management saw office automation as just a secretarial tool for producing documents faster. But office automation is also important as a management tool. Providing complete, quick, and accurate facts to management is an effective way of improving productivity.

Lack of Professional Supervision and Uneven Work Loads

In the traditional office most workers are supervised by the executive(s) for whom they work. In a large office one secretary may supervise several others in the department. In either case, the executive or senior secretary may not know how to supervise others well.

Also, it is unlikely that standard procedures have been adopted regarding the format of documents and handling priorities. More than likely, each executive has a personal preference for letter style, and two individuals may not agree on what task is most urgent.

Often production records are not kept on the work done by the secretaries. One secretary may be overworked while another has very little to do. Most offices have very busy periods (peak periods) as well as slack times throughout the year, which can be costly and can lower worker morale. During slack periods, both the employees and the company suffer. The employees become bored and believe that they are not needed because there is too little to do. The company suffers because costs are the same but

productivity has gone down. During peak periods there is the extra expense of paying overtime salaries or of hiring temporary help. During peak periods the high producer may become resentful of workers who do very little yet are paid the same. *Professional supervision* can spread the work loads evenly among the workers to bring about a more productive work force.

Inconsistent Career Paths and Misuse of Ability

A secretary in the traditional office performs all the secretarial work for one or more persons, such as typing, transcribing, filing, handling the mail, answering the telephone, and related duties. However, very few people are experts in every phase of secretarial work.

The secretary who enjoys typing may not have good filing skills nor be able to supervise others. Another secretary may have excellent skills that are not being put to use. This person is likely to become discouraged after the newness of the job wears off. Frustration will be reduced if the executive or supervisor knows the person's potential and provides a challenge and incentive for advancement. However, even when ability is known, the executive often will not recommend a promotion for the secretary.

Illus. 1-9 Uneven workloads cause frustration.

Illus. 1-10   Frustrations of the Traditional Secretary

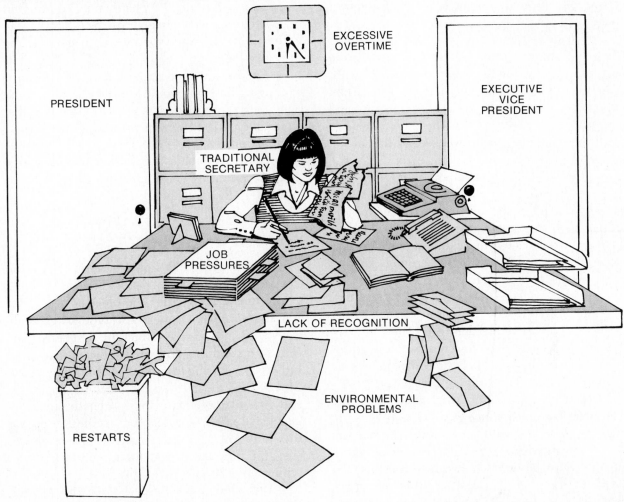

In the traditional office the secretary's **career path** (steps to a better paying job) is often determined by the executive's advancement. When the executive advances to a higher management position, the secretary is promoted as well. It is common to see a secretary to a vice-president enjoying higher status and pay than a secretary to a departmental manager, even though the lower level secretary may be better qualified and may produce more work.

When there is no relationship between secretarial qualifications and career paths, job dissatisfaction and low morale usually increase. The secretary may resign, and the company's *turnover* costs go up. Each year the average turnover rate for secretaries is about 30 percent. At this rate, hiring and training costs increase to between $1,500 and $2,200 a position.[13] Turnover

costs include advertising the position, interviewing and hiring the employee, training, and accepting a lower production rate while the new employee is learning the job.

Low Typing Production Rate of the Traditional Secretary

Imagine yourself as a secretary who does all the secretarial work for one or more executives. You answer the phone, type, run errands, keep the files in order, screen callers, process the mail, and carry out various other duties. If someone were to keep a record of the amount of time you spend actually typing, it would be only about 20 percent of your working hours.[14] During this period of time you produce many letters, memos,

[13]Leslie Petrovich, "The Million Dollar Answer in Word Processing," *The Office* (November, 1978), p. 70.

[14]Paul Truax and Jean Strong, "Think Before You Leap into Word Processing," *The Office* (November 1976), p. 75.

and statistical reports. If you are like the average typist, you can expect to make two errors on each page of typing.

A close-up of your transcribing a letter would go something like this: You are eager to get the last letter transcribed in time for the 3 PM mail. You quickly assemble the letterhead, carbon paper, and copy sheets. With a flick of your hand you put the carbon pack in the typewriter and type the current date. In the second line of the letter address you make a typing error. Since the correction will leave an obvious blemish, you remove the paper, insert a new carbon set, and start over. This time you get through the middle of the first paragraph and the phone rings. After taking the message, you take a moment to find your position and continue transcribing. Then in the next sentence you make another error, correct it, and continue **keyboarding** (typing). Just then the new secretary across the hall comes to your desk with a question. After this interruption you must again find your position. You go on. Along comes the word *occasion*, which you can never remember how to spell; does it have two *c*'s or two *s*'s? You better stop and check the dictionary for its spelling. Now you are close to the bottom of the page. You slow up a bit, for you know how difficult it is to correct an error where chances of realigning type properly are slim. You quickly proofread the letter and then remove it from the typewriter. You take it to the executive to sign. The executive scans the letter before signing it and spots a typing error in the second paragraph. In addition, the executive decides to change the wording of a sentence in the third paragraph. There is only one thing to do: retype the letter! And once again you can expect to have more interruptions. Even if the executive had made no changes and you could have corrected the error, chances are the correction would have downgraded the appearance of the letter.

How did you feel about the experience? In reviewing the entire process, what slowed your production? There were errors to be corrected; restarts; fear of making a mistake at the bottom of the page; interruptions caused by the telephone, the office visitor, and checking the dictionary; and the executive's revision. In addition, the pressure of trying to meet the 3 PM mail deadline probably caused increased anxiety and errors. These factors, in turn, affected the appearance of your letter and the time it took to produce it. Was the experience satisfying? Probably not. You wanted to produce an attractive, error free letter at an efficient rate, but you were frustrated by uncontrollable obstacles.

As though that experience was not discouraging enough, would you like to know what your actual production rate was? Assuming that you can type 70 to 80 wam on straight copy work, your *net production rate* in this situation was only about 5 wam. Such astonishing differences have been reported by consultants who have studied over 200 offices in the United States.

The Need for a System to Process Words

By the early 1960s offices were not able to keep up with the flood of paperwork and the costs of producing it. Neither the electric typewriter nor the automatic paper tape typewriter could meet the increased production demands. The MT/ST text-editing typewriter offered a solution, but it was suffering from a major stumbling block: Most offices did not see the machine's potential and would not lease or purchase such an expensive piece of equipment (selling price was $10,000). Many businesses could not defend its cost, for they knew that their secretaries were typing only 20 percent of the day.

When companies did acquire the MT/ST, they often placed it in the office of the senior secretary as a token of prestige. In many cases this was the office that did the least amount of typing. Some secretaries guarded the machine's use and made little effort to teach others to operate it. In turn, the machine was not used to its capacity and the expense of the investment could not be justified.

A WORD PROCESSING SYSTEM IS BORN

As a result of the problems offices were having and the lack of acceptance of the MT/ST, concerned office managers, efficiency consultants, and equipment manufacturers took an in-depth view of office practices to see what could be done.

It soon became clear that to successfully market text-editing typewriters, a new *system*

Illus. 1-11   Reorganization of Secretarial Duties

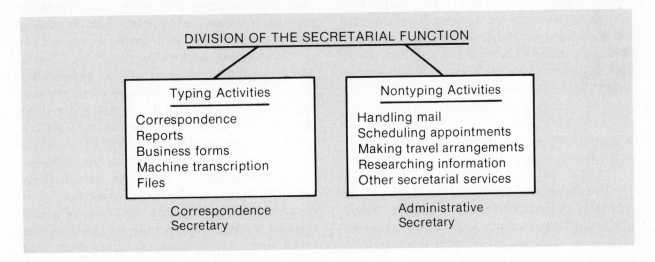

DIVISION OF THE SECRETARIAL FUNCTION

Typing Activities

Correspondence
Reports
Business forms
Machine transcription
Files

Correspondence
Secretary

Nontyping Activities

Handling mail
Scheduling appointments
Making travel arrangements
Researching information
Other secretarial services

Administrative
Secretary

would also have to be sold. The organization of secretarial services would have to be changed so that this powerful text-editing typewriter could be used as much as possible.

Office managers were encouraged to divide all secretarial duties into two areas—typing and nontyping. Using the text-editing typewriter, the typing specialist would do the typing, transcribing, revising, and proofreading tasks for two or more people. This secretary was given the title of *correspondence secretary*. Nontyping tasks, such as handling the mail, filing, telephoning, arranging appointments, and serving as a receptionist, would be done by the *administrative secretary* (or administrative support secretary). By 1969 this marketing idea began to gain acceptance. Office managers could better understand how the machine could increase production enough to justify its cost.

The pioneers who supported this new way of organizing secretarial services took even more steps. They promoted more efficient ways to manage an entire office system so that both the advanced equipment and the specialized people were well coordinated. Each of these correspondence and administrative secretaries, or specialists, worked with others as a team to serve several executives. Advancement was determined by a person's skill and ability rather than by the executive's promotional pattern. Each team of secretaries was supervised by a qualified supervisor. This system became known as a word processing system.

Word Processing Matures

The emphasis in the 1970s was to increase the productivity of secretaries. The 1980s will see the work of managers and executives become more automated. Efforts are being made to help them become more productive. New machines with even greater capabilities than those presently used are being developed. Various types of machines along with more efficient procedures make up systems that will automate the processing of information in the office.

Information can be in the form of text (words), data (numbers), voice (sound), and/or images (pictures). A total information processing system is built by linking subsystems (small systems), each of which has a certain purpose. For example, word processing is the system that prepares *text*, such as letters and reports. *Data processing* is the system that works with numbers for such tasks as accounting and payroll. There are also systems that reduce documents to microfilm, make copies of documents, send information, and prepare information to be printed in brochures and books.

Information systems will be used by both secretaries and managers. As a result, businesses will be able to communicate much faster. But it will take time to link the various subsystems to form a complete information processing system. During this period of development, the term *word/information processing* is often used to describe the system that processes text.

As a result of advancements in office machines and systems, many challenging and exciting career doors are opening. How can you find your place and reach your greatest potential within this office structure? You will find out in Unit 9, where you will learn about career opportunities in word processing.

Questions About Modern Word/Information Processing

You have seen how the development of machines and systems led to modern word processing. The idea was born and it began to catch on. As we come to the end of this unit, let's pause to answer some questions that are often asked.

Are handwriting and typewriting considered word processing? They are methods of processing words; however, until 1964 (the invention of the MT/ST) the term "word processing" was not used in conjunction with these functions. The term "word processing" implies the use of a text editor.

Is word processing the same as data processing? No. Word processing specializes in handling text, as in letters and reports; data processing deals with numbers, as in inventory control.

Is word processing a machine? No. That is like saying traffic management is an automobile, or data processing is a computer. Word processing is a system of which a text editor is a part. However, the word processing system began as a result of a new machine—the MT/ST.

Is word processing equipment fully automatic? No. That is like saying a car can drive itself. As you will learn in the next unit, the word processing system directs the flow of paper through a cycle. A machine by itself cannot create, type, and revise words. The system must work through PMPE—its main parts. You will find out what PMPE means in Unit 3.

Throughout this book you will see how word processing concepts grew and took on new dimensions until word/information processing has become one of the most exciting areas in office administration. Word processing is one of the key systems that helps process information.

Review Exercises

Completion

Complete the following sentences by filling in the blanks.

1   Writing or printing by hand is a ___manual___ method of processing words.

2   The first automated typewriter recorded the typed copy on ___paper___ tape.

3   The invention of the ___MT/ST___ by IBM in 1964 marked the beginning of modern word processing.

4   ___Magnetic___ tape can be corrected by putting a new recording on top of another.

5   Word processing is a/an ___system___ rather than just a machine.

6   Of all white-collar workers, the ___managers, executives, professional___ group accounts for the largest part of labor costs.

7   The person who performs the typing duties within a word processing system is called a/an ___correspondence secretary___.

8   The person who performs the nontyping functions within a word processing system is called a/an ___administrative secretary,___

9   The largest part of office costs is for ___labor___.

10 While data processing handles mostly numbers, word processing handles mostly ___text___.

Short Answers

Indicate your answers by filling in the blanks.

1   Why did the automatic paper tape typewriters never catch on and become important in the development of modern word processing systems?

___Corrections + revisions were difficult to make on paper tape.___

13

They frayed easily.

2   Name the four main methods of processing words (from the
    earliest to the most recent):

    a manual   c automated

    b mechanical   d electronic

3   Describe five office practices that point to the need for a modern
    word processing system:

    ① Increase in paperwork.
    ② Rising cost of producing letters.
    ③ Uneven work load.
    ④ Misuse of secretarial skill.
    ⑤ Interruptions during transcription.

④   To successfully market text editors, it was discovered that the
    traditional office system would have to change. Explain three
    features of the new word processing system that came about:

    ① Two separate parts of secretarial jobs,
        typing, + non typing.
    ② Advancement would be determined by individual
        skill + ability.
    ③ Each secretary would serve 2 or more executives.

5   Various office-related positions need an understanding of basic
    word processing concepts. Name three of them:

    a correspondence secretary

    b supervisor.

    c executive

Name **Kathy Lawrence** Date_____ Section_____

Multiple Choice

Select the letter that best completes the sentence, placing it in the space provided in the right column.

1   Using a typewriter to prepare a report is an example of which word processing method? (A) automated, (B) manual, (C) mechanical, (D) electronic, (E) none of these.

_C_

2   An electronic method of processing words is (A) taking shorthand notes, (B) using an electric typewriter, (C) using an automatic paper tape typewriter, (D) using a text editor, (E) both B and C.

_D_

3   Which of the following features describes the MT/ST: (A) corrects errors by backspacing and striking over, (B) records on paper tape, (C) manufactured in 1946, (D) plays back recorded material at 90 wam, (E) both A and B.

_A_

4   The traditional secretary (A) is a specialist, (B) is professionally supervised, (C) is promoted independent of the executive, (D) performs both typing and nontyping functions, (E) is all of these.

X~~E~~ (D)

5   Two new titles created by word processing are (A) computer operator and computer programmer, (B) executive assistant and communications consultant, (C) correspondence secretary and administrative secretary, (D) executive secretary and office supervisor, (E) none of these.

_C_

6   Word processing came about because there was a need to process written communications with (A) greater speed, (B) better accuracy, (C) lower cost, (D) more effort, (E) A, B, and C.

_E_

7   In breaking down the cost of a letter, the largest factor is (A) postage, (B) salaries of the word originator and transcriber, (C) paper and typewriter ribbons, (D) filing, (E) equipment.

_B_

8   The cost of replacing a secretarial employee includes (A) advertising the position, (B) interviewing and hiring, (C) training the new employee, (D) allowance for reduced rate of production, (E) all of these.

_E_

9   While typing a report, the traditional secretary can expect (A) few interruptions, (B) no changes that require retyping the page, (C) no errors to be corrected, (D) another secretary to type some of the pages, (E) none of these.

_E_

10 Successful marketing of the MT/ST required (A) selling a better office system, (B) reorganizing secretarial services, (C) getting approval from traditional secretaries, (D) both A and B, (E) both B and C.

_D_

True or False

*Indicate your answer by placing a **T** or **F** in the right-hand column blanks.*

1   Preparing 15 letters each with the same body but with different names and addresses is faster on an electric typewriter than on a word processor.   *False*

2   Word processing first became automated with the invention of the paper tape typewriter in the 1930s.   *True*

3   Corrections can be made easily on documents recorded on paper tape typewriters.   *False*

4   Office costs have increased to about 50 percent of a company's costs.   *True*

5   The traditional secretary spends about 20 percent of the working day typing.   *True*

6   Most secretarial employees are experts in all phases of office work.   *False*

7   Studies have shown that secretaries who can type 70 to 80 words a minute on straight copy work have a net production rate of about 60 wam.   *False*

8   Traditional secretaries are usually not supervised by a professional who knows how to coordinate people and machines well.   *True*

9   Management personnel are productive enough; therefore, word processing hardly affects their performance.   *False*

10 Word processing and data processing are subsystems of a total information processing system.   *True*

Instructions for Job 1a

MATERIALS NEEDED
8½" x 11" plain paper
Typewriting eraser
Clock with 60-second sweep hand or stopwatch
Dictionary
Telephone book

Assume you are secretary to Mr. Gary Randolph, project consultant with Hawthorne Traffic Control Systems. After dictating the letter you are about to type (Job 1a) he was called away from the office. Type the letter on page 18 that follows these instructions.

As you are transcribing, certain situations occur. These situations are explained in italics at the point at which they happen. Follow these instructions as you come to them; do not read ahead. Take the necessary time to handle these interruptions, and continue to type the letter.

Name_____ Date_____Section_____

Mr. Randolph prefers the block letter style with open punctuation. (See the model below.) Set 1½-inch margins and begin the current date on Line 16. Correct any mistakes you make with a typewriting eraser. Continue to work on the letter until it is mailable—even if you have to start over again.

Using a stopwatch or a clock with a 60-second sweep hand, record the exact time you begin and finish this letter. Figure the time it took you to type the letter—including the interruptions and restart(s). Do not look ahead at Job 1b until you have recorded the start and stop times.

STARTING TIME: min.   sec.

STOPPING TIME: min.   sec.   TOTAL TIME: min.   sec.

Illus. 1-12   Model: Block Letter Style with Open Punctuation

```
┌──────────────────────────────────────────────────────────────┐
│                                                              │
│     ┌─────┐                                                  │
│     │SCCC │  St. Clair Community College                     │
│     └─────┘  Business and Office Administration Department    │
│     200 Bedford Lane  ■  Montgomery, AL 36109-2401  ■  (205) 793-2212 │
│                                                              │
│                                                              │
│  LINE 16 September 18, 19--                                  │
│           │                                                  │
│           │ 4                                                │
│           ↓                                                  │
│         Mr. George Adams                                     │
│         Administrative Services Manager                      │
│         Rehmer Laboratories, Incorporated                    │
│         2844 Woodland Street                                 │
│         Montgomery, AL  35202-2110                           │
│         DS                                                   │
│         Dear Mr. Adams                                       │
│         DS                                                   │
│         Because of your experience and demonstrated competency in the │
│         field of business, we extend an invitation for you to serve │
│         on our Business Advisory Committee.                  │
│         DS                                                   │
│         We believe that advisory committee members can help us to be │
│         aware of the local community needs in the area of secretarial │
│         training and office management.  The meeting of the committee │
│         will deal with curriculum content, equipment, facilities, and │
│         placement of graduates.  Carl Brown, program coordinator, will │
│         conduct most of the discussion.                      │
│                                                              │
│         Will you accept and plan to attend our first meeting?  We will │
│         meet on Tuesday, October 21, from 7:30 to 9:30 p.m. in Main │
│         Hall, Room 30, at St. Clair Community College.  A reply card │
│         is attached for your answer.                         │
│         DS                                                   │
│         Sincerely                                            │
│           │                                                  │
│           │ 4                                                │
│           ↓                                                  │
│         Miss Irene Francka, Chairperson                      │
│         Business and Office Administration Department         │
│         DS                                                   │
│         ds                                                   │
│         DS                                                   │
│         Enclosure                                            │
│                                                              │
│                                                              │
└──────────────────────────────────────────────────────────────┘
```

Current Date

Mr. Jay *Davis*
Supervisor of Transportation
City Utilities of San Carlos
P.O. Box 6514 *(No. He said P.O. Box 614. Remove your paper and start over.)*
San Carlos CA 94070-3702 *(Squeeze in a comma between the city and state.)*

Dear Mr. Davis

Hawthorne Traffic Control Systems has been retained to conduct a brief survey of transit properties throughout the nation and in other countries. The purpose is to determine the needs and concerns of management in automating the transit environment.

In the current economic climate, cost reduction *(The telephone rings. "This is Miss Rita Saeger of the Word Processing Association. We would like to invite the person in charge of teaching word processing at a local school to our next meeting. Who was your business teacher? May I have the correct name and address, including zip code?" Provide the information; you may have to check a reference, such as the telephone directory.)* programs have become paramount objectives. Computers are tools that can provide the power to accumulate *(Is "a-c-c-u-m-m-u-l-a-t-e" the correct spelling? You had better check the dictionary.)* data, process it, and evaluate the management information required to achieve those objectives.

The enclosed survey will give you the opportunity to assist in the design of a system specifically for transit needs. By participating in the research you will receive a copy of the report. To ensure that your responses are included in the results and that you will receive your free copy, please respond within two weeks.

Your time, effort, and contribution to this project will be appreciated.

Sincerely

Gary Randolph
Project Consultant

Your initials

Enclosure

Instructions for Job 1b

MATERIALS NEEDED
8½" x 11" plain paper
Paper cover-up material
Clock with 60-second sweep hand or stopwatch

Name_____ Date_____ Section_____

You are still secretary to Mr. Randolph. Type the letter that follows these instructions. Correct any errors that you make with correction fluid, correction paper, or a lift-off tape/ribbon. Work on the letter until it is mailable.

With a stopwatch or a clock with a 60-second sweep hand, record the exact time you begin Job 1b and the exact time you finish. Figure the time it took to type the letter—including the interruptions and restart(s) if there were any.

STARTING TIME: min.   sec.
STOPPING TIME: min.   sec.   TOTAL TIME: min.   sec.

_____

Current Date

Mr. Jay Davis
Supervisor of Transportation
City Utilities of San Carlos
P.O. Box 614
San Carlos, CA 94070-3702

Dear Mr. Davis

Hawthorne Traffic Control Systems has been retained to conduct a brief survey of transit properties throughout the nation and in other countries. The purpose is to determine the needs and concerns of management in automating the transit environment.

In the current economic climate, cost reduction programs have become paramount objectives. Computers are tools that can provide the power to accumulate data, process it, and evaluate the management information required to achieve those objectives.

The enclosed survey will give you the opportunity to assist in the design of a system specifically for transit needs. By participating in the research you will receive a copy of the report. To ensure that your responses are included in the results and that you will receive your free copy, please respond within two weeks.

Your time, effort, and contributions to this project will be appreciated.

Sincerely

Gary Randolph
Project Consultant

Your initials

Enclosure

_____

Questions to Ask Yourself upon Completing Jobs 1a and 1b_____

1   Which job took the least amount of time?

2   What was the difference in time?   min.   sec.

3   Which job was easier to type?

4   Which job caused you the most frustration?

5   Which job had the better appearance/quality?

6   Can you see why one's NET PRODUCTION RATE is slower than GROSS SPEED? Producing a letter involves more activities and time than merely keystroking.

7   Can you see why the traditional secretary does not produce as much typewriting as the correspondence secretary in a word processing environment?

UNIT TWO.

The Cycle of Word Flow

The purpose of an office is to process information in a timely and usable form. As information in the form of typed words is being processed, it goes through various steps of a cycle. The result is text (words) that appears as a letter, a memorandum, a report, or another business document. This unit explains each step within the word processing cycle.

The invention of the text-editing typewriter was the major force behind the development of modern word processing. Once text has been recorded in a word processing system, it can be further processed by other information processing systems. Some of these systems include micrographics, reprographics, and electronic mail.

Most offices are still organized around separate systems, whereby each system acts alone or independent of any other system. However, the trend is toward connecting these systems into a total information processing system. Working with another system to process information is called *interfacing*. Many attempts are being made to interface data processing and word processing systems. One goal of interfacing is to avoid having to retype (or rekeyboard) text.

To understand how a word processing system can interface with other systems for a total information processing system, one must first study the word processing cycle.

WORD PROCESSING CYCLE

Words go through various steps to form a cycle. The five basic steps that make up the cycle are input, output, revision, distribution, and storage. Short descriptions of each term are given to help you learn their meanings:

Input—originating (typing, writing, or dictating) words to be processed.

Output—producing typed or printed text.

Revision—changing, correcting, or editing the text.

Distribution—sending or delivering the document.

Storage—filing and keeping the paper copy as well as the medium on which the document is recorded for easy retrieval.

Table 2-1 helps you identify each step in the word processing cycle. Trace the flow of words in that example through the flowchart (a diagram of steps of the cycle) in Illustration 2-1. As you do, keep in mind that for each part of the cycle there are different ways to perform that step. Office systems vary in the ways of processing words and other types of information. Illustration 2-2 represents a modern approach to handling each of these steps.

An optional step, *reproduction*, is often considered a step within the cycle. Should copies of the original document be necessary, the original is reproduced. However, additional copies are not always required.

21

TABLE 2-1   Tracing the Steps of Word Processing

DESCRIPTION	*STEP*
Keith Tate is a student who has been assigned to write a report on word processing for his English class. After studying and doing research on the topic, Keith composes his thoughts using pen and paper. When he changes his mind about some of the phrases or sentences, he merely scratches out the line and starts over on a line below. Since the report is to be submitted in typed form, Keith pays a fellow student, Cindy Hendrix, to type it for him. On Friday he takes his typed report to class.	→ *INPUT—Thoughts put into words by longhand.* → *REVISION—Changes made during input.* → *OUTPUT—Typed report.* → *DISTRIBUTION—Paper hand delivered to teacher.*
A week later the teacher returns the reports to the students with helpful suggestions on how they can improve their papers for a higher grade. Some of the paragraphs of Keith's report need to be changed, and there are some typing and spelling errors to be corrected. Keith marks these changes on the copy with his pen. Then he asks Cindy to retype all seven pages of the report. She makes one copy using carbon paper, which is to be retained in Keith's class notebook. The original, turned in to the teacher, will ultimately be filed in the English Department of the school.	→ *REVISION—Changes to be made after output.* → *OUTPUT—Report retyped.* → *DISTRIBUTION—Revised paper delivered to teacher.* → *STORAGE—Original filed at English Department; copy filed in Keith's notebook.*

Illus. 2-1   Flowchart of the Word Processing Cycle

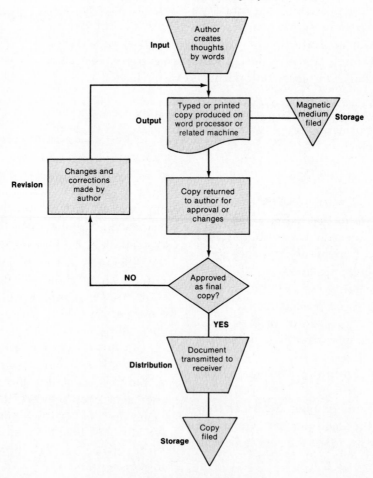

Illus. 2-2   Steps in the Word Processing Cycle

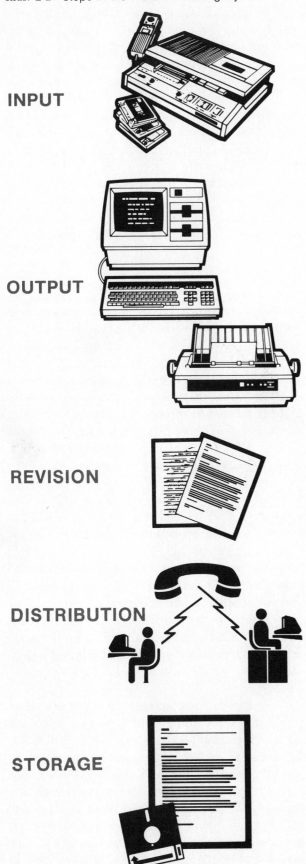

INPUT

OUTPUT

REVISION

DISTRIBUTION

STORAGE

Input: Putting Thoughts into Words

As an author puts ideas into words, the word processing cycle begins. Common ways to present the words to the secretary who will type them are longhand, shorthand dictation, machine dictation, and rough draft. These are methods of word origination or input methods.

Keith Tate, in the example in Table 2-1, used longhand to compose his report. The writer may also compose words at the typewriter and then use longhand to mark the corrections and changes; the result is called a *rough draft*. An executive might dictate letters to a secretary who records each word in shorthand. Or the executive may use a dictation machine.

A recent input method uses **optical character recognition (OCR)** equipment. Shown in Illustration 2-3 are characters that can be read by OCR equipment.

Illus. 2-3   OCR Characters

Alphabet

ABCDEFGHIJKLMNOPQRSTUVWXYZ

Numerics

0123456789

If you have a credit card, you have probably noticed your name and number embossed on the card. When you charge a purchase, the credit card number and sometimes the amount of the purchase are printed on the sales slip in OCR characters. This data can then be read directly into the company's computer system without the salesperson having to enter the information.

Perhaps you have seen the OCR scanners in supermarkets that read identification labels as shown in Illustration 2-4. One part of the label shows the manufacturer and the other part gives the product number. Instead of the salesperson having to manually key in the numbers on the cash register, the OCR scanner reads them. As it does, it causes the cash register to print the price of the product on the receipt. At the same time it updates the inventory of the product for that store. This is an example of using OCR as a data processing function.

Illus. 2-4   Labels are read directly into computers.

Illus. 2-5   OCR reads typewritten copy directly onto the magnetic medium.

In like manner, typed information can be read by an OCR scanner and then processed by a text editor. For example, after typing a rough draft the secretary feeds the pages into an optical scanner. The scanner reads the copy very fast, puts it in machine language, and duplicates the copy onto a *magnetic medium*. At this point the recorded material can be read and processed by a text editor. In short, the OCR machine can turn one type of input (typed copy) into another (recorded magnetic medium). An OCR machine saves keyboarding the information on a text editor.

These and other input methods are further described in Unit 4, "How Words Originate."

Output: Producing Text

The next step in the word processing cycle is getting the input into readable form by typing or printing. Transcribing from longhand, shorthand notes, rough draft, or machine dictation to produce typed or printed text is called *output*. The most common tools used in a word processing system are word processors and transcribing machines. The typewriting tool of the traditional office has been the electric typewriter, but it is being replaced by the electronic typewriter.

Producing words on a typewriter goes on today much as it has for years. However, correcting typing errors or making changes in the text on even the finest electric typewriter is not easy. Imagine yourself in the process of typing a ten-page report. Halfway through the report the author decides to add (insert) or remove (delete) a few paragraphs and rearrange some others. You must retype all the pages affected. You still must be able to handle the problems of word division, tabulations, even margins, and numbered pages. How does a word processor make this task easier? Let's see.

Going from an electric typewriter to a word processor is like going from an automobile with standard transmission to one with automatic transmission, power brakes, and power steering. As the operator types on a word processor, the text is recorded on a magnetic medium such as a *floppy disk*. (Illustration 2-6 shows an operator inserting a floppy disk in a word processor.) If an error is made, the operator just backspaces and retypes over the mistake. The floppy disk is

Illus. 2-6 Word Processors record text on a floppy disk; text can then be printed on paper or stored on disk.

corrected automatically. Words or entire paragraphs can be inserted or deleted with as much ease. When all text is typed and the magnetic medium corrected, the operator can direct the printer to play back the text on paper. These printers are at least eight times faster than the normal typing rate. The magnetic medium can then be filed for future use. On which machine would you prefer typing a ten-page report?

The result of producing words from longhand, shorthand, rough draft, or machine dictation is also called *output*. Output may be printed on paper, stored on the magnetic medium, or sent across telephone wires to another machine.

Revision: Editing Words

How often does your day turn out exactly as you had planned that morning? Probably not too often, for things happen that cause you to change your mind about what is urgent. In turn, you change your schedule. This also happens during the cycle of processing written communications. After a document has been typed, usually errors are found and writers change their minds about what is most important to include in a document. Word processing personnel refer to changes as revision.

Revision means that words are corrected, inserted, deleted, or replaced to improve the document. *Editing* is another word for this process. Of course, revision can take place as the author composes the input or as the secretary types the initial output. Such changes are generally minor and take just a little time to correct. To revise a document that has already been printed is a major task; it is a separate step within the cycle.

During input when an author wishes to make a revision, the correction is usually made at that moment. For example, Keith Tate scratched out and inserted different terms as he composed his report. Had he dictated his report on a machine, he could have erased the incorrect terms by dictating the new terms over the original recording.

Revision is also a part of initial output. As Cindy Hendrix typed Keith's report, she no doubt made some errors and corrected them by using either a cover-up or a lift-off material. Had Cindy used a word processor, she could have corrected the text by merely backspacing and striking over.

One of the unique features of a word processing system is that even after the words are produced the text can be revised without retyping the entire document. When the author receives the typed copy to proofread, the corrections and changes are marked with pen. The edited copy is then returned to the secretary.

Illus. 2-7 Only corrections or changes need to be keyboarded when copy is revised on a text editor.

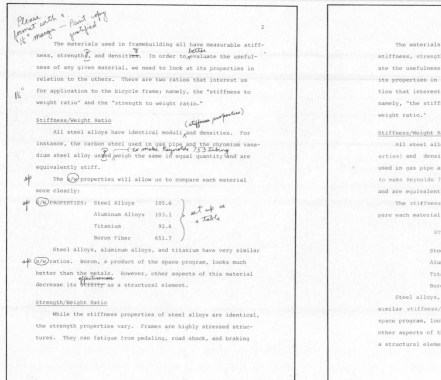

Rather than retype the entire document as Cindy had to do for Keith, the secretary using a word processor just keyboards the changes to be made. The magnetic medium is placed in the word processor. Within seconds the document to be revised can be searched by the system. The operator can quickly locate the places where corrections must be made. Once all the revisions have been made, the entire document can be played back and a final copy produced at high speed. This process is shown in Illustration 2-7.

With more advanced word processors, additional revision features are available. For example, after editing a document of 15 pages, the pages may have to be renumbered. Some word processing machines can renumber pages automatically. Or perhaps a particular word has been abbreviated throughout the text. Now the writer wants it to be spelled out. With one command, the text editor can search for the abbreviation and change it to the complete spelling wherever it appears in the text. This search and replace feature can also be used to correct the spelling of a word throughout the text.

Distribution: Sending Words

When you have good news to relate, you are eager to tell your friends. Or when you are expecting a check, you are eager to receive it as quickly as possible. The business person feels the same way about sending and receiving an important message. Distribution is the process of putting the item into the hands of the receiver.

The document may be a letter offering a contract to a business associate. It may be an article for a sales brochure to be delivered to the publications department for printing. It can be a memorandum announcing a price change to be sent over the telephone wires from a home office word processor to the word processors of all branch offices. It can be a medical report to be reduced to microfilm size and kept in the medical records department of a hospital. It can be a letter with an architect's drawing that must reach a customer in another state within four hours. In each situation, with all revisions having been made, the copy is in final form and ready to be sent to its destination.

Mailgram. Mailgram is an overnight delivery service that combines the services of Western Union and the U.S. Postal Service. A Mailgram is sent through Western Union's computer over their communication networks to a teletypewriter located at the post office nearest the receiver. The post office physically delivers the message the next business day. A Mailgram is used mostly for short messages. It provides speed, economy, and a written record to customers, suppliers, and employees in branch offices.

Illus. 2-11   A Mailgram and a Terminal

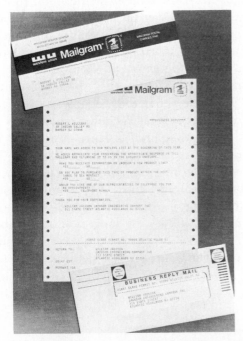

Computer-Based Message System. One of the problems in office communication is what is known as "telephone tag"—trying to catch the receiver by telephone. It is not often that the sender can catch the receiver on the first attempt. Instead, either the message is left with the secretary or a request for a return call is made. In either event, getting back to the original caller involves the same risk of information being delayed and/or lost.

With a *computer-based message system (CBMS)* the sender and receiver do not have to talk at the same time as in a telephone conversation. Instead, the computer system is the message sender, carrier, receiver, and filer. Each user is assigned an *electronic mailbox.* To send a message to another user, you do not have to be concerned that the user is in his or her office. The message is left at the user's mailbox. The receiver gets the message when he or she makes an inquiry. Making an inquiry (accessing one's mailbox) can be done from any terminal that can connect to the computer system. Thus, the mailbox can be checked even when away from the office.

Advantages of Electronic Mail. Why do companies choose a form of electronic mail in place of the postal service, carrier service, telephone calls, or face-to-face communication? The following are among the reasons:

- The speed of sending information is as fast as direct dialing a long-distance call.

- Messages can be sent at any time of day. Thus companies can take advantage of the lowest telephone rates by sending documents in batches at night.

- Because there is no rekeying of information, errors are reduced.

- The cost of sending information is cheaper and more reliable than other methods. (This assumes the initial cost is justified by the volume and type of information being sent.)

- Paperwork is greatly reduced, for a hard copy is made by the receiving unit only if it is needed.

Storage: Filing and Keeping Words

As a student, you no doubt have a special place for notes from class lectures so that you can find them when it is time to study for a test. If so, you have developed a method of filing and keeping words—a storage plan. Storage involves filing documents so that they can be found easily. In the word processing cycle, there are two items that require storage—the typed or printed page (hard copy) and the recorded medium (for example, floppy disk). With hundreds of letters, memorandums, reports, and forms produced each week, employees must be able to find a copy of any one of them at a moment's notice.

The records management department of a company generally is in charge of classifying, arranging, and storing paper records. One way to reduce storage space is to use *microfilm*, which is the process of making miniature copies of paper records on film. The science of microfilming is called *micrographics*. Micrographics has made it possible for words recorded on magnetic media to be converted directly to microfilm without first being printed on paper. Microfilming will be discussed in detail later.

Another part of storage concerns storing and finding what has been recorded on magnetic media. For example, a floppy disk on which standard form letters have been recorded needs to be stored where any secretary can find it. However, a floppy disk on which individually dictated letters have been recorded will probably be stored in the transcriber's immediate work

area. This floppy disk will be kept for two or three days, because the author may request a revision of the letter. After the hold-for-revision period, the transcriber erases the floppy disk so that it can be used for new recordings.

INTERFACING WORD PROCESSING WITH OTHER SYSTEMS

In reviewing the word processing cycle—input, output, revision, distribution, and storage—you no doubt noticed that several machines other than word processors are used. Once words have been recorded on magnetic media by a word processor, they can be handled by other office machines. To describe this ability, terms such as *capturing keystrokes, interfacing, integrating word processing with . . . ,* and *interrelation of word processing with other systems* are used.

The interaction between word processing and other systems can occur during any part of the word processing cycle. Here are some short examples: As one INPUT method, a word processor can interface with OCR equipment to accept typed copy from a typewriter. A word processor can interface with another text editor for the REVISION of lengthy documents. In DISTRIBUTING words, a word processor with the communication feature can send recorded words

Illus. 2-12   Storage involves filing the paper copy and the magnetic media.

over the telephone system or by satellite to another word processor or to a computer. Words recorded on a magnetic medium can be converted to microfilm for STORAGE without having to be printed on paper.

Another function, which is sometimes a step within the word processing cycle, is reproduction. The term *reprographics* is used to describe processes of reproducing copy. The basic machines used are photocopiers and duplicators. For each letter or report produced by the word processing department, at least one copy is generally made before the document is distributed or stored. For only one copy, a carbon copy is the most economical way; but for two or more copies the photocopier is usually preferred. For large numbers of duplicated copies with quality appearance, companies often choose to use offset duplicators. Word processors are instrumental in producing error free masters for offset machines. In addition, technology is developing word processors that can be interfaced with intelligent copiers. This would allow text keyboarded in one location (St. Louis) to be printed in another location (Chicago).

This unit briefly tells how word processing can be integrated with other systems—optical character recognition, data processing, electronic mail, micrographics, and reprographics. You can hardly discuss word processing without being

Illus. 2-13 Keystrokes captured on magnetic media can be used by other information systems.

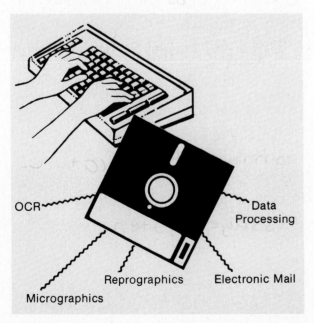

OCR

Data Processing

Reprographics

Electronic Mail

Micrographics

aware of its "cousin" systems. The interfacing of these systems is made possible by the captured keystroke.

All word processing keyboards have a storage medium that records (captures) each keystroke. Once words have been recorded, the medium can be used to produce more playbacks of the document on the word processor or to interface with another system of information processing. The operator of the word processor never has to rekey the strokes. Also, the operators of the other information processing systems do not have to rekey the text that was first captured by a word processor.

CASE SITUATION

Now visualize yourself in the following office scene, which summarizes the word processing cycle:

You are a correspondence secretary for Eagle & Flynn Associates. The word processor that you use records on floppy disks. The group of people with whom you work serves two departments— the personnel department and the public relations department.

At 11:30 on Monday morning, Fran Haug, director of personnel, picks up the microphone of his dictation machine to dictate a memorandum on absenteeism.

At 1:00 PM, after your lunch break, Jose Felipe, the supervisor of the word processing department, hands you two cassette tapes to transcribe. One of the tapes contains the memorandum on absenteeism dictated by Fran Haug.

You place the first cassette tape in your transcription machine. Then you listen to the recorded message while you type. As you transcribe the documents, the words are being recorded on the floppy disk of your word processor. (A floppy disk will hold up to about 100 pages.)

As you transcribe each document, you label the document so you can find it later. Then you file the disk in the special disk file on your desk. The documents that are ready to be returned to the authors are placed in the out basket. A delivery person will pick them up at 2:30 PM.

When Mr. Haug receives the memo on absenteeism that you transcribed, he reads it

Illus. 2-14 The Word Processing Cycle

INPUT

OUTPUT

REVISION

DISTRIBUTION

STORAGE

carefully and makes one editing change. He also decides to add another paragraph at the end of the memo. Then he returns the memo to the word processing department.

Recognizing your initials on the memo as the person who transcribed it, Mr. Felipe gives it to you to key in the changes.

Within a few seconds you have retrieved from your disk file the diskette on which the memo was recorded. To prepare the revised memo, you insert the diskette and direct your word processor to play back the original recording. As it types (plays back) the last word of the last original paragraph, you stop it and key in the change and the paragraph that Mr. Haug has added. Having corrected the magnetic diskette, you are ready to print a perfect copy.

The revised memo is routed back to Mr. Haug, who reads it and signs it. He then sends it to Mrs. Carolyn Trimble, an administrative secretary in the reproduction services department, and requests that a photocopy be sent through company mail to each of the 15 office workers listed on an attached sheet of paper.

The original, along with the list of employee names, is then returned to the personnel department for filing. By 4:15 PM the job is done and the word processing cycle completed.

Wouldn't it be exciting to work in a modern word processing office? By the time you finish reading this text and doing the projects, you will have a good background in word processing concepts.

Review Exercises

Completion

Complete the following sentences by filling in the blanks.

1   Typing or printing a document describes the _output_ step in the word processing cycle.

2   Another term for changing, correcting, or editing a document is _revision_.

3   Federal Express and Emery Air Freight are two _private carriers_ of mail.

4   The process of getting the message to the receiver is the _distribution_ step in the word processing cycle.

5   Electronic equipment made to send charts, drawings, graphs, and photographs over a distance is called _facsimile_ equipment.

6   A computer-based message system involves sending messages by keying them in on a/an _terminal_.

7   Two types of materials that must be filed and stored within a word processing system are the hard copy and the _recorded medium_.

8   A step that is sometimes considered a part of the word processing cycle, depending on the need for copies, is _reproduction_ _____.

9   Interfacing machines and systems to process information is possible because of _captured_ keystrokes.

10 The diagram showing the steps of the word processing cycle is called a/an _flowchart_.

33

Short Answers_____
Indicate your answers by filling in the blanks.

1   Name the five basic steps in the word processing cycle. List them
    in the order that they usually take place.

    a _input_____   d _Distribution_____
    b _output_____   e _Storage_____
    c _Rivision_____

2   List three ways that words originate.

    a _longhand_____
    b _shorthand_____
    c _rough draft_____

3   List three basic ways of sending typed information.

    a _company mail_____
    b _private carriers_____
    c _electronic mail_____

4   How does a word processor differ from an electric typewriter in
    processing words?

    Keystrokes are not recorded on any medium
    _____except a paper copy._____
    Corrections must be made by erasing on typewriter.
    _____
    _____
    _____

5   Name three types of electronic mail methods.

    a _word processors with communications feature_
    b _facsimile_____
    c _computer based message system_____

6   Name three systems that can be interfaced with word processing
    to process information.

    a _Data processing_____

Name_____ Date_____ Section_____

b _electronic mail_____

c _micrographics_____

Multiple Choice

Select the letter that best completes the sentence, placing it in the space provided in the right column.

1   A teletypewriter exchange service provided by Western Union is (A) OCR, (B) CPU, (C) TWX, (D) FAX, (E) none of these. ___C___

2   Electronic mail can be sent by (A) telephone and telegraph lines, (B) satellite networks, (C) offset duplicators, (D) both A and B, (E) both B and C. ___D___

3   *Revision* means (A) duplicating, (B) editing, (C) microfilming, (D) photocopying, (E) storing. ___B___

4   *Distribution* refers to (A) recording, (B) sending, (C) transmitting, (D) both A and B, (E) both B and C. ___E___

5   Methods of electronic mail are (A) communicating word processors and facsimile equipment, (B) OCR and U.S. Postal Service, (C) offset and photocopy, (D) microfilm and typesetting, (E) none of these. ___A___

6   A Mailgram is (A) processed through the telephone switchboard of the receiver, (B) ordered through a private carrier, (C) an overnight delivery service, (D) not processed by a computer, (E) used mostly for multipage documents. ___C___

7   Micrographics refers to the processing of (A) microphones, (B) microfilm, (C) microwaves, (D) microclines, (E) none of these. ___B___

8   The word that does *not* describe the relationship of word processing to other systems is (A) interfacing, (B) interrelating, (C) integrating, (D) intercepting, (E) captured keystrokes. ___D___

9   Photocopying and duplicating functions are included in the area of (A) reprographics, (B) data processing, (C) micrographics, (D) OCR, (E) both C and D. ___A___

10   Electronic mail can be sent by (A) telephone lines, (B) microwave, (C) fiber optics, (D) satellite, (E) all of these. ___E___

True or False

Indicate your answer by placing a T or F in the right-hand column blanks.

1   The input step in the word processing cycle refers to originating words. ___True___

2   An OCR scanner generally interfaces with the storage step in the word processing cycle.   *False*

3   Word processors cannot connect with high-speed printers or computers.   *False*

4   An electronic mailbox is a box in the company mail room that automatically opens after an electric switch is pressed.   *False*

5   Hard copy refers to the paper copy of written, typed, or printed material.   *True*

6   Word processors can be ordered with or without the communicating feature.   *True*

7   The basic machines used in reprographics are terminals and couplers.   *False*

8   Microfilming is usually a function of the records management department of a company.   *True*

9   Interaction between word processing and other systems happens only during input and output.   *False*

10   The purpose of interfacing machines and systems is to allow the operator of each system the chance to key in the entire document even if it has already been recorded by one system.   *False*

Instructions for Job 2_____

The following flowchart shows the word processing cycle that was described in the Case Situation at the end of Unit 2. Assume that you are the correspondence secretary in the word processing department.

Identify the missing parts of the flowchart by filling in the blanks to the left of the symbols.

Then fill in the blanks to the right which describe each step of the cycle.

Name_____ Date_____ Section_____

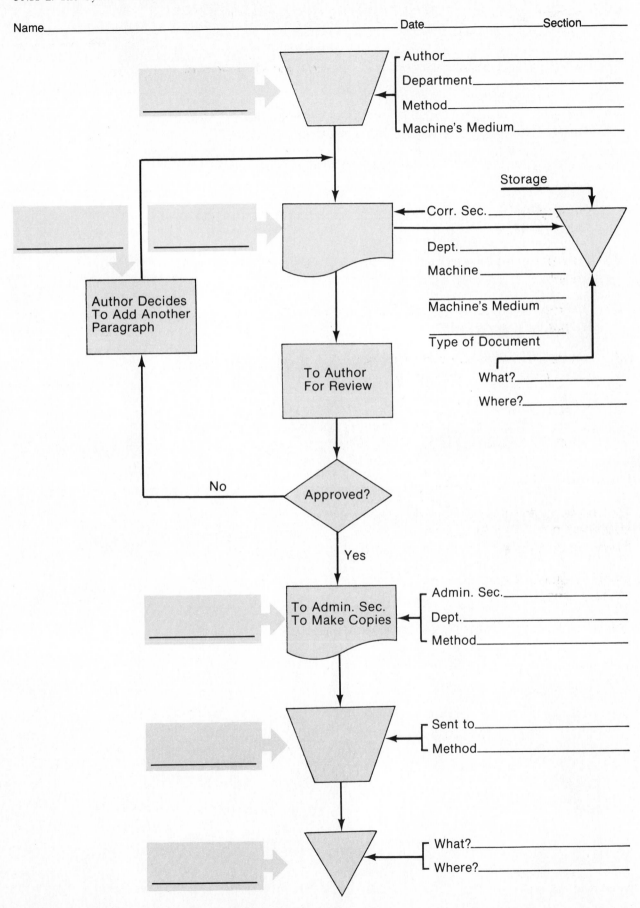

Author_____
Department_____
Method_____
Machine's Medium_____

_____

Storage

Corr. Sec._____

Dept._____
Machine_____
_____
Machine's Medium
_____
Type of Document

What?_____
Where?_____

_____   _____

Author Decides
To Add Another
Paragraph

To Author
For Review

No   Approved?

Yes

To Admin. Sec.
To Make Copies

Admin. Sec._____
Dept._____
Method_____

_____

Sent to_____
Method_____

_____

What?_____
Where?_____

_____

UNIT THREE.

The System Involves "PMPE"

Word processing involves more than a text editor. In order for words to flow through the cycle most efficiently, a system is needed. A word processing system is made up of specialized *People*, sophisticated *Machines*, efficient *Procedures*, and a pleasing, comfortable *Environment*. A word processing system coordinates these elements to process written communications. These four parts —PMPE—can be seen in other systems as well.

THE PMPE OF ANOTHER SYSTEM

Before you learn about the PMPE of word processing, take a look at another type of system—a food service system—that coordinates the same four parts. A food service system is a restaurant, a cafeteria, or a fast food chain. Some of the people employed are the cook, the waiters/waitresses, and the manager. The machines include ovens, a grill, refrigerators, a dishwasher, an ice-making machine, a beverage fountain, and heat lamps. The restaurant uses certain procedures to seat people in the order in which they arrive and to time the preparation of each item offered on the menu. Procedures help to serve customers a quality meal within a short period of time. The environment has comfortable seating, an attractive atmosphere for the patrons, and a well-arranged working area for the employees.

No one part of this food service system can be successful without the other three. Take a moment to imagine four restaurants, each lacking in one of the PMPEs. You no doubt would rather eat at a restaurant that is superior in all four areas.

Although all four elements are important, the one that is most important to the success of a business is people. Without well-trained employees who are friendly and courteous to other workers as well as to customers, the system cannot perform at its best. A restaurant may have the latest models of machines for preparing food, well-defined procedures, and a charming atmosphere. But if the employees are impolite, unfriendly, or do not follow procedures, customers will not return. If the manager does not work effectively with the personnel and does not pay a reasonable wage, the workers will seek employment at other places where their abilities will be better appreciated and financially rewarded.

These four elements—people, machines, procedures, and environment—form a system. Each system has its own unique features. The goal of a food processing service is to prepare delicious food that is served to the customers promptly. The goal of a word processing service is to prepare a quality document that is delivered to the executive promptly. This unit describes the four parts of a word processing system in general terms. When you have completed Unit 3, you will have a broad idea of what word processing means and how it works.

PEOPLE

People are the most important part of any system. Successful word processing systems have a well-trained staff led by a professional supervisor who is backed by top management. On the other hand, most word processing failures are caused by human failure in one way or another.

Illus. 3-1   Word processing includes: people, machines, procedures, and environment.

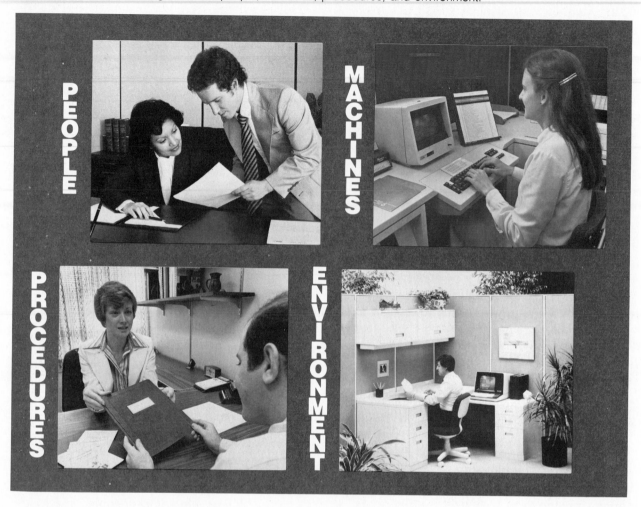

The titles of people working in a word processing system vary from one organization to another. Yet the nature of each person's work is similar to that done by someone in another word processing system. The same is true in other systems. For example, the maintenance system of one company has custodians, while another gives the same type of worker the title of sanitary engineer. Let's meet the people involved in word processing and learn about their roles.

Originators or Principals

One who uses secretarial services is an originator of information. These persons are also known as principals, authors, or users.

Word originators can be at any level on the organization chart. They are sometimes called executives or managers, but those who dictate letters do not necessarily manage other people.

Illus. 3-2   Word Originator

Originators/principals initiate work that is done by secretarial support. The work may involve transcribing and typing or administrative duties.

Each executive who formerly had a personal secretary now shares the services of a secretarial team (or teams) with other executives. Each team specializes in certain services. Thus, principals can expect to have all secretarial services provided at the highest level. The top managers set the example by their support of the word processing concept.

Correspondence Secretaries/Word Processing Operators

The person who is trained to type and transcribe documents (such as letters) is called one of the following: correspondence secretary (CS), word processing operator, word processing secretary, or word processing specialist. In this book the term correspondence secretary (CS) will often be used. However, you should be familiar with the other titles.

The CS's main duty is to transcribe the text dictated or written by the word originator. This means keyboarding the text, proofreading and correcting typing errors, and editing the text. The final document should have no errors. Types of documents processed include letters, memorandums, reports, tables, and catalogs. Much text will be taken from machine dictation, which requires careful listening. In operating the text editor, the CS must be able to understand and follow instructions. In addition, excellent communication skills (grammar, spelling, punctuation, and knowledge of company vocabulary) are needed. Proofreading skills are also very important. To be a technical specialist, the CS must enjoy working with machines.

Administrative Secretaries/Administrative Support Secretaries

Secretaries who handle the nontyping tasks for more than one principal are called administrative secretaries or administrative support secretaries (AS). This book will often refer to the administrative support secretary as the AS.

The needs of an individual department or company will determine the types of services provided by the AS. The most common nontyping tasks include scheduling appointments, making travel arrangements, filing, receiving callers, answering the telephone, handling the mail, and composing *routine correspondence*. An administrative secretary may act as a liaison (one who works between groups) between the transcribers and the principals. This is considered a paraprofessional position in some firms.

Illus. 3-3   Correspondence Secretary

Illus. 3-4   Administrative Secretary

Supervisors

In a word processing system each group of secretaries works as a team to support a group of principals. Each team of secretaries is supervised by one person other than a principal. This person might be called a coordinator, a manager, or a supervisor. The term "supervisor" will be used most often in this book. In a large word processing organization there can be two managers—one over correspondence support and one over administrative support.

The role of the supervisor is to help the people and procedures work in harmony. Together with top management, the supervisor creates procedures for both the authors and the word processing staff. The goal is to assure a smooth flow of work. It is then up to the supervisor to see that policies and procedures are followed on a daily basis. As problems arise, it is up to the supervisor to resolve them. In Unit 9 the specific duties of the supervisor are discussed.

Illus. 3-5 Supervisor

Other Personnel and Career Opportunities

Other personnel of a word processing system can include a receptionist and a delivery person. The receptionist screens and welcomes office visitors, handles telephone calls, and may help with administrative support tasks. In some firms one of the administrative secretaries serves as the receptionist. The delivery person picks up and delivers mail to and from the departments. This allows the correspondence secretaries to remain at their work stations. However, some firms have each correspondence secretary take a turn at picking up and delivering documents to be filed or mailed. In this way the CSs may become acquainted with the principals they serve.

There are opportunities in word processing for careers in selling, consulting, marketing support, and training. Companies that sell information processing equipment hire sales representatives to sell the equipment. The work of the sales representative is to interest potential customers in the company's products and to demonstrate the equipment. After the customer expresses interest in the products, a *consultant* may be called in to help determine the customer's needs and to design a system which will best meet those needs. After the equipment has been sold, most vendors will train a limited number of the customer's employees to use it. This is the job of a *marketing support representative (MSR)*—also called a customer support representative (CSR). This person teaches customers to operate the equipment and suggests applications for its best use.

Some companies also hire an in-house instructor or trainer who is responsible for

Illus. 3-6 Marketing support representatives train users.

conducting training programs for people at all levels. Examples of topics covered are machine dictation, operating word processors, designing efficient procedures, and improving writing skills. Unit 9 discusses career opportunities and suggests ways to find a satisfying career.

MACHINES

The two most important kinds of machines in a word processing system are dictation equipment and typewriting equipment. Dictation equipment provides the input, or the means to record the spoken word. Typewriting equipment produces output, the printed word. The use of dictation equipment and word processors provides the basis for modern word processing systems.

Dictation Equipment

Dictation equipment has three parts: the dictation unit, the recorder, and the transcribing machine. The dictation unit allows the originator to dictate, review, and correct the message. This unit is also called the *dictation station* or input station. The *recorder* actually places the dictation onto the magnetic medium. The recorder may be part of the dictation unit or it may be a separate machine. The *transcribing machine* plays back the recorded words for the operator to transcribe.

Dictation equipment is usually classified by its location and by the way it is used. Units may be portable, desk top, or centralized.

PORTABLE

The hand sized, battery operated portables are useful for the executive who travels. A portable can be used in a car, in an airplane, or wherever it is convenient to dictate.

DESK TOP

Desk top units are used most often in companies that do not have a large number of originators. These units are also used in firms that have centralized dictation equipment by those who do more than the average amount of dictating.

Illus. 3-7   Portable dictation units are convenient in the office or on the road.

Desk top equipment consists of a dictation unit and a transcription machine. The dictation unit is located at the executive's desk, and the transcription machine is at the secretary's desk. Desk top equipment can also be purchased as a combination unit. One piece of equipment acts as both a dictation unit for the originator and a transcription device for the secretary. In this case, the machine has to be moved from the executive's desk to the secretary's desk.

Illus. 3-8   Desk Top Dictation Unit

Illus. 3-9   Parts of a Centralized System: Dictation Station (top), Recorder & Optional Supervisor's Console (middle), & Transcribing Machine (bottom)

CENTRALIZED

With centralized dictation equipment, the dictation stations, recorders, and transcription machines are separate units. The dictation units are either desk microphones or telephone receivers. These are located throughout the company so that it is convenient for executives to use them. Each dictation station is connected to the recorders. Housed in one central place, the recorders are located in the same room as the transcribing units.

When there are many originators, a centralized system is less costly than a desk top system because each dictation station does not have to have its own recorder. A centralized system is also easier to control.

Typewriting Equipment

Once ideas have been created on paper or dictation equipment, a readable copy needs to be made. Equipment that will produce a typed page can be as simple as an electric typewriter or as sophisticated as a word processor that connects to a high-speed printer or to a computer system.

Word processing equipment allows the user to create, store, edit, and print text. As text is keyboarded, it is recorded inside the machine's memory or on a magnetic medium. A simple command allows the operator to remove a word, a sentence, or a paragraph. The machine automatically closes up the space. If words are to be added, a command opens up space so that text can be inserted. Changes can easily be made after the text has been recorded. Once the copy has been stored in the machine's memory or on the magnetic medium, it can be played back quickly to produce a typed document. Each of the following types of machines can perform these text-editing functions.

ELECTRONIC TYPEWRITER

An electronic typewriter is a cross between an electric typewriter and a word processor. It automates some of the manual functions of typing such as underscoring and centering. It stores a limited amount of text in an internal memory. An electronic typewriter is able to perform the basic text-editing functions of editing and printing copy. This one piece of equipment is used for keyboarding and printing. However, only one of these functions can be done at a time. Electronic typewriters are sometimes called intelligent typewriters or memory typewriters. Some people consider them low-level word processors.

STANDALONE WORD PROCESSOR

A standalone word processor operates without help from any other machine. Its main parts include the electronic keyboard for entering the instructions and the text, the recording medium for storing the text, the *logic/intelligence* or brain for managing the operations of the machine, and the printing device for converting the stored text into print. Nearly every standalone today has a *visual display* screen that looks similar to a TV screen. One of the first types of visual display screens was the cathode ray tube (CRT). Thus, the term *CRT standalone* is sometimes used.

As the operator keyboards onto a standalone with a visual display, the text appears on the screen. This allows the operator to see the document as it is being prepared, spot errors, and revise text—all before it is printed on paper. An indicator, called a *cursor* or pointer, marks the place of action (position of text entry) on the screen. As text fills the screen, the upper lines *scroll* (move) off the screen. Once all editing is finished, the text is moved from the screen to the recording medium or memory for storage. When the copy is to be printed, playback occurs from an attached *printer* at more than 420 wam.

Some standalones can handle both data and word processing functions, for they are made like small computers. Others have more limited data processing capability.

Illus. 3-10 Electronic Typewriter

Illus. 3-11 Standalone Word Processor

MULTISTATION SYSTEMS

Two or more stations (keyboard and visual display) may share the use of another device such as a printer, a storage medium, or a computer. This arrangement is called a multistation system.

By sharing certain functions, each station does not have to have all the parts of the whole, or all the parts of a standalone. For example, three or four word processors can share one printer. Or several word processors can share the master file (information about customers, products, employees, and so forth) that is on another storage medium. Each station may have its own intelligence, or it may depend on another station or a computer for its intelligence. By sharing the intelligence of a computer, complicated math calculations done by the computer can be added to a report being processed on a text editor.

Illus. 3-12   Two stations are sharing the use of a printer and a storage device.

By sharing certain functions, the average cost of each word processor is less than that of a standalone system. However, if one part of a multistation system is down (out of order) the other parts that depend on it are unable to do that function. Also, for certain functions of multistation systems only one station at a time can perform those functions.

Multistation systems that share are generally housed within one building or in nearby buildings. The entire system is usually owned or rented by one company.

TIME SHARED SERVICES

Time shared services allow a number of companies having word processors to share the services of a large computer system. Few companies can afford to own such a powerful computer, nor can they use all its capabilities. Time shared services allow each user to pay for just the services it needs. Each user pays monthly charges based on the length of processing time, the amount of storage required of the computer system, and the output.

The user needs only a word processor or a computer terminal that is able to access (directly reach records in) the large computer. Because the user's terminal is in a different location from the computer, it is called a *remote* terminal. Communication between the computer and the text editor is by way of telephone lines or satellite.

Word processing service bureaus operate in a similar way. They perform word processing functions for companies that do not have enough work or cannot afford to have a word processing system of their own. Instead they pay for whatever service is needed. Work orders can be sent by the public postal service or electronic mail, or they can be delivered in person.

PROCEDURES FOR CONTROL

Procedures are guides that help people work and use machines most efficiently. They bring order to a system. Even though most traditional offices have certain procedures for controlling costs and improving efficiency, they are less structured. A word processing system is more formal and uniform in practicing control techniques. A discussion of several basic control procedures follows.

Logging Work

In order to keep an accurate record of the work done by word processing specialists, most

Illus. 3-13   A log sheet provides a record of a secretary's daily work.

COPPUS ENGINEERING CORPORATION
TYPING CENTER
DAILY LOG SHEET

DAY **FRI**

DATE **8/31/--**

OPERATOR **EMC**

WORK TYPES
L = Longhand
D = Dictation
R = Revision
S = Stat./Other

ORIGINATOR		DAY IN	TIME IN	TIME OUT	WORK TYPE	LINE COUNT
DEPT.	INIT.					
812	RCM	8-30	4:15	9:20	D	42
781	BS	8-31	9:20	10:55	L	66
811	JL	8-31	10:35	11:35	L	25
811	RCM	8-31	1:45	1:50	R	39
521	DS	8-31	1:50	2:05	R	90
501	EDM	8-31	2:40	2:50	L	26
803	EB	8-31	2:45			
781	JFP	8-31	3:10			
812	LLM	8-31	3:20			

companies require their secretaries to log their work. This means that as typing or any other task is completed, the information about what was done and for whom is recorded on a log sheet. The log sheet provides a record of all dictation, longhand, revision, and statistical work done by the secretary.

Log sheets provide a means for easily tracing a document from the time it enters the system until it is completed. Also, log sheets supply a place on which to record the number of lines or pages that have been keyboarded. Illustration 3-13 shows an example of the type of information recorded on a log sheet. Daily information is then transferred to weekly and monthly reports, which summarize the office's production.

Measuring Production and Setting Standards

Keeping track of how much work is done by each secretary and by the work force as a whole is called measuring production. Work is measured for many reasons: Employee's work can be evaluated so that high producers can be rewarded and slow producers can be helped to improve. Keeping production records helps the supervisor prove the need for more machines and staff. Standards of performance can be set. Any dips below the standard signal that there may be a problem. Measuring production allows the department using the services to be charged for the work produced.

A *standard* is a rate of production that the average worker can meet. It establishes certain periods of time for the completion of various tasks. By keeping records, departmental and individual standards can be set. Comparisons can then be made from one month or quarter to another.

Setting Priorities and Scheduling Turnaround

A secretary may be asked by two principals to do two separate tasks immediately. In a traditional office, the secretary feels pulled between two equal forces. In a word processing system, the work is done according to set priorities. The *priorities* are based on what the principals have earlier agreed to be the order of urgency of office tasks.

Illus. 3-14 Work is scheduled according to set priorities.

Most word processing operations schedule work so that each job is completed and returned to the originator within a reasonable time limit. This is known as scheduling *turnaround*. A turnaround goal serves as an incentive for prompt service to the principals. It also gives the employee a realistic goal for self-evaluation. Turnaround goals depend on the type of assign-

ment. For example, the turnaround goal for a memorandum may be four hours, while the time limit for a nine-page report may be eight hours.

Standardizing Formats

The simplest way to type a document takes the least amount of time. Therefore, it costs less to produce a document with a simple format (style) than one with a complicated format. Rather than allowing many styles to be used for the same type of document, word processing systems generally use one format.

When a standard format is used for each type of document, there are fewer opportunities to make mistakes. In addition, it takes less time to train employees and to keyboard the documents because there is less decision making. For example, if only one letter style is used in a company, it is much easier and faster for the secretary to transcribe a number of letters for several executives from different departments.

Managing Prerecorded Media Files

As a document is recorded, it is given a label (code number or short name) indicating where it is stored on the magnetic medium. The recording medium is labeled as well. **Document labels** allow both word originators and secretaries to easily refer to or find documents again.

Since each magnetic medium can store many documents, the following questions must be answered: Which types of documents should be

Illus. 3-15 Procedures are needed for filing the magnetic and paper copy of documents; the magnetic copy is later erased.

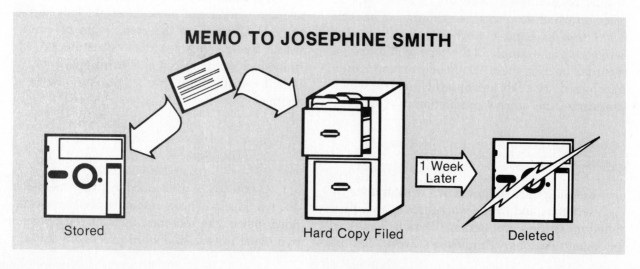

MEMO TO JOSEPHINE SMITH

Stored   Hard Copy Filed   1 Week Later   Deleted

stored on each? Which information should be temporarily stored in memory, and which documents should be permanently stored on a removable medium? When and how should documents be erased (destroyed) from the file? These duties are all part of what is called *file management*.

Maintaining Quality Printout

A quality document is one that has no errors and is printed with clear, dark characters. Letter quality print should look as though it were typed without error on a typewriter with a carbon ribbon.

To be sure that there are no errors in grammar, spelling, punctuation, or word usage, someone other than the operator must proofread the document. Final proofreading may be done by the supervisor, by an experienced CS, or by a person who is hired just to proofread.

In order to have quality printing, the printing device needs to be watched carefully so that the paper feeds evenly and the print is evenly dark and clear. Since the printing device is a separate piece of equipment, in many large word processing centers one person oversees the printing of documents.

Writing Procedures Manuals

A procedures manual is a handy reference that tells workers how to do basic tasks. It is especially helpful to new employees who are learning how to perform certain tasks. A procedures manual saves their having to interrupt other workers to ask questions. Each company should design and write its own manuals to fit its individual needs.

Information likely to be in the manual for correspondence secretaries includes the following: a list of originators and job titles; instructions with samples of the standard format used for letters, memorandums, and reports; recorded form letters; instructions for logging and measuring work; and ZIP Code information.

Training Personnel

You may feel that once you have completed high school, vocational school, or college that you are through learning. Not true. In most occupations, technology is constantly changing procedures and challenging you to keep up. To keep pace with progress, many companies offer in-service training programs to help train or retrain their employees in certain areas.

Illus. 3-16   Through in-service training, employees learn about new equipment and procedures.

Training for correspondence secretaries includes learning how to operate word processors and reviewing grammar, spelling, and punctuation. For administrative secretaries there are programs on mail processing, telephone communication, and records management. The principals often need help in improving their dictation techniques, in organizing their work, and in delegating tasks to secretaries.

Not only new employees need to be trained. All employees can improve the quality and quantity of their work through advanced training.

Unit 7 covers procedures for controlling word processing services.

ENVIRONMENT

In order to be productive, people must feel compatible with the equipment they use and with their surroundings or environment. Without a proper environment machines do not work well, procedures are inefficient, office costs rise, and people feel uncomfortable. A good environment requires careful planning.

To choose the proper environment for yourself, the following questions should be answered: Where would I fit within the company? What would my work area and surroundings be like? Let's find a brief answer to these questions.

Word Processing Within the Organization

Where would you fit within the company? The importance given to word processing within the organization usually determines the location of word processing equipment and personnel. This is often revealed by the organization chart of the company. The organization chart lists all the jobs within a company and shows the lines of authority. The position of word processing within the company structure depends on how secretarial services are organized and where the operation will work best for those using the services. Thus, word processing operations have been designed and placed within various companies in different ways.

The abbreviations *AS/CS* and *WP/AS* imply that secretarial services are formally organized into specialized teams within the company. CS or WP represents the correspondence support team. AS represents the administrative support team. One supervisor can control both the AS and CS teams, or each team can have its own supervisor. In any case, the secretaries are professionally managed. Career paths allow employees to advance according to their skills and abilities.

Some companies have organized only the CS side of secretarial services. The other secretaries function as traditional secretaries but are relieved

Illus. 3-17   An organization chart shows the position of word processing in an organization.

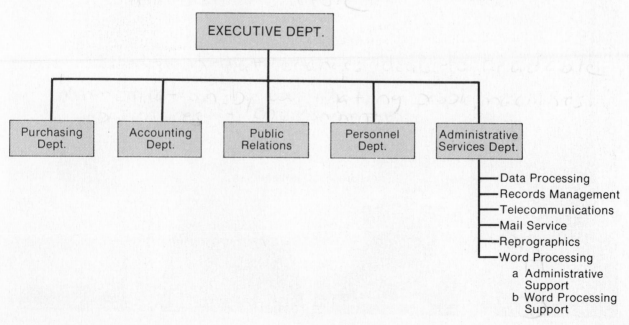

of heavy typing and transcribing. They serve one or more principals and are supervised by them.

WP/AS can be a department of its own. It can be a part of a large department, such as an administrative services department. It can be spread throughout the company in small groups serving divisions of the company. When the whole company is served by one center, the physical layout is *centralized*. A system of several small centers, called minicenters or *satellite centers*, is said to be *decentralized*. The size of the company and the nature of the work usually determine how word processing services are organized and physically located.

Some firms add word processing equipment to their offices without reorganizing the secretaries. Even though a formal word processing system does not exist, word processing equipment is being used.

Reading about word processing structures can be confusing. Some speakers and writers assume that word processing refers only to correspondence support. Others think that word processing implies that the CS team performs the typing tasks and that the AS team performs the nontyping tasks.

Physical Characteristics

What would your work area and surroundings be like? Years ago most office employees were assigned a desk of fairly standard design, and the employee made the desk fit his or her needs. Today the office environment is designed by studying the needs of the employees and the requirements of the equipment. These needs include providing proper seating and work space; controlling the lights, noise, humidity, and

Illus. 3-18   Open landscaping includes work stations designed to meet our needs for proper lighting, space, noise and air control, and privacy.

temperature; and allowing for privacy. *Ergonomics* is the science of planning the work environment with human comfort and efficiency as its main goals.

As a result of viewing the office as a total environment, several changes are being made. Rather than having work areas divided by permanent walls and doors, *open landscaping* is used. Open landscaping has movable partitions rather than walls. The partitions may house electrical wires and limit the exposure of cords and wires.

A small work area or *work station* provides each employee with everything that will be needed. *Modular furniture* replaces the stationary desk. The work surface, counters, overhead storage, and shelves can be rearranged quickly and inexpensively as the need arises. Chairs adjust for the comfort of the worker. The employee has space for plants, pictures, or other items to personalize the work station.

Unit 8 describes in more detail the necessary environment for word processing services.

SUMMARY

Word processing can be defined as a system that changes ideas to readable communication by coordinating people, machines, procedures, and environment. As one of the systems that processes information, word processing specializes in the handling of text (documents such as letters, memorandums, and reports).

Review Exercises

Completion

Complete the following sentences by filling in the blanks.

1   Secretaries in a word processing system work as a/an ___team___ to support a group of principals.

2   A word processor with a screen on which to see the text is called a/an ___CRT___ standalone.

3   An arrangement that allows many companies to pay for only the time and services needed of a large computer system is called ___time shared services___.

4   When all dictation units placed throughout a company are connected to recorders housed in one area, the firm has ___Centralized___ dictation equipment.

5   Keeping a record of all the typing and transcribing that is done for principals is called ___logging___.

6   As documents are recorded, they are ___coded___ so that they may be found quickly.

7   A handy reference to answer questions the employee may have on how to do a task is a/an ___procedures manual___.

8   The abbreviation ___AS/CS___ indicates that all secretarial services are specialized (typing or nontyping) with a professional supervisor over each group.

9   The work area that has all the furniture, machines, and accessories the employee needs to do his or her work is called a/an ___work station___.

10 A system in which two or more text-editing machines can be connected to each other, to a printer, to a storage medium, or to a computer is called a ___multistation system___.

Short Answers

Indicate your answers by filling in the blanks.

1 Name the four basic parts of a word processing system.

a _people_   c _procedures_

b _machines_   d _Environment_

2 Identify the three main types of dictation machines.

a _portable_   b _desk top_   c _centralized_

3 Briefly describe five procedures for controlling a word processing system.

a _logging work_

b _measuring production_

c _setting standards_

d _setting priorities_

e _scheduling turnaround_

4 Name four physical characteristics that are part of a word processing environment.

a _open landscaping_

b _movable partitions_

c _work stations_

d _modular furniture_

5 Define *word processing*.

A system that changes ideas to readable communication by coordinating people, machines, procedures, + environment.

Multiple Choice

Select the letter that best completes the sentence, placing it in the space provided in the right column.

1 The PMPE of a word processing system stands for (A) people, machines, procedures, and environment; (B) people, methods, psychology, and equipment; (C) personnel, materials, procedures, and environment; (D) partitions, materials, principals, and editing; (E) none of these.   _A_

2 Another name for supervisor is (A) manager, (B) coordinator, (C) principal, (D) both A and B, (E) both B and C.   _D_

Name_____ Date_____ Section_____

3   In a WP/AS organization (A) the ratio of secretaries to principals is 2 to 1, (B) WP refers to the correspondence support and AS stands for administrative support, (C) WP refers to word processing and AS stands for auxiliary services, (D) each secretary is supervised by a principal, (E) both A and B.   _____B_____

4   A standalone (A) is generally shared by several companies, (B) is connected to a minicomputer, (C) can do text editing and printing without connecting to a computer, (D) does not usually have a screen, (E) both A and B.   _____C_____

5   Another term for the "brain" of text-editing equipment is (A) storage, (B) logic, (C) intelligence, (D) both A and B, (E) both B and C.   _____E_____

6   The three basic parts of dictation equipment are (A) belt, card, and disk; (B) dictation unit, recorder, and transcribing unit; (C) keyboard, screen, and printer; (D) collator, binder, and punch; (E) none of these.   _____B_____

7   Electronic typewriters are also known as (A) intelligent typewriters, (B) memory typewriters, (C) low-level word processors, (D) both A and B, (E) all of these.   _____E_____

8   Word processing services within a company can be (A) a separate department, (B) a part of the administrative department that serves the entire company, (C) divided into small centers placed throughout the company to serve groups of principals, (D) only correspondence support, (E) all of these.   _____E_____

9   The organization of word processing services within a company (A) is not affected by its importance within the company, (B) is about the same for all companies, (C) is usually centralized to serve the entire company, (D) depends on the size of the firm and the nature of the work, (E) both A and B.   _____D_____

10   In a modern word processing environment, one would generally *not* find (A) open landscaping, (B) a work station for each employee, (C) a separate office with permanent walls and doors for each employee, (D) movable partitions or screens, (E) any of these.   _____C_____

True and False_____
Indicate your answer by placing a T or F in the right-hand column blanks.

1   A model word processing system would have all levels of management, including top management, using word processing services instead of individual traditional secretaries.   _True_

2   The term *word processing* in one company can mean only correspondence services, while in another it can mean processing information by both administrative and correspondence services.   *True*

3   The abbreviations WP/AS and AS/CS refer to two different methods of organizing secretarial services.   *False*

4   When a company has several satellite centers, the word processing layout is said to be decentralized.   *True*

5   With centralized dictation equipment, all the dictation stations (dictation units) are placed in a central area.   *False*

6   A standalone word processor must connect to a computer mainframe (main part of a computer system).   *False*

7   Turnaround goals are based on priorities of documents that have been established by the principals and supervisor.   *True*

8   Allowing each principal or department to choose its preferred letter style is an efficient procedure.   *False*

9   In most companies each type of personnel, including word originators, can improve performance by training or retraining.   *True*

10 Environment has little effect on the functioning of machines and people.   *False*

Instructions for Job 3_____

From the following alphabetic list of words taken from Unit 3, write each term under one of the five appropriate headings given. List the word under the heading with which it is normally associated.

AS
author
chair
combination unit
consultant
correspondence secretary
CRT
CS
cursor
desk top unit
dictation station
electronic typewriter
ergonomics
file management
humidity
labeling documents
lighting
logging

noise control
open landscaping
partitions
pictures and plants
portable
principal
printing device
procedures manual
production standards
recorder
sales representative
scrolling
setting priorities
standalone
standardizing formats
supervisor
temperature
text editor

Name_____ Date_____ Section_____

maintaining quality printout
manager
marketing support representative
measuring production
microphone
modular furniture
multistation system

time shared services
training program
transcribing unit
turnaround goals
visual display terminal
word originator
work station

PEOPLE

AS
author
consultant
correspondence secretary
CS
manager
marketing support manager
principal
sales rep
supervisor
word originator

MACHINES—TYPEWRITING

CRT
cursor
electronic typewriter
multistation system
printing device
scrolling
standalone
text editor
time shared services
visual display terminal

MACHINES—DICTATION

combination unit
desk top unit
dictation station
microphone
portable
recorder
transcribing unit

PROCEDURES

file management
labeling documents
logging
maintaining quality printout
measuring production
procedures manual
production standards

setting priorities   temperature
standardizing formats   workstation
   training program

ENVIRONMENT

chair

ergonomics

humidity

lighting

modular furniture

noise control

open landscaping

partitions

pictures + plants

How Words Originate

How exciting it is to see how words are used to communicate thoughts. The sending of words is vital to your personal and academic life as well as to business, to government, and to the professions.

Information is transmitted orally or in writing. The oral method—for example, by telephone—may be more convenient, faster, less costly, and more personal for many situations, especially for those that require discussion. However, there is usually no record of oral communications.

The written message may be handwritten, typed, printed, or shown as a picture, chart, or graph. Whether the output is a sheet of paper, a microfilm, a visual display on a screen, or a form of electronic mail, it is read rather than heard. The written message provides a permanent record and allows both the sender and the receiver to handle the communication when it is most convenient.

This unit explains the methods of originating thoughts to be processed in readable form. The input methods for originating words are longhand, rough draft, shorthand dictation, machine dictation, work request for a prerecorded document, optical character recognition (OCR), recording from another text editor, and voice recognition.

LONGHAND AND ROUGH DRAFT

Longhand is the slowest and most expensive method of originating words, but it is still the most widely used. Why? Handwriting is easy and convenient. Whether longhand should or should not be used as a form of input depends on the situation and the type of material being processed.

Advantages of Longhand

There are times when longhand has advantages over other methods.

CREATIVE WORK

For composing creative work many authors prefer writing by hand. They need only a pencil or pen and paper. With these simple tools they can compose at a place and time of their choice. There is no need to coordinate machines and people. In composing creative work such as reports or short stories, many writers need to be able to see the words. The copy can be revised by simply crossing out words or lines and adding new text.

COMPLICATED TABULAR MATERIAL

Reports or financial statements that have four or more columns are difficult to dictate and to transcribe. Complicated tables should be given to the transcriber in longhand.

REVISION WORK

In revising a typed document, the author generally uses longhand. Handwriting can fit into any space, and using colored ink makes the changes stand out. Many originators will compose a speech or a report at the typewriter and then revise it using longhand before giving it to the secretary to type in final form.

The term "rough draft" may refer to text that is to be revised or to copy that already has the revisions marked on it. Thus, a rough draft can be either input or output.

ANNOTATING AND OUTLINING

When reading letters or memorandums that have just arrived, a principal or an administrative secretary can save time by annotating. By underscoring key words or sentences to be answered and by writing comments in the margins, one saves having to reread the document. The author in Illustration 4-2 is annotating a document.

It is easy to dictate a reply from an annotated document. The underscored parts are also visual reminders of key points for future reference.

Disadvantages of Longhand

In spite of the ease and convenience of longhand, it has some major disadvantages.

1 Handwriting is slow. At top speed one writes only about 40 wam. When composing in longhand, the rate drops to only 10 or 15 wam.

2 Longhand is often difficult for others to read: the more illegible the script, the slower the transcription rate.

3 Because longhand is slow and often difficult to transcribe, it is a costly method of processing words. Imagine the cost of a 200-word letter handwritten at 10 wam by an executive earning $35,000 a year. Twenty minutes of writing would cost the company $5.60. Add to this the secretary's time for deciphering and typing, and you have a very costly letter.

SHORTHAND DICTATION

Office dictation may occur in several ways; namely, by dictating to one who writes shorthand, by using dictation equipment, or by dictating to a typist who transcribes at a typewriter. Because shorthand and machine dictation are the most common methods of dictation, they will be discussed in further detail.

Illus. 4-1   Longhand makes revision and tabular work

Illus. 4-2   Annotating a letter makes it simple to reply.

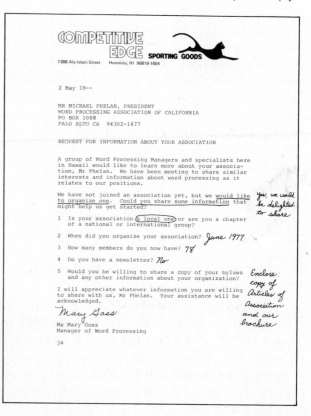

Since the rate of speech is much faster than the ability to write in longhand, shorthand became a needed office skill. Compared to writing longhand at 30 to 40 wam, shorthand can be written easily at 80 to 120 wam.

The main advantage of shorthand has been the increased speed of recording spoken words. However, as word processing concepts have developed, the use of dictation equipment has increased and the importance of shorthand has been challenged. For most letters and memos the shorthand method is slower and more costly than the machine dictation method. Yet shorthand is a valuable skill for many administrative support tasks.

Recommended Uses for Shorthand

Shorthand is recommended for the following administrative support tasks:

WRITING INSTRUCTIONS

As the principal gives instructions about tasks to be done or reviews the daily agenda, the secretary can take notes using shorthand.

RECORDING TELEPHONE MESSAGES

Messages and notes often have to be taken from telephone conversations. Considering the cost of long distance rates as well as the caller's and receiver's time, both time and money can be saved by recording the messages in shorthand.

TAKING MINUTES OF A MEETING

No machine is able to sit in on a meeting; summarize the main points of discussion; and then organize, transcribe, and duplicate the minutes. Only a person with shorthand as a tool can do this task.

ASSISTING AUTHOR IN COMPOSITION

Although shorthand dictation is not recommended for originating most letters and memos, there are situations in which an originator wants the administrative secretary to assist in composing certain messages. As the author dictates, the secretary uses shorthand to take the dictation and to help compose.

Illus. 4-3 Shorthand is vital for taking minutes.

SUMMARIZING INFORMATION FROM OTHER SOURCES

Shorthand is an efficient method for summarizing the key points of an article or report. This is especially true when a photocopying machine is not available.

Why Shorthand is Not Recommended for Most Correspondence

For letters and memos that can be easily dictated on machine, shorthand is inefficient and costly. Here are the reasons:

1 Shorthand dictation can be given only at the office when the secretary is on duty. The secretary is generally not available after working hours, although the author may wish to dictate.

2 Shorthand dictation ties up the time of both the author and the secretary. Also, the secretary's other duties must be neglected during dictation.

3 Because two people are being paid to originate the document, shorthand dictation (averaging 30 wam) is half the rate of machine dictation (averaging 60 wam).

4 Interruptions during dictation slow down the process. At such times the secretary

will review and punctuate notes but then have to sit and wait. Dictation speed is also slowed while the executive recalls his or her thoughts at the time of the interruption.

5 The cost of the dictator's and the secretary's time (taking the shorthand notes and then transcribing them) accounts for about 65 percent of the cost of a letter. Thus, a letter that originates by shorthand dictation costs more than one originated by machine dictation.

6 Unless shorthand notes are transcribed immediately, they often become difficult to read. If the secretary becomes ill, another person could have difficulty reading the notes.

MACHINE DICTATION

For the reasons just given, machine dictation has been encouraged. It is being used more and more by productive and cost-conscious executives.

Two developments increased the use of dictation equipment. The first was the invention of magnetic media, which allowed the recording medium to be erased and reused. Principals were thus able to correct their dictation by backing up the tape and dictating over the error. Also, the mechanical features of the equipment were improved, which made transcription easier.

The second major influence on dictation equipment was the development of word processing concepts. Word processing systems that combined the use of dictation equipment and text editors proved to be the most efficient and least costly means of processing correspondence.

Advantages of Machine Dictation

Originating correspondence by machine dictation has the following advantages:

FLEXIBLE TIME AND PLACE

A dictation machine can be available whenever and wherever the executive wants to dictate. Dictation equipment can be used during or after office hours. It can be used at the office, at home, in a car, or at the airport.

FASTER ORIGINATION AND TRANSCRIPTION

Machine dictation, at an average rate of 60 wam, is twice as fast as shorthand dictation and four to six times faster than longhand. Transcription from machine dictation, at an average rate of 30 to 35 wam, is faster than from shorthand notes, 20 to 25 wam, or from longhand, 10 to 15 wam.

LOWER COST

Since machine dictation offers faster origination and transcription and involves only one person's time during dictation, the cost of producing a letter is less. According to the Dartnell Survey in 1983, the average cost of a letter dictated and transcribed by the use of dictation equipment was $5.70. This represents a 25 percent savings over the shorthand method.

FLEXIBLE TRANSCRIPTION

Machine dictation can be transcribed by any trained word processing specialist; however, shorthand notes and longhand are not easily read by others.

MACHINE CONTROLS

Dictation equipment has many features that make the dictator's, transcriber's, and supervisor's work easy. The basic controls are for speed, tone, and volume. More sophisticated features are explained later in this unit.

Dictation equipment allows the principal and the secretary to use their time more productively. Each can work at his or her own pace with fewer interruptions. Such flexibility gives the secretary more time for other tasks.

Potential Problems with Machine Dictation

Companies that choose to use dictation machines are likely to face certain problems. But these problems can be overcome by proper planning, training, and supervision.

1 Since most originators will not have had training on dictation machines, they must be taught how to dictate and how to use the equipment. Standard procedures for

dictation and transcription must be understood and followed by all users and transcribers.

2 The cost of buying machines, installing them, and training people to use the dictation system is expensive. However, the cost is offset by the time saved during word origination and during transcription. Another way to justify the cost is to compare it with the cost of hiring more personnel to keep up with the paperwork.

3 Selecting the wrong dictation equipment results in added expense and frustration. An example of an unsatisfactory selection is the purchase of equipment that is not compatible with other dictation equipment in the office. If the new equipment records on a different size or type of magnetic medium than the other equipment that will continue to be used, there will have to be two types of transcribing machines. The result is added equipment costs and less flexibility in distributing dictation.

4 Even the best machine needs repair at times. A guarantee of good service from the vendor is important.

5 Many people resist change. Some authors feel that dictating on a machine is impersonal. Others believe that having a personal secretary to take dictation is an indication of their status. Secretaries may fear that machines will replace them.

6 Without proper procedures and supervision, dictation can get lost. Even though the fault is likely to be human error, users can quickly lose confidence in the system and drop back into their former inefficient patterns.

By being aware of possible problems, word processing supporters can take steps to avoid or eliminate hazards and weaknesses that hinder the adoption of a word processing system.

Categories of Dictation Equipment

Dictation machines come in many brands, shapes, and sizes. Common features allow the user to dictate, review what has been dictated, make corrections, mark the end of dictation, and give the transcriber instructions.

Dictation equipment is classified by its use and location. The three main groups are portable units, desk top units, and centralized systems.

PORTABLE UNITS

Portable units are very useful for people who travel frequently. They may be used in a car, in a hotel, or in an airport. Portable units are hand sized, battery powered, and designed to be placed in a pocket or briefcase. Should the executive be on a long trip, the recorded tape can be mailed to the office for immediate transcription.

The portable unit has a combined microphone and recorder that is easy to operate with one hand. Magnetic recording media used by portables include standard cassettes, minicassettes, and microcassettes. Most companies purchase portables that use the same recording media as their desk top or centralized systems.

Illus. 4-4 Portable Dictation Unit

DESK TOP UNITS

Desk top units appeal to companies that do not have enough dictation volume to justify the cost of a large centralized system. In companies that do have centralized dictation systems, those authors whose dictation volume is high may be asked to use desk top machines so that they do not tie up the centralized lines. Some desk top units are small enough to be stored in desk drawers or under the telephone. With built-in speakers for group listening and very sensitive microphones, they work well for recording meetings.

Illus. 4-5   Desk top units are good for low-volume users.

The latest models have some interesting capabilities. Some have a one-line visual display. This provides information regarding the number of instructions and the length of each document. Some models allow users to record telephone messages. The dictating machine becomes a telephone answering device whenever the user chooses. Callers leave messages on the recording medium, and the receiver can listen to the recording upon returning to the office.

Desk top machines are available in three units—a unit for dictating only, a unit for transcribing only, or a combination unit for both dictating and transcribing.

Desk top units use the same kinds of recording media as portables. The transcribing unit will accept tape that is dictated on a portable unit if that tape is the same size or if an **adaptor** (a device that makes media compatible) is used.

CENTRALIZED DICTATION SYSTEMS

With centralized dictation systems, the recorders are located in a central place—the transcription area. Although all dictation is recorded in the central transcription area, it originates at many different locations throughout the building. Dictation may also originate from telephones outside the building. Centralized systems are generally found in large organizations. A centralized system is the most cost-effective way to serve a large number of dictators who have a light or medium volume of dictation.

Basic Parts of a Centralized System. A centralized dictation system is easy to understand when you look at the individual parts.

Dictation Station (also called Dictation Unit or Dictation Terminal). This is the unit into which the author dictates. It may be a hand microphone or a telephone receiver. Because the dictation stations and the recorders are in separate locations, dictation is said to be remote.

Recorder. This is the unit that records the dictation onto magnetic tape. Generally there are many more dictation stations than recorders, since it is not likely that all executives will be dictating at the same time. The number of principals who can dictate at one time depends on the number of recorders available.

Transcription Machine (or Transcribing Unit). This is the unit that plays back the recorded text so that it can be transcribed. It is equipped with a headset for listening and a pedal for controlling the tape.

Supervisor's Console (or Supervisory Monitor). This is an optional unit that helps the supervisor manage the work flow. Documents to be transcribed can be given to the word processing operator who can provide the fastest turnaround time. The supervisor's console provides information such as date and time transcription begins, author of document, length of document, the transcriber, the time the job was completed, and turnaround time.

Illus. 4-6 A Centralized Dictation System

Dictation Station

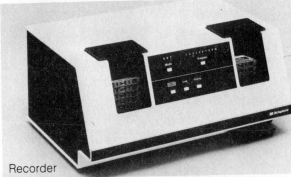

Recorder

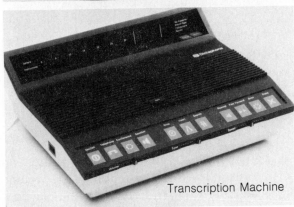

Transcription Machine

Supervisor's Console

The console also prepares a record of the dictation transcribed for management reports. These productivity reports can be used by supervisors and managers to evaluate operator and machine performance.

Two Types of Media: Discrete Media and Endless Loop. Centralized dictation systems record on either discrete media (individual cassette tapes) or on endless loop (a continuous loop). The major difference is how recorded dictation is given to the secretaries for transcription. With *discrete media* systems, the supervisor physically removes the cassette tapes and gives them to the transcribers. *Endless loop* systems, however, eliminate the handling of tape. A long and continuous loop of tape is permanently housed in a tank (the recorder). The tape passes from the part that records to the part that plays back. Both the dictator and the transcriber can use their units at the same time, but no one handles the tape. This prevents lost or misplaced dictation—a problem that can happen with the handling of cassettes.

Although endless loop systems offer the advantage of not having to handle the tape, they are not flexible. Let's assume a tape has 90 minutes of dictation. Only one person can transcribe at a time, and the documents have to be transcribed in the order that they were dictated. With discrete media systems, the 90 minutes of dictation can be recorded on four separate cassette tapes. These four tapes can be given to four transcribers. This helps to divide the work load and reduces turnaround time, which is important when priority work is involved.

Wire Connections of Centralized Systems. The dictation stations, recorders, and the supervisor's console are all connected by wires. Thus, they are said to be *on-line*. The wiring of the system may be done in one of two ways:

Private Wire. This is a separate system of wires within the company. Its only purpose is to connect the parts of the dictation system. Although some dictation stations look like telephones, they are privately wired and not linked to telephone lines. A privately wired system is expensive to install and is limited to accepting dictation from within the building. However, there is no monthly expense for leasing telephone lines, and heavy dictation does not tie up the telephone lines.

Illus. 4-7   Inside the recorder, the endless loop travels between the recording and transcribing heads.

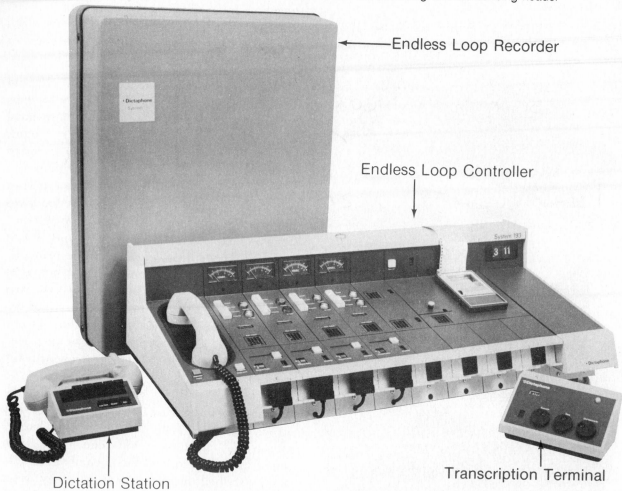

Endless Loop Recorder

Endless Loop Controller

Dictation Station

Transcription Terminal

Telephone Lines. A system that is wired through the telephone lines allows any telephone to be used as a dictation station. Dictation can be phoned in from outside the building as well as from within. By dialing the assigned number, the executive gains access to a recorder. By pressing certain buttons on the telephone the executive can start and stop the recorder, review the dictation, make corrections, or give instructions. Although the installation cost is less than for a privately wired system, there is the monthly cost for leasing the telephone lines.

To offer the advantages of each type of wire connection, some companies choose to have at least one or possibly all recorders wired both ways. Those who dictate within the building use their privately wired dictation stations without tying up the telephone lines. Principals who are away from the office can dictate directly into the center by telephone.

Features Offered on Dictation Equipment

The new models of dictation equipment are easy to use. The standard controls are volume, speed, tone, rewind, fast forward, and playback. The following features are also offered on many machines:

1 Voice operated relay causes the tape to stop when the author stops talking and to start up again when speech begins.

2 Speech compression removes pauses.

3 *Electronic queue tones* and visual display show where a document begins and ends and where special instructions are given by the author. Older models of equipment give this information on paper index slips.

4 Words can be added in the middle of a sentence without the dictator having to erase any words he or she wants to keep.

Magnetic tape is low in cost, has high storage capacity, and can easily be erased and used again. Cassettes are available in standard, mini, or micro sizes. The size and capacity of each is shown in Illustration 4-10.

Illus. 4-8   Index slips indicate length and instructions.

Illus. 4-10   Standard Cassette: 30-45 Minutes Per Side; Minicassette: 15-30 Minutes Per Side; Microcassette: 30-60 Minutes Per Side

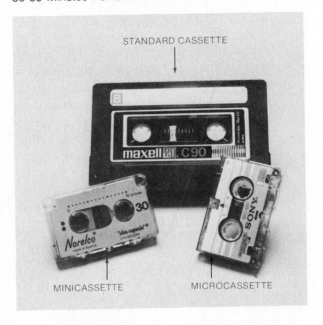

STANDARD CASSETTE

MINICASSETTE   MICROCASSETTE

Illus. 4-9   Visual display shows length and instructions.

WORK REQUEST FOR PRERECORDED DOCUMENT

5   Originators have control over where documents are recorded (for example, a particular recorder). This allows dictation to be distributed by priority, by type of document, or to a specific transcriber.

6   Dictation and transcription can take place at the same time.

7   Telephone-answering options allow the public and co-workers to leave messages and the principals to get the information from remote stations. Individually assigned codes prevent unauthorized people from being able to acquire this information.

Dictation Media

Most dictation equipment records on some type of magnetic tape. (Earlier models recorded on magnetic belts and disks.) You are probably familiar with the magnetic tape that is used in cassette tape recorders and tape decks of stereos.

Another way of originating work is to give a *work request* to the word processing center. It describes the work an originator wants done. A work request is turned in for a *prerecorded document*, which is a document that has already been recorded on a magnetic medium. A form letter is an example of a prerecorded document. A *form letter* is composed for one purpose but is sent to many people. It can be originated either by dictation or by rough draft copy. In either case the author must signal where the variables (data such as names or amounts that change from one letter to another) will be added during playback on the word processor.

Standard documents are recorded on the magnetic medium of the word processor. Once recorded they can be played back whenever needed. Labels are assigned to documents so that they can be referred to easily and quickly located. To initiate a form letter, the originator merely needs to send the word processing operator a work request giving the label of the prerecorded document and the variable data, as shown in Illustration 4-11a. In some companies the work requests are dictated rather than given on a special form. An example of a form letter is shown in Figure 4-11b.

OPTICAL CHARACTER RECOGNITION

Optical character recognition (OCR) units can speed up the input step by reading material prepared on a typewriter and transferring it to the recording medium of a word processor. No rekeying of text is necessary. Once the copy is on the recording medium (for example, floppy disk), it can be edited and printed.

How OCR Aids Input

To better understand the interfacing of OCR with word processing equipment, let's follow a document through the OCR cycle.

1 The principal originates the document.

2 The secretary types a copy of the document at rough draft speed on a regular typewriter.

3 The typed document is given to the principal for approval. Changes are marked with a red pen.

4 The rough draft is then read by the OCR reader. During the scanning process the typewritten portion of the rough draft is duplicated onto a diskette. The OCR cannot read any changes that the principal made with the red pen.

Illus. 4-11b Form Letter

Letter AIC-04

Letter Address

AUTOMOBILE INSURANCE CLAIM # *Claim Number*

On *Date of Loss* your vehicle was involved in an accident with our insured, *Name of Our Insured* Our investigation reveals that your negligence was the cause of the accident. Therefore, *Name of Addressee*, you will need to provide the financial settlement.

I have enclosed a copy of the police report, a copy of the repair estimate, and a copy of the draft covering damages to the insured vehicle less the deductible.

Since you do not carry any liability insurance, we must ask that you sign the enclosed Promissory Note and return it to us by *Due Date*, with your first monthly payment. Make the check payable to American National Insurance Company.

Please reply soon, *Name of Addressee*

Name of Author
Title of Author

xx

Enclosures

Illus. 4-11a Work Request

WORK REQUEST FOR FORM LETTER

AIC-04

Variables to be Inserted

Letter Address: Mr R T Long
2609 Birthle Road
Albany NY 12207-3112

Name of Addressee: Mr Long

Claim Number: 25-184

Date of Loss: April 28

Name of Our Insured: Sara Schulte

Check Amount $ ____ Deductible Amount $ ____

Due Date: June 7

Name of Author: Mark Kastner

Title of Author: Subrogation Specialist

Illus. 4-12 The OCR Process

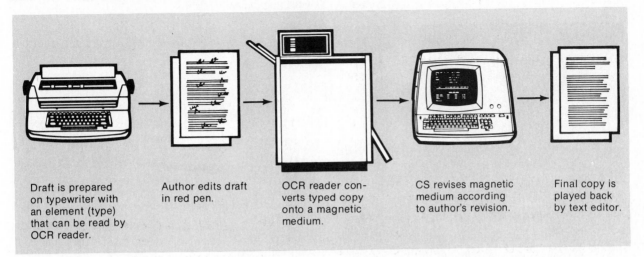

Draft is prepared on typewriter with an element (type) that can be read by OCR reader.

Author edits draft in red pen.

OCR reader converts typed copy onto a magnetic medium.

CS revises magnetic medium according to author's revision.

Final copy is played back by text editor.

5 The word processing operator inserts the diskette in the text editor and brings a page to the screen. The operator makes the changes shown in red ink.

6 The corrected document is ready to be printed.

Many people believe that OCR equipment makes better use of both equipment and employee skills. Secretaries with entry level skills can key in original copy on typewriters rather than use the more expensive word processors. This reduces equipment and training costs. Word processors can be used for the work they are designed to do best—revision work.

OCR manufacturers are developing machines that will be able to read anything on paper—typewritten or printed text, computer printout data, charts, or drawings. The information converted to recording media will then be input to word processors, computers, phototypesetters, and facsimile units. Other new trends will be in the design of scanners to read only areas highlighted by a special marker. This will allow only certain portions of text to be selected. The ability to read a variety of paper sizes, colors, and thicknesses is also being developed.

Problems of OCR

There are several problems that have prevented total acceptance of OCR in the office. OCRs are not 100 percent accurate; they make about one error (misreading) in every four pages.

OCRs do not accurately process paper that is creased and worn. Although OCRs may be able to handle most common type styles, having several type styles on one page can cause problems. OCR machines are costly. Some firms prefer to use this money to buy additional word processors.

RECORDING FROM ANOTHER WORD PROCESSOR

As described in Unit 2, word processors with the communicating feature are able to exchange information. As one word processor receives a recording from another word processor, this recording becomes a form of input. Information that is exchanged or communicated does not, of course, need to be rekeyed.

VOICE RECOGNITION

The terms *voice recognition, speech recognition,* and *voice input system* (VIS) relate to the technology that converts the spoken word to the typed or printed page. Once perfected so that it can be used for letters, memos, and reports, it will have a significant impact on the office.

How does it work? When an author speaks to a computer, the voice goes through a special type of processor that converts the speech to digital impulses or signals. The digital signals are then matched to the sound patterns stored in the computer's memory. When they match, the system recognizes the speech pattern and is able to print the word on paper.

Illus. 4-13   This voice input terminal is ideal for use in activities where the hands are busy. By speaking into the unit headphone, the sound becomes part of this system's 120-word vocabulary.

Some devices are able to recognize a limited number of single words such as *yes*, *no*, and *zero* through *nine*. This type of speech recognition equipment is used in activities where the speaker's hands are busy, as in stock inventory and placing orders.

The greatest challenge is continuous speech recognition. This means the machine understands the continuous flow of speech without pauses between words. This type of input is much more complicated to process than single words. With various users speaking into the system, voices can vary by pitch, dialect, loudness, and emphasis of words. As the size of the vocabulary increases, there is an increased chance for error. Words that sound alike but mean different things, such as *know* and *no* are a problem.

As voice technology becomes more sophisticated and lower in price, it will offer many advantages for word processing. Originators who cannot type, who are handicapped, whose eyes are busy, or whose hands are operating another piece of equipment will all benefit. Both time and human effort to produce a document will be reduced. However, these systems will not put secretaries out of work, because the output is only about 95 percent accurate. Secretaries are needed to make corrections and to see that final documents are mailable.

The 1980s will bring exciting advancements in voice recognition systems.

SUMMARY

You have studied the methods, proper uses, and problems of various means of originating words. The method that is chosen for an office will depend on the amount of input, the type of material being processed, the desired speed of turnaround, the organization of secretarial services, and the amount of money for equipment. As you have learned, the input method can affect the quality of output; so its control is important.

With this knowledge, you may be able to influence management to improve its methods of originating words. As an office employee, you will certainly have a better understanding of the input phase of the word processing cycle.

Review Exercises

Completion
Complete the following sentences by filling in the blanks.

1   For taking the minutes of a meeting, the recommended form of input is _short hand_

2   The recommended method for originating most correspondence is _machine dictation_.

3   The category of dictation equipment that is most cost effective in serving a large number of principals who have a light or medium volume of dictation is _centralized dictation systems_

4   Dictation media that have to be physically removed from the recorders and placed in the transcribing units are called _discrete_ media.

5   The wire connections of centralized systems connect the dictation stations to the _recorders_ and to the supervisor's console.

6   To have a prerecorded form letter sent to three people, the principal either dictates or fills out a/an _work request_ to give the label of the form letter and to supply the proper variables.

7   Units that can speed up input by reading material from standard typewriters onto magnetic storage media are called _scanners_

8   The slowest but most frequently used method of originating words is _longhand_.

9   Relating to the technology that converts the spoken word into the typewritten or printed page, the abbreviation *VIS* stands for _voice input system_

10 The method of input has a direct relationship to the accuracy and speed of _transcription_, which together deter-mine the cost of producing a document.

Short Answers

Indicate your answers by filling in the blanks.

1 Name three appropriate uses for longhand as a method of input.

a Creative work

b Four or more tabular columns

c Revision work

2 Name three recommended uses for shorthand as a form of input.

a Writing instructions from the principal

b Recording telephone messages

c Taking minutes of a meeting

3 Give five advantages that machine dictation has over either longhand or shorthand dictation.

a Dictation can take place any time or place.

b Word origination + transcription is faster.

c Only one person is involved at time of dictation.

d Cost is less.

e Transcription can be done by any trained transcriber.

4 Name the three basic parts of a centralized dictation system.

a Dictation Station

b Recorder

c Transcribing unit

d Supervisor's console/monitor (optional)

5 Name the two ways that centralized dictation systems are wired.

a Private wire

b telephone lines

6 Explain three reasons why a word processing system might choose OCR as an input device.

a Input time is reduced.

b Less expensive equipment is needed

c Word processors can do their best job of revision work.

Name_____Date_____Section_____

Multiple Choice_____

Select the letter that best completes the sentence, placing it in the space provided in the right column.

1   The slowest method of word origination is (A) longhand, (B) machine dictation, (C) optical character recognition, (D) voice recognition, (E) work request for prerecorded media to be processed.

A

2   For tabular material of five columns the best method of input is (A) voice recognition, (B) shorthand dictation, (C) longhand, (D) machine dictation, (E) none of these.

A̶ C

3   The fastest transcription rate can be achieved from (A) shorthand dictation, (B) machine dictation, (C) longhand, (D) hand printed, (E) both C and D.

B

4   Shorthand dictation (A) averages about 30 wam, (B) ties up the time of two people, (C) cannot easily be transcribed by anyone except the writer, (D) can be given only when the secretary is on duty, (E) can be all these.

E

5   With dictation machines (A) there is no possibility of their not working properly, (B) there is little expense involved, (C) communication between author and transcriber is personal, (D) equipment should be compatible, (E) none of these is correct.

D

6   Magnetic recording media (A) enables the author to correct dictation, (B) can be erased and reused, (C) does not have good tone quality, (D) both A and B, (E) both B and C.

D

7   Desk top dictation equipment (A) should be considered for high volume in-office dictation, (B) does not use the same type of recording media that portables use, (C) cannot accept media that was dictated on a portable unit, (D) can fit within one's pocket or briefcase, (E) is not described by any of these.

A

8   The problem with an endless loop system is (A) that the tape does not hold enough dictation time, (B) that dictation which is recorded on one tape cannot be given to several transcribers, (C) that the tape can easily be misplaced, (D) both A and B, (E) both B and C.

A̶ B

9   Which of the following is *not* a potential problem of OCR scanners for word processing? (A) high cost of reader scanners, (B) creased or worn paper, (C) high training costs, (D) several type styles on one page, (E) less than 100% accuracy in scanning.

C

10   Continuous speech recognition (A) has no long pauses between words, (B) is more complicated to process than single words, (C) cannot distinguish between words like *here* and *hear*, (D) is being developed for word processing applications, (E) is described by all these.

E

True or False

Indicate your answer by placing a T or F in the right-hand column blanks.

1 One advantage of written communication is that there is a permanent record of the conversation. **T**

2 One of the advantages of longhand and shorthand is that almost anyone can read another's writing with ease. **F**

3 Shorthand skill is more likely to be used for administrative support tasks than for correspondence support tasks. **T**

4 A message received from another word processor by telephone or by satellite is *not* a type of input. **F**

5 Desk top dictation units can be used to record telephone messages. **T**

6 The number of authors who can dictate at one time on central dictation systems depends on the number of recorders. **T**

7 A centralized dictation system that is privately wired allows the authors to dictate either within the office or outside the office building. **F**

8 Electronic queue tones and index slips serve the same purpose. **T**

9 OCR scanners can read the red pen marks that were used to edit the rough draft. **F**

10 The terms *voice recognition, speech recognition,* and *voice input system* relate to different and unrelated technologies. **F**

Instructions for Job 4

MATERIALS NEEDED
Typewriter
8½" x 11" plain white paper
Correction device (eraser, liquid cover-up, paper cover-up)
Pen
Carbon paper
Onionskin

This job requires that students work in pairs. If there is an uneven number of students in the class, the teacher may serve as one of the partners. As a team, one person acts as the author and the other person as the correspondence secretary (transcriber). After completing the first letter, the individuals will reverse roles.

Instructions for the Author (Word Originator)

1 Review the "Procedures for Dictation."

2 Position yourself behind your secretary (your partner) who is seated at a typewriter. Throughout the dictation process you

Name_____ Date_____ Section_____

cannot talk with or make any motions to the secretary, because you are simulating an executive who dictates using machine dictation equipment.

3 Dictate the letter addressed to Miss Penney on page 77. Note that different type styles are used to distinguish between the instructions of the dictator and the actual letter.

4 Once the rough draft has been typed and corrected by your secretary, proofread it carefully and mark any additional corrections to be made.

5 Return the rough draft to your secretary so that the final copy (with one carbon copy) can be typed.

6 Trade roles with your secretary and repeat the exercise.

7 Then dictate a personal thank you letter to a friend, a relative, or a teacher for a book or magazine you have received. Keep the letter short.

8 Reverse roles with your partner and perform the role of secretary.

Procedures for Dictation

1 Address the transcriber by his or her first name.
2 Identify yourself. Give your name and the name of your class.
3 Specify the type of document you are dictating: personal business letter, business letter, or memorandum.
4 Indicate whether you want rough draft or final copy form.
5 Request the desired number of copies beyond the file copy.
6 During dictation of the document, do the following:

a Indicate commas by pausing, periods by dropping your voice and pausing, and question marks by lifting your voice and pausing. Do not dictate the words *comma, period,* and *question mark.*

b Dictate the word *paragraph* between paragraphs.

c Dictate these punctuation marks: parenthesis, underscoring, semicolon, colon, hyphen, dash, quote, exclamation point.

d Specify capitalization by saying "All caps" or "Initial cap" before the word/phrases to be capitalized.

e Spell out proper names and unusual terms using the phonetic alphabet for any letters that sound similar to another—*p, b,* and *v; m* and *n;* for example, *P* as in *Peter, B* as in *Bertha,* and the like.

A	Alice	G	George	L	Lewis	Q	Quaker	V	Victor
B	Bertha	H	Henry	M	Mary	R	Robert	W	William
C	Charles	I	Ida	N	Nellie	S	Samuel	X	X-Ray
D	David	J	James	O	Oliver	T	Thomas	Y	Young
E	Edward	K	Kate	P	Peter	U	Utah	Z	Zebra
F	Frank								

7   For the closing lines, do the following:
　　a   Give your name.
　　　1)   Spell it.
　　　2)   Include your personal title (Mr., Miss, Mrs., or Ms.) if you:
　　　　　a)   are a woman.
　　　　　b)   have an uncommon or foreign name (Ho Sun).
　　　　　c)   have a name that could be male or female (Chris).
　　　　　d)   use only initials (H. P.).

　　b   Give your address.
　　　1)   Spell unusual names.
　　　2)   Include ZIP Code.

8   Specify *End of Dictation* or *End of Letter*.

9   Say *thank you* to the secretary.

Instructions for the Secretary/Transcriber

1   Review "Procedures for Transcription" below.

2   Be seated by a typewriter. Prepare to transcribe the author's dictation. While you cannot ask any questions (such as the spelling of a word or a request for punctuation), you are allowed to regulate the speed of dictation by saying "Please wait" or "Go ahead" or "Please repeat the last phrase."

Procedures for Transcription

1   Use the block letter style with open punctuation.

2   Estimate the margin sets so that there are about 1½ inches on each side.

3   Type the current date on Line 12. Correct errors.

4   For rough drafts use plain white paper. For the final copy of business letters and memorandums, use letterhead or interoffice paper; for personal business letters, use plain white paper or the executive's personal stationery.

5   Use a dictionary or spelling book to check any questionable spelling. Correct spelling should be checked while letter is being typed so that it does not have to be retyped.

6   For a personal business letter, the address of the author/dictator goes immediately below the name in the closing lines. This gives the individual who receives the letter a complete letter address.

7   Closing instructions: Use your reference initials and the name of your class (for example, *mjc/Office Procedures*).

8   Proofread the document and correct any errors overlooked.

9   Give the letter to the author.

10   When you receive the author's edited rough draft, type the final copy (including a carbon copy for the office files).

Name_____ Date_____ Section_____

(Name of Secretary), this is (Your Name) from (Name of Class) class.

I am dictating a personal business letter to be typed in rough draft form. After I have checked the rough draft, please type the final copy.

This letter is to:

Miss Angie *(spelled A, N as in Nellie, G, I, E)* Penney *(spelled P as in Peter–E–N as in Nellie–N as in Nellie–E–Y)*
Gulf Bicycle Shop
4236 Thomas Drive
Panama City *(two words)* Florida 32407–2107

Dear Miss Penney

When I visited your shop on Saturday, I overheard one of your customers talking about a bicycle tour. If I heard correctly, it was called *(initial cap)* Gulf Coast Tour. Will you please answer the following questions *(colon)*: *Paragraph*

(Secretary, please number these questions and double-space between each.)

1 What is the length of the route? *Paragraph*

2 Has a difficulty rating been given to the course? *Paragraph*

3 Has the tour been prepared according to the standard *(all caps)* TE *(resume lowercase)* format? *Paragraph*

Any information you can send me about the *(initial cap)* Gulf Coast Tour will be appreciated. If you know of any other tours, Miss Penney, please let me know about them.

Sincerely

(Your Name)
(Street Address)
(City, State, and ZIP)

End of Letter

Thank you (Name of Secretary)!

UNIT FIVE.

OUTPUT—How Text Is Recorded and Printed

The output step of the word processing cycle is made possible by the capture of keystrokes onto magnetic media. Once recorded, text can be revised and then played back in final form by a typewriting device. Unit 5 discusses the various types of word processing equipment—from the simple electric typewriter to the sophisticated word processors that interface with computers.

DEVELOPMENT OF TYPEWRITING EQUIPMENT

Of all machines in the history of office development, the typewriter holds the most distinguished position. Typewriting equipment has expanded office career opportunities, has streamlined the steps in office work, and has given a facelift to the office environment.

The first typewriting device was the manual typewriter that typed capital letters only. This "type-writer," invented by Christopher Sholes, was introduced in 1874 as the Remington Model 1. Soon other brands appeared on the market—Royal, L.C. Smith, and Underwood—and features improved. Manual typewriters dominated the office scene until the 1960s.

The first electric typewriter that was suitable for office use was introduced by IBM in 1934. In 1961 a new design, the IBM Selectric typewriter with a ball-shaped typing element, appeared on the market. Replacing the movable carriage, the element moved along the platen as keystrokes were made. This element could be easily changed to vary type styles and sizes. Other helpful features included the express backspace and the correction tape device. By 1970 most of the typewriters sold were electrics. The IBM Selectric was the basis for the development of text editors.

By 1980, interest had turned to word processing equipment. The interest had been

Illus. 5-1 Moving From the Antiquated to Today's Technology

79

ignited 16 years earlier by the historic MT/ST (Magnetic Tape Selectric Typewriter) that was introduced by IBM in 1964. For the first time captured keystrokes could be revised either during or after the text was recorded. Unlike paper tape, magnetic media was unique in that it could be corrected and could be reused. As Unit 1 explained, the birth of text-editing equipment resulted in a new arrangement of secretarial services.

The previous paragraphs have helped you quickly review over 100 years of progress in typewriting equipment. Now you will concentrate on the types of word processing machines that are used today.

WORD PROCESSING MACHINES

The brands, models, and features of word processing machines are too many and different to properly categorize. As technology advances, many hybrids develop and the problem becomes more difficult. This unit narrows the scramble of options to the following: electric typewriters, electronic typewriters, standalone word processors, multistation systems, computers with word processing software, and time shared services.

Electric Typewriter

Although not a text-editing machine, the electric typewriter still meets the needs of many office applications. For preparing short documents (a page or less) that are typed only once and that are not revised, the electric typewriter is used. The term *first-time/final copy* is sometimes used to describe this type of document. Examples would be a work request form, a check for travel reimbursement, a telephone message, and file labels. Most uses for electrics fall within the administrative support functions.

Some models have a type bar with keys that strike the paper; however, most electric typewriters have a single, ball-shaped element.

Electronic Typewriters

Electronic typewriters go beyond the capabilities of electric typewriters but are not as sophisticated as standalone word processors. Approximately 85 percent of the mechanical

(moving) parts have been replaced with electronic parts in an electronic typewriter. This is made possible by small electronic computer chips called *microprocessors* located within the typewriter. With fewer mechanical parts, electronic typewriters have fewer repair problems.

Illus. 5-2a   Electronic typewriters automate manual tasks.

Illus. 5-2b   With removable storage and a display screen, this same electronic typewriter is even more powerful.

FEATURES

Electronic typewriters automate several of the manual functions of the electric typewriter. Examples include the following:

Automatic Carrier Return. The carrier automatically returns within a certain number of spaces from the right margin.

Automatic Error Correction. Individual characters can be covered up or lifted off. Up to a full line of text can be erased with one keystroke.

Automatic Underscore. Words or phrases can be automatically underscored as they are typed.

Centering. Words or phrases can be automatically centered as they are keyed in.

Character Pitch/Type Style. Various type styles and sizes (10-, 12-, and 15-pitch, or proportional spacing) are available by changing the printing device.

Decimal Alignment. Columns of numbers can be automatically centered at the decimal point.

Format Storage. The most frequently used *formats* (line length, line spacing, and tab settings) can be stored for later use.

Line Memory. At least one line (the last line typed) is stored so that errors made within that line can be corrected before the line is printed on paper.

Phrase Storage. The most frequently used words or phrases (such as the dateline, standard closings, and long technical words) can be stored and played back without retyping.

All electronic typewriters have an internal memory or place where text is stored. Those with the most memory can store several pages. When the memory is full, it must be printed out or erased in order to receive new text. Some models, however, also have removable storage which increases their storage capability.

Many models have a one-line display. The printing device is usually a *daisy wheel* with output at the rate of 20 to 30 cps (characters per second)—about 360 wam. However, some models have a single element that prints at 15 cps, which is about 180 wam.

The options available on electronic typewriters are continually increasing. Removable storage, CRT display screens, more memory, and the ability to communicate are becoming common on many models.

APPLICATIONS

Electronic typewriters are designed for the secretary who handles short documents (under ten pages), memorandums, repetitive letters, or tables with light revisions.

Electronic typewriters are enough like electric typewriters that people do not feel frightened by them. Yet they increase the secretary's productivity, are affordable for all offices, and do not require the reorganization of secretarial duties. Electronic typewriters are replacing electric machines. Some experts believe that the use of electronic typewriters will decrease the resistance to more sophisticated equipment. Others believe their use will delay the change to real word processing concepts.

ADVANTAGES AND LIMITATIONS

Some electronic typewriters can be upgraded to increase the amount of memory and to add text-editing features. The machine then becomes a high-level model. Most electronic typewriters, however, have limited editing/revision capability. Except for the high-level models, the storage media cannot be removed and the display screen is limited to one line.

Standalone Word Processors

As the name implies, standalone word processors can "stand alone" without the aid of another machine (like a computer). The basic parts include a keyboard, a screen, a storage device, the logic/intelligence, and a printer. These parts may be separate but connecting, or some can be combined into one piece of equipment. For example, some models combine the keyboard and the screen, the screen and the storage device, or the storage and logic within a console.

THE SCREEN

The early standalone word processors did not have a screen; they were called blind standalones. Now, nearly all standalones have a screen. Systems with a visual (video) display screen allow the operator to see the text as it is being keyboarded. As text is keyed and appears on the screen, a cursor (indicator or pointer) marks the place of action. The operator moves the cursor to whatever point in the document that copy is to be added, omitted, or moved.

Illus. 5-3   The IBM Displaywriter has a dual disk drive.

The operator can key in new text while the previous page is being played out by the printer. Although the printer and the keyboard can operate independently of each other, they are both connected to and directed by the logic (brain) of the system. On the other hand, electronic typewriters without a screen or with only a one-line display (*linear display unit*) use the same device for typing as for printing. The operator has to wait for a page to be printed before beginning a new page of text.

Visual displays vary in the amount of text that can be seen on the screen at one time. Some are partial displays (as little as 6 lines) and others are full-page displays (54 lines). However, the most common display is about a half page.

Today's screens are designed for easier viewing. Many of them have an antiglare surface as well as brightness and intensity control. Some screens can be turned and/or tilted to avoid a glare from windows and overhead lighting.

THE KEYBOARD

The keyboard of a word processor looks much like that of an electric typewriter but with additional keys. Some keys are used to direct the movement of the cursor, and the others control the functions of the system—such as deleting or moving copy. Movable keyboards can be placed in a location that is most comfortable to the operator.

RECORDING/STORAGE DEVICE

Most standalone word processors have some internal memory that is used for *buffer* storage (temporary storage). As copy is typed on the keyboard, text appears on the screen and the computer (logic) of the system sends the information to temporary storage. However, if the word processor were shut off, information in the temporary memory would be lost. In order to save the information, it must be transferred to a magnetic medium for storage.

The storage medium used most often by standalones is a floppy diskette. It is covered with a magnetic coating that allows it to store information. Whether it is a standard diskette (about the size of a 45 rpm record) or a smaller minidiskette, it is kept in a square envelope that protects the surface of the diskette. The entire envelope is then inserted into a *disk drive*. The disk drive has a head similar to that on a tape recorder that reads the information on the diskette.

Because diskettes can be removed and stored away from the machine, they are considered to be *off-line storage*. The amount of storage is limited only by the number of diskettes.

PRINTING DEVICE

The printing device of a standalone word processor is a separate piece of equipment. Two or three word processors can connect to one printer and share its use. Or several word processors can each be connected to two different types of printers; for example, a slower, letter quality printer and a faster, draft quality printer. A more complete discussion of printing devices appears later in this unit.

INTELLIGENCE/LOGIC

What makes word processors work? The combined efforts of powerful microprocessors and software control the operating functions of a standalone system. A microprocessor is a small chip which gives computing power. (The term microprocessor is also used to mean small computer.) *Software programs* are instructions for special applications that have been placed on a floppy disk. When this disk is inserted into the disk drive, the functions of the word processor are expanded. Machines which are directed by software (and most are) are said to be *software programmable*. By inserting software to do math functions, standalone systems can then handle data processing applications.

APPLICATIONS AND FEATURES

Standalone word processors with a visual display are most effectively used to prepare documents of many pages that need heavy revision. Examples include legal documents, manuscripts, and reference manuals. Text can be scrolled page by page on the screen to quickly view or revise any part of the text. Entire paragraphs or pages can be added, omitted, or moved. Even columns of words or numbers can be moved. The system can search for a word or phrase and then replace it with another. The format can be changed within one document. Text that has already been recorded can be adjusted to fit the dimensions of a new format.

Some display screens are divided either vertically or horizontally so that an operator can work on two pages at once. Pages can be automatically numbered. As text is added or removed, the system will automatically adjust the text to full pages and renumber all pages (called *repagination*). Any heading or footing to be put on each page of a document (called *headers* and *footers*) can be done automatically. Several format settings can be stored and used within a document. Some systems have spelling dictionaries that aid in proofreading. However, incorrect word usage (such as "their" for "there") goes unnoticed by the system.

Software expands the capability of these systems. Figuring mathematical calculations, sorting lists either alphabetically or numerically, filling in forms, and communicating with similar machines or computers are examples of expanded capabilities. However, the communications feature, which allows machines to exchange information, is a standard feature on some machines.

RANGE OF CAPABILITY

Standalone word processors are often grouped into low- and high-level models. Low-level models usually have only one disk drive

Illus. 5-4   The Wangwriter has a single disk drive.

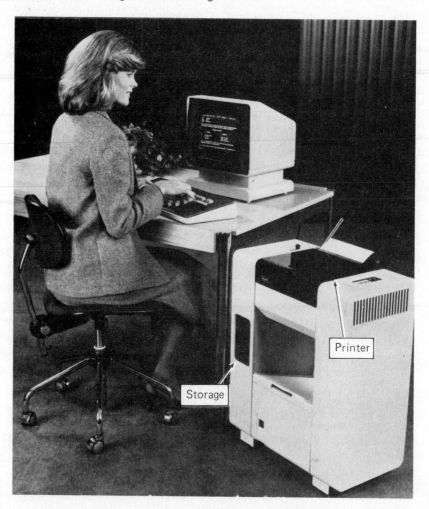

which houses either one floppy diskette or one or two minidiskettes. These low-level machines are sometimes called "writers," for many vendors have added that word to the model name. Examples include: Magna-Writer (A. B. Dick), OFISwriter (Burroughs), Infowriter (Honeywell), Omniwriter (Royal), and Wangwriter (Wang).

The more sophisticated, high-level standalones can offer additional features because of expanded storage. The storage capacity might be increased by double density (twice as many characters as a standard diskette), double-sided (can record on both sides) floppy diskettes, as well as *hard disks*. Larger internal (buffer) memory makes it possible to store some text within the memory rather than have to record and recall it from floppy disks.

Standalone systems can also become more powerful by interfacing them with other word

processors or information processing systems. This is made possible by the communications feature which allows one machine to "talk" or communicate with another machine.

Even though standalone systems vary in the size of their displays, amount of storage, and software capability, they all can be used alone. Each standalone word processor has its own logic (brain or intelligence) without being connected to another device.

Multistation Systems

As you know, homes and offices can have two or more telephones connected to one line. Each phone shares the communication capability of one line and one number. The cost per phone set is less than if each had its own line and number. Yet, if the line malfunctions, no phone can be used. To have your own telephone line and number gives you more independence, but the cost is higher. Similar options are available with word processing equipment.

The term "multistation system" is general enough to include various types of system arrangements. Other terms that are used to describe the same concept are "multiterminal system," "clustered text-editing system," and "multiwork station system." A multistation system offers the same functions and features as a standalone system, but the design and arrangement of parts are unique.

A multistation system has more than one terminal, and each terminal shares something from another device. Either term, "station" or "terminal," may be used to describe both the screen and keyboard. Several stations might share one printer, a storage disk, or the logic/intelligence of the system. Several terminals might share two printers—one that produces letter quality print and another that prints faster but sacrifices quality (used for rough drafts). Terminals may be either smart or dumb. A *smart*

terminal has some intelligence and can do some functions on its own. A *dumb terminal* has no intelligence but depends on the **central processing unit (CPU)** for its logic capabilities. Several dumb terminals can connect to one CPU, a minicomputer. Some systems are designed with paired terminals, whereby the dumb terminal connects to and depends on the smart terminal for its intelligence capabilities. The intelligence (logic) is made possible by powerful microprocessors, just as you find in electronic typewriters, standalone word processors, and computers.

ADVANTAGES AND LIMITATIONS

Multistation systems offer two basic advantages over standalone systems: (1) By allowing several stations to share at least one other device, the average price of each station (including the sharing of the cost of the printer, CPU, and/or storage disk) is less than for the same number of standalone word processors. This reduces the cost of the entire system. (2) Several operators on the

Illus. 5-5a   Three stations are sharing the central processor, which gives them additional storage and intelligence.

Central Processor

Illus. 5-5b   Stations in Lanier's Shared System use the same printer and central processing unit.

system can share the master files (common data base) that are stored on a hard disk in the main storage device. This eliminates the need for each station to have a diskette (or several diskettes) in order to have the same master files. The entire system has greater capabilities.

The main limitation of multistation systems is that when either the CPU or smart terminal is "down" (malfunctioning) all stations that depend on it are also down. In the event of CPU failure, the terminals that have some intelligence of their own can perform some work even though another part of the system is down.

OTHER TERMS

There are some other terms used to describe certain types of multistation systems. Here is a brief review:

Shared-Logic System. Several dumb stations (no intelligence) are connected to and depend upon a central processing unit (CPU). The stations also share a printer.

Distributed-Logic System. Each terminal has some intelligence but uses the CPU to increase its capabilities. Printers and hard disk storage are also shared.

Shared-Resource System. Several stations, each having its own maximum intelligence, share the printing device(s) and possibly hard disk storage.

Multi-Function Systems. Systems which offer more than word processing are called multi-function systems. A good example would be a system that can perform both word processing and data processing functions.

Characteristics of Standalone and Multistation Systems

Characteristics that are common among standalone and multistation systems include recording and storage media, printing devices, basic features, and major uses.

RECORDING AND STORAGE MEDIA

The kinds of media used most often today are floppy diskettes and hard disks, which are housed in disk drives. Floppy diskettes provide off-line storage (removable). This means the diskettes can be stored away from the machine. Some hard disks can be removed from the disk drive. Others are permanently mounted in the disk drive, providing *on-line storage* (nonremovable). Floppy diskettes are flexible, whereas hard disks are rigid.

Floppy Diskettes. These come in two sizes—standard or mini. Each is kept within a square envelope that protects it from frequent handling. A single-sided standard diskette (data recorded on one side only) holds about 100 pages; a minidiskette holds about 30 pages on one side. Floppy diskettes (standard or mini) can be double-sided for recording on both sides. They can also be made with double density, which gives them the ability to hold twice as many characters.

Floppy diskettes provide low cost storage that is easy to use. However, a floppy diskette used by one brand of equipment cannot be used with another brand, even if the diskettes are the same size. Each vendor has different ways of storing the information on the diskette.

Illus. 5-6 Standard and minidiskettes are in envelopes.

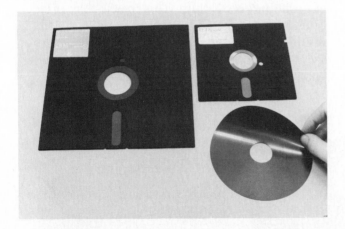

Hard Disks. These are rigid rather than flexible. They are sealed inside a casing that protects them from dust, dirt, and smoke but provides air circulation. The Winchester disk is a deluxe hard disk. (The size could be 14″ or 8″ or 5 1/4″ in diameter). Compared to a standard

diskette which can store 312,000 characters, the same size Winchester disk can store up to 8.4 million characters and can operate more than 17 times faster.

Illus. 5-7a A hard disk is sealed inside a casing.

Illus. 5-7b An operator inserting a hard disk pack.

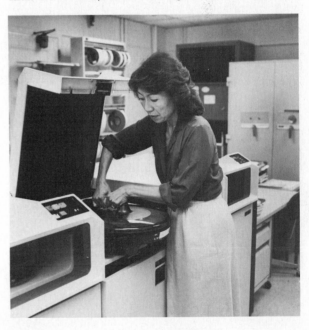

Bubble Memory. Developed by Bell Telephone Laboratories, bubble memory offers a new type of storage. A bubble memory is a tiny, mass storage device (a chip) that is made from a synthetic garnet. When viewed under a magnifying lens, it looks like a liquid bubble. When the power goes off, no information is lost in bubble memory. Unlike disk technology, bubble memory is completely electronic and has no mechanical parts to suffer wear and tear. Bubble memory is the more reliable kind of memory. Bubble memories are also faster, more compact, and require less power than disk storage.

Optical Disk. Another approach to storage is the optical disk. It is shaped like a magnetic disk but is not magnetic. Information is stored on an optical disk by a laser beam that burns tiny holes in the disk's coating. Information is also retrieved (or read back) with a laser. The laser reflects light back according to the presence or absence of holes in the disk. Optical disk has the potential to offer much more storage at a lower cost than magnetic media. For example, a single optical disk might be able to hold the images of about 10,000 letter size documents as compared to about 100 documents on a floppy disk. However, technology must be further developed to improve accuracy before this type of storage becomes practical for text processing. Because data recorded on optical disk cannot be erased, long-term storage (archival storage) is about the only practical use for this type of recording media.

Illus. 5-8 Optical Disk: Technology of the Future

PRINTING DEVICES

The printing device converts the copy on the magnetic medium into printed form. The printing device can be either an impact printer or a nonimpact printer. Impact printers physically strike the paper, whereas nonimpact printers do not.

Impact Printer. An impact printer is either a serial printer (prints a character at a time) or a line printer (prints a line at a time).

Serial printers come in four styles: ball-shaped element, daisy wheel (printwheel), thimble, or matrix. The first three are similar in that the device rotates to the correct position and a hammer drives the character against a ribbon. This action provides letter quality print. This means the print is comparable to that of an electric typewriter. These devices come in a number of print styles and sizes, including 10-, 12-, 15- pitch, and proportional print. The ball-shaped element contains 88 characters and prints at a speed of 15 cps (or 180 wam). The *daisy wheel* printer looks like a wheel with 96 spokes each having its own character. Some printwheels have two rows of 96 characters (for a total of 192 characters and symbols). They can print at the rate of 30 to 55 cps or 360 to 669 wam; the highest rate is 75 cps. Although shaped differently, the *thimble* is similar to a printwheel. It has 64 petals each with 2 characters, for a total of 128 different characters. Most daisy wheel and thimble printers print *bidirectionally*. This means they print from left to right and then from right to left, resulting in a faster speed. Daisy wheel printers are the most common printer for word processing applications.

Illus. 5-9 Printing Devices: Ball-Shaped Element, Daisy Wheel, and Thimble

Illus. 5-10a   Impact printers provide letter quality print.

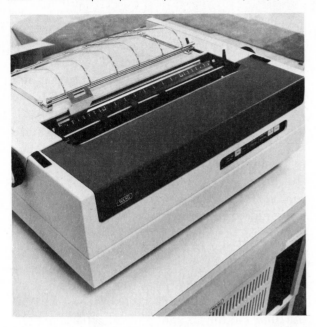

Illus. 5-10b   Inserting a daisy wheel into a printer.

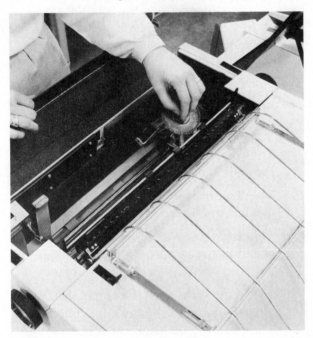

Matrix printers form the characters out of a cluster of dots. They are faster, quieter, and able to produce graphics. On matrix printers, it is easier to change type styles and sizes than on the daisy wheel printer. Matrix printers can create anything from a company logo to a personal signature. The speed of a matrix printer may be from 50 to 600 cps (600-7,200 wpm). The disadvantage is that the quality of print is not letter quality as produced by daisy wheels.

Line printers print a line at a time. Just picture a thin conveyor belt carrying the letters of the alphabet at high speeds. When each letter is in its proper place, a hammer strikes the chain and the line of letters hits the paper, printing the entire line at once. The speed of line printers may be as high as 20,000 lpm (lines per minute). Although faster than serial printers, most line printers do not offer letter quality print. They are used mostly for data processing or for rough draft documents.

Nonimpact Printer. Nonimpact printers are clean, quiet, and fast. Other advantages include their ability to produce graphics and varying type faces and sizes. A form and the data to be inserted can be printed on plain paper, making preprinted forms unnecessary. The disadvantages, however, are high cost and loss of letter quality print. Nonimpact printers use techniques such as ink jet, thermal, laser, ion deposition, or combinations of technologies to form an image on paper.

Illus. 5-11   A Nonimpact Ink Jet Printer

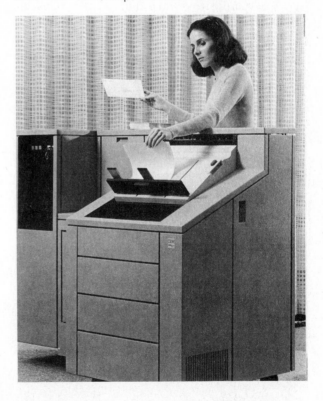

MAJOR USES

Visual display equipment, whether a stand-alone or a multistation system, is very useful for revising lengthy documents. Also, repetitive documents are quickly produced by merging the variables with the prerecorded standard text. These machines can interface with other electronic equipment. You will become more aware of their sophisticated features as you read about applications of word processing in Unit 6.

Standalones and multistation systems are also called *dedicated word processors*, for they are specifically designed to do text-editing functions. In contrast are computer systems that were originally designed to perform data processing functions but that can perform text-editing functions by the insertion of word processing software.

Computers with Word Processing Software

Computers of any size can perform text-editing functions by the insertion of word processing software. Gaining in popularity are the small computers known as personal computers (PCs).

Companies that have more data processing work than word processing work and that want to perform both types of work on one machine go this route. The word processing software may be limited to only basic word processing functions and may require more keystrokes for each feature than dedicated word processors. The users must shop for the software program that will perform the word processing functions desired and that will work on their company's computer.

Illus. 5-12   The Apple Lisa does word processing.

Time Shared Services

Sharing the cost of a large, powerful computer among many users in various locations is called time shared services. The user needs only a word processing terminal or a computer terminal with communications capability to access the computer of the service company.

To use the time shared service the terminal is connected to a telephone line. An ordinary telephone receiver is placed in a coupler that is attached to the terminal. The operator dials the computer's telephone number and gives the proper identification. From that point the operator can use the full power of the large computer. Recent developments in satellite communication networks offer another means of connecting terminals with a computer in another city.

With a time shared system, the user pays for the time and the amount of service that it needs. Costs for the time shared service include charges for terminal connection, storage at the computer center, processing time on the computer system, output (printing), and telephone wire use (or satellite transmission).

ADVANTAGES

Time shared services are attractive to companies in the following situations:

1 The company cannot afford to buy or lease the equipment needed to produce the work.

2 The amount of work does not justify the cost of such sophisticated equipment.

3 Before ordering equipment, the company would like to sample what can be done and how such applications can best be produced.

4 A specific task must be done that is not possible on the company's own equipment. For example, the user might need to use a certain library of construction specifications, standard legal documents, or other information.

APPLICATIONS

In addition to common text-editing tasks, special applications are possible through time shared services. Examples include sorting long lists in two or more ways at a time, doing library research, and merging many variables into

Name_____ Date_____Section_____

Instructions for Job 5_____

MATERIALS NEEDED
8½" x 11" plain paper—3 sheets
correction device (eraser, liquid cover-up, paper tape)

The supervisor of the Word Processing Services Department of Parkview Hospital handed you the work request shown on page 98. Type Form Letter 109 (shown on page 98) to the three people listed on the work request. Fill in the proper variables that appear in italic type. Assume you are using letterhead stationery and type each letter in the block letter style. Should you make any errors, correct the copy so that all three letters are mailable.

Record the exact time you begin and the time you complete all three letters.

STARTING TIME: hour   min.
STOPPING TIME: hour   min.   TOTAL TIME: hour   min.

Compare the amount of time it took you to produce the three mailable letters with the secretary who performed the same job on a word processor. By using a word processor with a daisy wheel printer, a secretary can produce all three letters in *6 minutes and 45 seconds*. This includes both keyboarding the standard text and variables and printing the three letters.

To produce these letters on a word processor, the secretary records the letter and the list of variables in two different locations on the diskette or on two separate diskettes as shown in Illustration 5-16. The secretary then directs the system to merge (combine) the form letter with the list of variables. Between letters only one key needs to be depressed to signal the system to continue playback. This brief stop allows the operator to insert a new sheet of paper in the printer.

FORM LETTER 109

Current Date

Letter Address
_____

Dear Name in Body

WELCOME TO THE SCHOOL OF X-RAY TECHNOLOGY

Congratulations, Name in Body , on being accepted into the School of X-ray Technology of Parkview Hospital.

Our students must attend classes at the University for three months. As part of the educational program, you will work 15-20 hours in the X-ray Laboratory. You are required to wear a white uniform and white shoes at the hospital.

Your meals at the hospital are free. You will be issued a hospitalization insurance plan (Blue Cross-Blue Shield) at no cost to you.

Please keep me informed of your intentions. If you have any questions, Name in Body , please contact me.

Sincerely yours

Mrs. Shirley Claybough
Supervisor of X-ray Technology

xx

Request for Form Letter _____109_____

Requested By _Shirley Claybough_

Department _X-ray Technology_

Time In _____   Time Out _____

Letter Address	Name in Body
1. Mr. Jeff Shin	Mr. Shin
4261 West Grandview	
Kansas City, MO 64113-0923	
_____	
2. Miss Julie Wasson	Miss Wasson
Wellshire Apartments, #207	
1736-88 Street West	
Omaha, NE 68107-1240	
_____	
3. Mr. Manfred Asu	Mr. Asu
859 Launer Drive	
Lincoln, NE 68506-2411	
_____	

Name_____ Date_____ Section_____

Illus. 5-16 The word processor merges the form letter and the list of variables to form multiple documents.

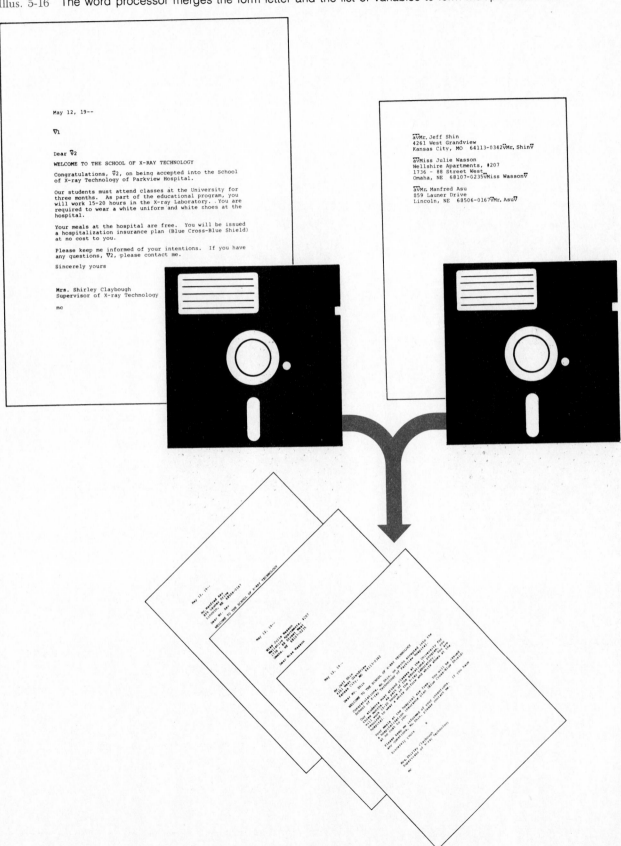

UNIT SIX.

Applications of Word/Information Processing

Having learned some basic word/information processing concepts, you are ready to see how people and machines work together to produce attractive, quality documents. In this unit you will visit typical word processing users and see some common applications. Your tour will include visiting an educational institution, a law firm, an industrial corporation, a telephone company, a utility company, a hospital, an accounting firm, and a savings and loan institution. At the end of the unit you will perform an application for an insurance company. Throughout your tour, you will see how word processing relates to other systems in processing information.

Whether large or small, firms that process a lot of paperwork have the need for a word processing system. At each stop during the tour you will see how word processors are helpful tools in processing information. The features of the equipment that are shown are examples of those that are common to most standalone word processors and multistation systems.

EDUCATIONAL INSTITUTION—BUILDING A FORM LETTER

Your first stop is at the department of office administration and business education of a university. This office answers many letters of inquiry from teachers and from potential students. The goals are to answer promptly and to produce high quality letters that appear to be individually dictated and transcribed.

One type of letter that is often received asks about the department's word processing classes. Since one or two of these letters must be answered each day, standard paragraphs have been developed from which individual letters can be built. Table 6-1 is taken from the reference manual used by authors who originate correspondence. It shows the document label (WP-206), the standard paragraphs, their code numbers (1, 2, etc.), and the purpose of each paragraph.

TABLE 6-1 Prerecorded Standard Paragraphs—Dept. of Office Administration & Business Education

DOCUMENT LABEL: WP-206

CODE	SUBJECT LINE AND INITIAL PARAGRAPH	PURPOSE
1	OUR WORD PROCESSING CURRICULUM It was a pleasure, *Name in Body,* to hear that your school is developing a word processing curriculum. Here are the course titles and descriptions among those required for our Word Processing program that you requested:	To a teacher
2	CONTINUING YOUR WORD PROCESSING EDUCATION Thank you, *Name in Body,* for inquiring about our word processing major. According to your background, you would want to enroll in one of the following courses next term:	To a potential student

Continued

CODE	MIDDLE PARAGRAPHS	PURPOSE
3	**OBE 195 Introduction to Word Processing** The objectives of this course are to develop an understanding of WP concepts and how they fit into a total information processing system of handling paperwork. Students will learn the basics of operating text-editing equipment.	Introductory course
4	**OBE 293 Word Processing Transcription** The purposes of this course are to review basic language skills, to review formats of written documents, to operate machine transcription equipment, to produce mailable transcripts from various input methods, and to experience a variety of business, government, and professional applications.	Machine transcription course
5	**OBE 295 Text Editing** This course provides basic operator training on two types of WP equipment—standalone text editors and a multistation system that shares.	Text-editing course
6	**OBE 395 Word Processing Applications and Procedures** The content of this course includes further development of WP concepts, introduction to supervisory techniques, and advanced applications on text editors. The WP cycle is simulated with the use of centralized dictation equipment and text editors.	Advanced applications and procedures course
7	**OBE 495 Word Processing Systems Management** Advanced WP concepts and management techniques are given to include: conducting a feasibility study, designing a system, implementing WP, and managing the WP system.	Systems management course
8	Samples of our course outlines and departmental brochures describing our two-year and four-year WP programs are enclosed. Should you have specific questions after reading these materials, *Name in Body,* please telephone me. Sharing with fellow business teachers is a privilege.	To a teacher
9	The departmental brochures that describe our two-year and four-year WP programs are enclosed. Should you have any questions after reading them, please contact me. It would be a pleasure to chat with you about your career opportunities in word processing and to show you our department. Give me a call, *Name in Body,* and we will schedule a time for you to visit.	To a potential student

SIGNATURE BLOCK

o	Dr Arnola Ownby Department Chairperson	Dr Ownby
s	Dr Sarah Shin Professor	Dr Shin
t	Tom Trimble Assistant Professor	Mr Trimble

ENCLOSURE NOTATION

y	Enclosures: Brochures on 2-year and 4-year WP programs	WP brochures
z	Enclosures: Brochures on 2-year and 4-year WP programs Course outlines	WP brochures & Course outlines

The document label and the standard paragraphs and their codes have also been prerecorded on a floppy disk. In paragraphs 1, 2, 8, and 9, you see *Name in Body,* a variable. Variables are those parts of the form letter that change from one letter to another. The machine stops during playback at these points so that the operator can manually type the name. (In recording the standard paragraphs, the correspondence specialist (CS) used the *Auto Underscore* feature. As each course number and title was keyed, the text was automatically underscored.)

The AS selects the appropriate standard paragraphs and lists the variables on a work request. For example, Illustration 6-1a shows a work request for a letter to a potential student who plans to transfer to a university that offers a word processing major. This student has had an introductory course at another college. Note the paragraph codes. The work request is sent to the CS who then prepares the form letter.

To prepare form letters from the standard paragraphs, the CS follows these steps:

1 Places the floppy disk with the prerecorded document (WP-206) in one disk drive and a second floppy disk on which the new document will be recorded in the other disk drive. (The disk drive houses the floppy disks.)

2 Touches two keys that direct the machine to instantly recall the top margin, dateline, and blank lines that follow. The current date is

Illus. 6-1b Only the variables in this form letter were keyboarded.

Illus. 6-1a The standard paragraphs and variables are listed on a work request.

REQUEST FOR FORM LETTER

Source *WP-206*

Letter
Address *Miss Carla Volovsek*
1304 Weeks Avenue
Superior, WI 54880-2101

Name in
Body *Carla*

Para-
graphs *2, 4, 5, 9, 5, y*
Codes

Requested by *Cyndie Metcalf*

Department of Office Administration and Business Education
2129 Highview Road East
Peoria, IL 61611-3415

DuBoise College

16 June 19--

MISS CARLA VOLOVSEK
1304 WEEKS AVENUE
SUPERIOR WI 54880-2101

CONTINUING YOUR WORD PROCESSING EDUCATION

Thank you, Carla, for inquiring about our word processing major. According to your background, you would want to enroll in one of the following courses next term:

OBE 293 Word Processing Transcription

The purposes of this course are to review basic language skills, to review formats of written documents, to operate machine transcription equipment, to produce mailable transcripts from various input methods, and to experience a variety of business, government, and professional applications.

OBE 295 Text Editing

This course provides basic operator training on two types of WP equipment--standalone text editors and a multi-station system that shares.

The departmental brochures that describe our two-year and four-year WP programs are enclosed. Should you have any questions after reading them, please contact me. It would be a pleasure to chat with you about your career opportunities in word processing and to show you our department. Give me a call, Carla, and we will schedule a time for you to visit.

Sarah Shin
Dr Sarah Shin
Professor

mh

Enclosures: Brochures on 2-year and 4-year WP programs

stored within the system; it does not have to be manually keyed. This feature is known as ***program, glossary,*** or ***phrase storage.***

3 Types the letter address and returns that follow.

4 Directs the system to automatically play back Paragraph 1. The system stops and displays a "prompt," *Name in Body*. (A ***prompt*** is the system's way of telling you it needs more information.) The CS types the name and directs the system to continue playback.

5 Touches two keys that cause the system to play back Paragraphs 4, 5, and 9. The system stops at the position *Name in Body;* the CS types the name.

6 Directs the system to play back Paragraphs s and y and to print the document.

To prepare the letter, the CS uses several time saving steps. A standard line length is used for all letters and memos so that margins do not have to be changed. The dateline and letter address are positioned so that window envelopes can be used. This saves typing individual envelopes.

LAW FIRM—REVISING A DOCUMENT BY REPLACING VARIABLES

Your next stop is at a law firm. The receptionist takes you to the CS who is preparing a legal document on a standalone word processor. The document is an agreement with an author to have a training manual written.

Since this agreement is similar to one that was recently prepared for Susan Patton, time can be saved by revising the old document. The attorney pulled out the Patton document from the file to see what needs to be changed for the agreement with Chris Dickinson. Illustration 6-2a is the first page of the document. The highlighted words and phrases are the variables that will need to be changed; the parts which remain are the ***standard text.*** The attorney then

Illus. 6-2a The variables are marked to be changed.

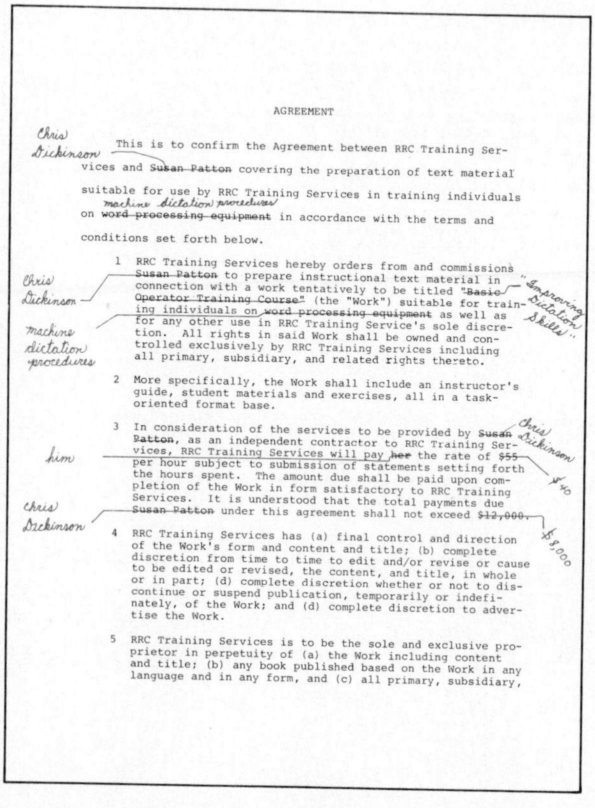

AGREEMENT

This is to confirm the Agreement between RRC Training Services and ~~Susan Patton~~ covering the preparation of text material suitable for use by RRC Training Services in training individuals on ~~word processing equipment~~ in accordance with the terms and conditions set forth below.

1 RRC Training Services hereby orders from and commissions ~~Susan Patton~~ to prepare instructional text material in connection with a work tentatively to be titled ~~"Basic Operator Training Course"~~ (the "Work") suitable for training individuals on ~~word processing equipment~~ as well as for any other use in RRC Training Service's sole discretion. All rights in said Work shall be owned and controlled exclusively by RRC Training Services including all primary, subsidiary, and related rights thereto.

2 More specifically, the Work shall include an instructor's guide, student materials and exercises, all in a task-oriented format base.

3 In consideration of the services to be provided by ~~Susan Patton~~, as an independent contractor to RRC Training Services, RRC Training Services will pay ~~her~~ the rate of ~~$55~~ per hour subject to submission of statements setting forth the hours spent. The amount due shall be paid upon completion of the Work in form satisfactory to RRC Training Services. It is understood that the total payments due ~~Susan Patton~~ under this agreement shall not exceed ~~$12,000.~~

4 RRC Training Services has (a) final control and direction of the Work's form and content and title; (b) complete discretion from time to time to edit and/or revise or cause to be edited or revised, the content, and title, in whole or in part; (d) complete discretion whether or not to discontinue or suspend publication, temporarily or indefinately, of the Work; and (d) complete discretion to advertise the Work.

5 RRC Training Services is to be the sole and exclusive proprietor in perpetuity of (a) the Work including content and title; (b) any book published based on the Work in any language and in any form, and (c) all primary, subsidiary,

Illus. 6-2b Revised variables are now in the agreement.

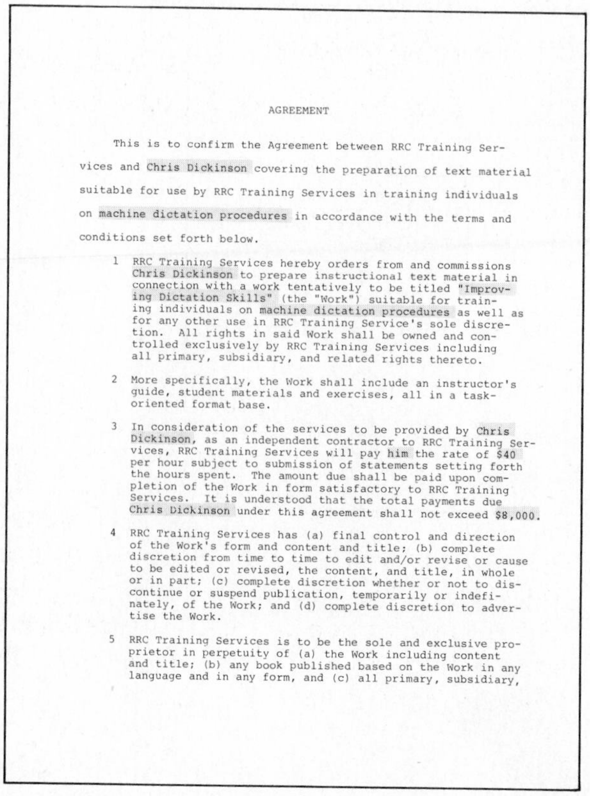

AGREEMENT

This is to confirm the Agreement between RRC Training Services and Chris Dickinson covering the preparation of text material suitable for use by RRC Training Services in training individuals on machine dictation procedures in accordance with the terms and conditions set forth below.

1 RRC Training Services hereby orders from and commissions Chris Dickinson to prepare instructional text material in connection with a work tentatively to be titled "Improving Dictation Skills" (the "Work") suitable for training individuals on machine dictation procedures as well as for any other use in RRC Training Service's sole discretion. All rights in said Work shall be owned and controlled exclusively by RRC Training Services including all primary, subsidiary, and related rights thereto.

2 More specifically, the Work shall include an instructor's guide, student materials and exercises, all in a task-oriented format base.

3 In consideration of the services to be provided by Chris Dickinson, as an independent contractor to RRC Training Services, RRC Training Services will pay him the rate of $40 per hour subject to submission of statements setting forth the hours spent. The amount due shall be paid upon completion of the Work in form satisfactory to RRC Training Services. It is understood that the total payments due Chris Dickinson under this agreement shall not exceed $8,000.

4 RRC Training Services has (a) final control and direction of the Work's form and content and title; (b) complete discretion from time to time to edit and/or revise or cause to be edited or revised, the content, and title, in whole or in part; (c) complete discretion whether or not to discontinue or suspend publication, temporarily or indefinately, of the Work; and (d) complete discretion to advertise the Work.

5 RRC Training Services is to be the sole and exclusive proprietor in perpetuity of (a) the Work including content and title; (b) any book published based on the Work in any language and in any form, and (c) all primary, subsidiary,

wrote in the changes as shown. The CS works from this rough draft to prepare the new document.

The CS explains how the word processor helps prepare the agreement for Chris Dickinson. Since the name is used several times in the document, "Chris Dickinson" is recorded in the buffer (internal) memory of the word processor. Then any time the name is needed, it can quickly be recalled by just touching two keys.

The CS inserts the diskette on which the agreement with Susan Patton was recorded and calls it up on the screen. When revising the old document to produce a new document, the replace feature and the adjust feature are helpful.

The *replace* feature allows the operator to quickly delete old text and replace it with new text. For example, *Susan Patton* can be deleted and replaced by *Chris Dickinson* throughout the document. Usually the new copy is longer or shorter than the old copy. The *adjust* feature adds or closes up the space needed by the new text and adjusts the line endings so the right margin is as even as possible. The right margin is ragged (not perfectly even).

If this particular agreement is to be used often by the firm, the CS will record the standard text with stop codes wherever variables are to appear. *Stop codes* instruct the system to stop so that the operator can type the variables. Stop codes save having to first delete the old variables before adding the new variables. The method of revising text and of recording standard documents depends on the number of times the document will be printed.

INDUSTRY—BROCHURE THAT IS TYPESET IN-HOUSE

In visiting a company that manufactures stainless steel products, you will see how a brochure is prepared by word processing equipment and typesetting equipment without the CS having to rekey the text. Examples are shown of the auto centering, search and replace, and the superscript/subscript features. The word processing specialist explains how in-house publications are processed by reviewing how one page of a brochure is prepared.

The word processing specialist transcribes the document as shown in Illustration 6-3a. To *automatically center* a heading, the CENTER key is depressed just before typing the heading. The word processor automatically determines its correct position. This saves the time of tabbing to the center of the page and backspacing once for every two characters in the heading.

Another feature of the word processor is the *superscript/subscript* feature. At the point of the degree symbol (°), the machine is given the command to automatically raise the printing device when the superscript is printed. A command must follow to return the print to the normal line. The screen does not show the raised symbol; however, when the document is printed, the hard copy will show the raised superscript.

Illus. 6-3a   The original document is transcribed.

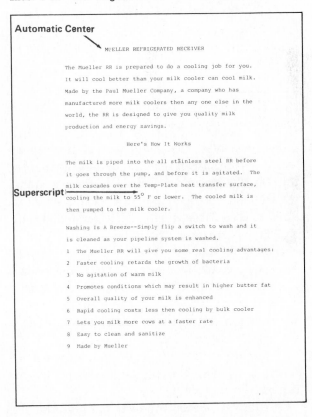

After the author revises the first draft, the CS revises the recording on the floppy disk by keying in only the changes made by the author. Text that is longer or shorter than the original recording can easily be inserted or deleted.

Illus. 6-3b   The author revises the original document.

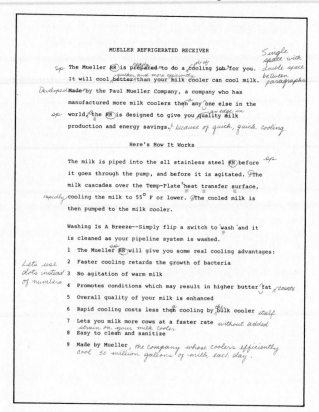

Illus. 6-3c   The final document is ready to be typeset.

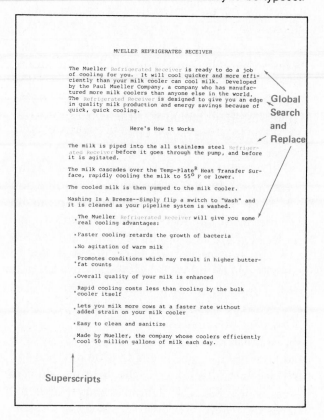

To change each instance of "RR" to "Refrigerated Receiver" the *global search and replace* feature saves a lot of time. With the cursor at the top of the document, the machine searches throughout the document for each instance of "RR" and replaces it with "Refrigerated Receiver." However, if the situation had called for only certain "RRs" to be replaced, the machine would have been given the *selective search and replace* command. In this command, the cursor stops at each instance of "RR" and the operator decides whether to replace it with "Refrigerated Receiver."

The dots that replace the numbers will be made by having the period (.) raised by the superscript feature.

After the author approves the revision, the document is ready to be sent to the phototype-setting department by electronic mail. The text is arranged and typeset by adding commands but without retyping any text. Artwork is prepared by the art department and is positioned with the typeset copy. The printed brochure appears in Illustration 6-3d.

Illus. 6-3d   The document is typeset and printed.

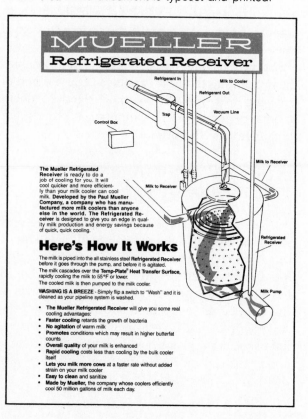

The company has many brochures, technical publications, business forms, newsletters, quarterly and annual reports, price lists, and catalogs to print. Such a large number of printing applications certainly justifies that printing be done in-house rather than be sent to a commercial printer. At this manufacturing company you were able to see how word processing, electronic mail, and phototypesetting systems interface to produce quality products.

TELEPHONE COMPANY—ANNOUNCEMENT WITH COLUMNS OF NUMBERS AND EVEN RIGHT MARGINS

As you arrive at the telephone company, the word processing supervisor greets you and takes you on a tour of the word processing center. One of the operators is preparing an announcement to be enclosed with next month's telephone bill. The process of preparing this document is explained as follows:

The author used longhand to create this report since it is short and contains a rather complicated table.

Illus. 6-4a The original document is in longhand.

Telephone Rate Change

Effective the first of this month, changes in rates for residential telephone service and other products and services have been approved by the Public Service Commission.

Monthly charges for telephone equipment were increased by an average of 6.5 percent.

Telephone Equipment Charges

Monthly Rate

Type of Instrument	New Rate	Old Rate
Standard Rotary set	$1.75	$1.30
Standard Touch-Tone set	2.80	2.00
Princess Rotary set	3.10	2.70
Princess Touch-Tone set	3.90	3.40
Trimline Rotary set	3.40	3.20
Trimline Touch-Tone set	4.45	4.20

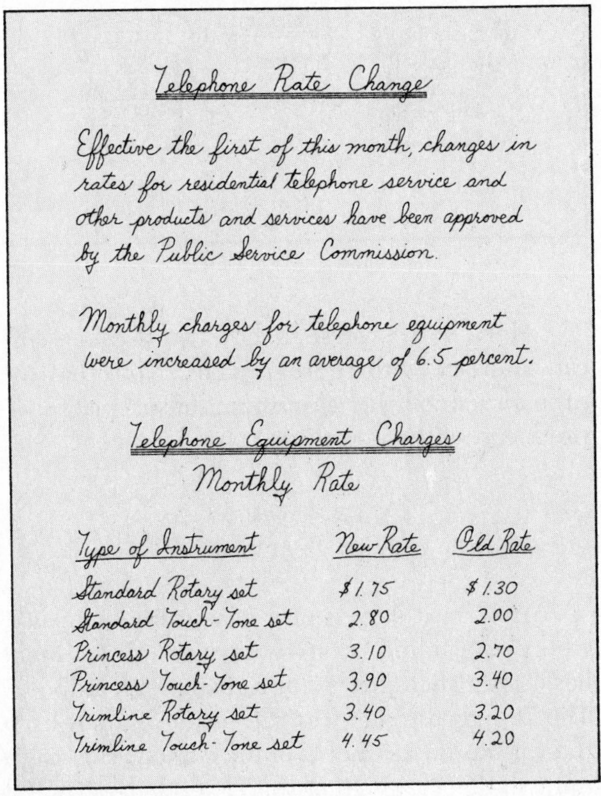

The operator set the format line for typing the report which included the following: line spacing, single spacing; line length, 48 spaces; tabs, beginning of second and third columns. The CS then typed the report up to the point of the column entries.

Illus. 6-4b A format line gives margins, spacing, and tabs.

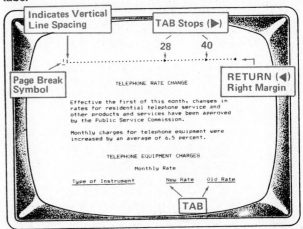

After typing the column headings, the operator made the following changes in the format line: line spacing, double spacing; tab stops, moved tabs 2 spaces to the right in Columns 2 and 3 so that the tabs are set at the decimal points. Before typing each number in the columns, the operator hit the DEC TAB key. The ***DEC TAB*** (decimal tab) feature aligns numbers at the decimal point even when the numbers are of a different length as shown below:

7.09
.095
2,466.51

Illus. 6-4c Spacing and tabs are changed for the table.

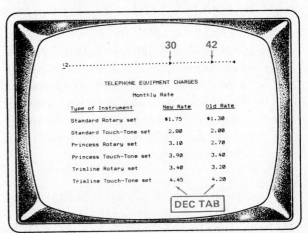

The report was then printed and returned to the author to proofread and edit. The author requested that the right margin be *justified* (even) and that the table be single spaced to give more room for an illustration to be added at the bottom of the page.

Illus. 6-4d   Author revises the original printed document.

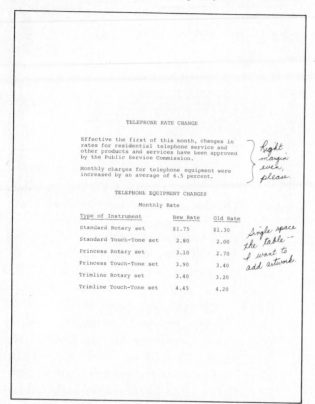

To prepare the final copy, the operator merely had to call up the second format line on the display and change the line spacing to single spacing and command the printer to "Print—Justified." Both of these changes were made without rekeyboarding any of the copy.

The printed copy is now ready for the illustration to be added. The hard copy will be sent to the reprographics department, which will use a camera to take a picture of the page. From the negative an aluminum plate will be made. From the plate thousands of copies can be duplicated by offset press.

A complete brochure is shown in Illustration 6-4e. For brochures, policy booklets, and other documents that are duplicated or

printed in multiple copies, usually the right margin is justified. However, for letters and memorandums that are to appear individually dictated and transcribed, the right margins are ragged—but as even as possible.

Illus. 6-4e   The revised brochure is now printed.

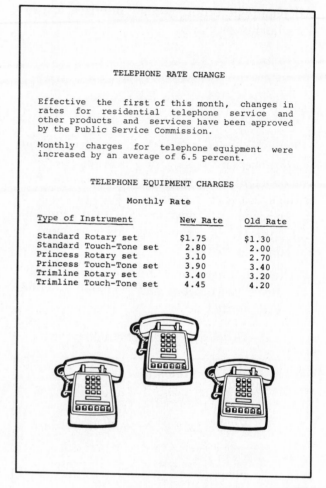

Here you have seen how word processing can interface with reprographics. Note that the preparation of the aluminum offset plate was produced without retyping the document.

CITY UTILITY COMPANY— CUSTOMER HANDBOOK

Your next stop is at a city utility company, where the administrative services department has just finished producing a customer handbook. The 78-page project was the result of input from the various departments of the company. Using a multistation system that shares, each department

Name_____ Date_____ Section_____

TABLE 6-2   Prerecorded Standard Paragraphs—Claims Department

DOCUMENT LABEL: AIC-04

CODE	SUBJECT LINE	PURPOSE
s	AUTOMOBILE INSURANCE CLAIM # *Claim Number*	Subject line

FIRST PARAGRAPH

| 1 | On *Date of Loss* your vehicle was involved in an accident with our insured, *Name of Our Insured.* Our investigation reveals that your negligence was the cause of the accident. Therefore, *Name of Addressee,* you will need to provide the financial settlement. | To person causing the accident |

MIDDLE PARAGRAPHS

2	Enclosed are copies of the police report, the repair estimate, and the draft covering damages to the insured vehicle less the deductible.	Proof of negligence and $ of damage
3	Our loss report indicates that you do not carry liability insurance. Thus, you will need to personally pay for the cost of repairing our insured's vehicle. Please send a check or money order made payable to Continental Insurance Company in the amount of $ *Check Amount,* which includes our insured's $ *Deductible Amount* deductible.	Damages under $500 not covered by insurance; request for payment.
4	Since you do not carry any liability insurance, we ask that you sign the enclosed promissory note and return it to us by *Due Date,* with your first monthly payment. Make the check payable to Continental Insurance Company.	Damages $500 or more not covered by insurance; promissory note

LAST PARAGRAPH

| 5 | Please reply right away, *Name of Addressee.* | Within area code |
| 6 | If you wish to discuss this settlement with me, you may call our toll free number 1-800-836-5372. Please reply soon, *Name of Addressee.* | Outside area code |

SIGNATURE BLOCK

| k | Ms. Sandra King
Subrogation Specialist | Ms. King |
| r | James Rogers
Subrogation Specialist | Mr. Rogers |

ENCLOSURES

| y | Enclosures: Proof of negligence | Proof of negligence |
| z | Enclosures: Proof of negligence
Promissory note | Proof of negl. & promissory note |

Illus. 6-10 This sample letter results from merging the variables with the standard paragraphs.

 CONTINENTAL INSURANCE COMPANY

416 Plaza Towers, Suite 1266 · Syracuse, NY 13225-1408 · (315) 722-1600

June 16, 19--

Ms. Dono Zoro
1125 - 124 Street West
Syracuse, NY 13238-1308

Dear Ms. Zoro

AUTOMOBILE INSURANCE CLAIM #6506

On May 27 your vehicle was involved in an accident with
our insured, Janet Carlberg. Our investigation reveals
that your negligence was the cause of the accident.
Therefore, Ms. Zoro, you will need to provide the financial settlement.

Enclosed are copies of the police report, the repair
estimate, and the draft covering damages to the insured
vehicle less the deductible.

Since you do not carry any liability insurance, we ask
that you sign the enclosed promissory note and return it
to us by June 30, with your first monthly payment. Make
the check payable to Continental Insurance Company.

Please reply right away, Ms. Zoro.

Sincerely yours

James Rogers

James Rogers
Subrogation Specialist

nb

Enclosures: Proof of negligence
             Promissory note

Name_____ Date_____Section_____

3   Fill out the two requests for form letters provided on page 124 for both Case 1 and Case 2 listed below. Remember, Continental Insurance Company is located in Syracuse, New York. These work requests will be forwarded to the word processing department.

Case 1

Mr. Rogers wants a letter from AIC-04 sent to Mr. Juan Salez, 809 North Grant, Syracuse, NY 13247-1151. Mr. Salez was negligent, as proven by the support documents, in an accident that occurred one month ago today and which involved our insured, Joyce Sheffield. The claim number is 6725. The damages, although under $500, were not covered by insurance. A check for $425.65, which includes the $250 deductible amount, should be sent to Continental Insurance Company.

Case 2

Ms. King wants a letter for claim number 6803 sent to Miss Mimi Cheung, 1677 West St. Clair, Boston, MA 02147-3026. Supporting documents are being enclosed that prove Miss Cheung's negligence in an accident that occurred three weeks ago today involving our insured, Michael Parks. A promissory note is also being enclosed that should be returned within two weeks from today; the damages exceed $500. A letter can be built from AIC-04.

Part B

As a correspondence specialist in the word processing department, you are to process requests for form letters. Many of the work requests are prepared by administrative secretaries for their principals.

4   Type a letter for each of the two work requests that were in Part A. Use the block letter style. Use the company's standard letter placement, which is 1½-inch side margins and the date on Line 13. Supply an appropriate salutation and complimentary close; add your reference initials. A sample letter is shown in Illustration 6-10 which was prepared from the work request on page 120. Proofread and correct all mistakes you may make.

Summary of Benefits

Without standard paragraphs, the authors would have to either individually dictate each letter or design form letters to fit each situation. Building a letter from standard parts and paragraphs saves time and effort for all people involved. It allows administrative secretaries to relieve executives of timely and routine tasks. It saves hours of keyboarding time for the correspondence secretaries.

REQUEST FOR FORM LETTER
Claims Department

Label _____

Letter
Address _____

_____

_____

Claim
Number _____

Name of
Addressee _____

Paragraph
Codes _____

Date of Loss _____

Name of
Our Insured _____

Check Amount $_____

Deductible
Amount $_____

Due Date _____

Requested by _____

REQUEST FOR FORM LETTER
Claims Department

Label _____

Letter
Address _____

_____

_____

Claim
Number _____

Name of
Addressee _____

Paragraph
Codes _____

Date of Loss _____

Name of
Our Insured _____

Check Amount $_____

Deductible
Amount $_____

Due Date _____

Requested by _____

UNIT SEVEN.

Procedures for Control

Procedures are methods of doing tasks that help people and machines work most efficiently within the environment. Let's take the example of buying a lawn mower and mowing a lawn. The size of the lawn, its terrain, and the number of obstacles to mow around (environment) help determine the kind of lawn mower (machine) to buy. The guidelines to follow in keeping the mower clean and in good working order, the methods of buying and storing fuel, and the pattern of cutting the grass are procedures. Efficient procedures can lessen the time it takes to do a job, eliminate unnecessary physical and mental effort, lengthen the working life of machines, improve the quality of the finished job, and enhance the employee's satisfaction. Procedures have a similar effect on a word processing system.

WHY PROCEDURES?

Expensive word processors and personnel need to be coordinated and used to their greatest potential. A word processing system has five goals. Compared to a traditional office system, a word processing system should process paperwork as follows:

Faster—greater speed; increased production rate

More Accurately—fewer errors; better proofreading

With Improved Quality—professional type; no signs of error correction; better composition; and more personal approach

With Less Effort—physical: no retyping of correct text; minimum of keystrokes; simple formats —mental: avoid time-consuming decision making

At Lower Cost—the least expensive

Certain factors that determine the cost of a document do not change. Examples are the cost of paper, stamps, overhead, and equipment. Factors that vary from one company to another are called variables. Table 7-1 shows how a 250-word document might cost $12 in one company but only $6 in another.

The cost of a document goes up as each of the following factors increases: the amount of time used by the originator and secretary, the number of errors to be corrected, the number of revisions, the difficulty of the format, the rekeying of correct portions of the text, and the poor appearance of the document. Labor (salaries of personnel) has the greatest impact on the cost of a document. Thus, the more time used by the author and secretary, the higher is the cost of the document.

WHAT ARE PROCEDURES?

Procedures are like a formula for the right answer or prescriptions for success. They help

TABLE 7-1 Variables that Determine the Cost of a Document

FACTORS	INEFFICIENT PROCEDURES MOST COSTLY LETTER—$12	EFFICIENT PROCEDURES LEAST COSTLY LETTER—$6
Method of Input	Words are composed by longhand (15 wam) or shorthand dictation (30 wam). Transcription rate is only 15 wam from longhand and 20-25 wam from shorthand. Labor costs are high.	Words are composed by machine dictation at the rate of 60-80 wam. Transcription rate is about 35 wam. Labor cost is kept at minimum. Prerecorded form letters are used for routine letters.
Method of Output and Further Revision	Electric typewriter may result in unattractive error correction. Repetitive typing and revisions involve time and effort in rekeying correct portions of text and in proofreading.	Word processors print letter quality type without a blemish. Once the standard text of repetitive letters has been proofread, only the variables need to be checked in each letter. For revisions, correct text is never rekeyed.
Organization of Secretarial Services	Each secretary does both typing and nontyping tasks. Interruptions slow the rate of transcription and increase the chance of error. Not all secretaries are expert typists and proofreaders.	Each secretary specializes and becomes an expert in a task—typing or nontyping. Typing is done without interruption for the maximum rate and with less chance of error. Typewriting and proofreading are done by experts.
Format of Document	Variable placement is time-consuming and often inaccurate. Needless centering and tabulating take more time and slow revision. Inconsistent punctuation after abbreviations and numbered items lowers quality.	Standard placement reduces decision-making time, increases production rate, and lowers chances of error. Blocked headings and paragraphs reduce time in keyboarding and in revising. Consistent punctuation after abbreviations and numbered items shortens keystroking and revision.

Illus. 7-1 An efficient secretary follows procedures for cost-effectiveness; an inefficient secretary increases costs.

determine how well the five word processing goals (speed, accuracy, quality, minimum effort, and low cost) are met. The most sophisticated word processors and the most skilled secretaries can exist in chaos without meeting these goals. Or they can be well managed and work to their greatest potential. Procedures help the supervisor control the word processing system. In turn, the users are pleased with the quality of service and the secretaries are more likely to be satisfied with their careers.

The procedures that are used within a word processing system are listed in Illustration 7-2. They are used by both correspondence support and by administrative support. As you might expect, not all companies practice all the procedures that are discussed. However, you will find that the most efficient systems include all of them.

Logging Work

Recording facts about work as it comes in and goes out of a work area is called logging. Each employee might keep a separate log sheet for each day of work, or all secretaries might record on one log sheet. There are various ways to log work.

LOG SHEET

The type of data that is commonly recorded on a log sheet includes:

1 Name or initials of the secretary

2 Date received

3 Time received

4 Input identification: number of the dictation recorder, cassette tape, or work request

5 Name and department of the word originator

6 Type of document—letter, memo, report, or statistical table

7 Method of input—dictated, longhand, prerecorded, or rough draft

8 Draft or final copy to be produced

9 Document label

Illus. 7-2 Procedures Used in a Word Processing System

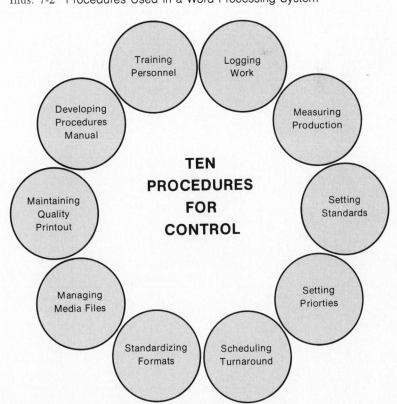

TEN PROCEDURES FOR CONTROL

- Training Personnel
- Logging Work
- Measuring Production
- Setting Standards
- Setting Priorties
- Scheduling Turnaround
- Standardizing Formats
- Managing Media Files
- Maintaining Quality Printout
- Developing Procedures Manual

10 Number of lines, pages, or units produced

11 Errors found by the proofreader

12 Time completed

13 Number of minutes used

Only data that provide meaningful information should be included. The log sheet should be designed so that the effort and time used in filling it out are kept to a minimum. An example of a daily log sheet is shown in Illustration 7-3.

WORK REQUEST

Some companies use work request forms. On these forms the principal describes the work to be done and gives special instructions. These forms are especially needed for work that originates some way other than machine dictation (for example, rough draft, longhand, or prere-corded form letter). They are also needed for work that must be further processed by another system, such as reproduction services or photo-typesetting. An example of a work request is shown in Illustration 7-4.

Some work request forms are designed so that the instructions from the originator and logging data from the transcriber are combined on one form. There might even be added instructions from the supervisor. This type of form is also known as a *job ticket*. At the end of the day all the forms are tabulated onto a summary report and totaled.

REASONS FOR LOGGING

There are several reasons for logging work as it enters and leaves the center.

1 A log sheet enables the supervisor to quickly find a document at any time. For example, the author may need to add a paragraph.

Illus. 7-3   Sample Daily Log Sheet

WORD PROCESSING LOG

Date 9/5/--
Secretary Denise Payne

	Time In	Input ID	Author's Name	Dept ID	Doc	Input Form	Output Form	Doc Label	Total Lines	Errors	Time Out	Total Min
1	9:10	B1	Leta Torres	11	L W R S	D L P RD	FC RD	05-lt-01	31		9:26	16
2	9:28	012	John Scott	14	L M R S	D L P RD	FC RD	05-js-02	115		9:34	6
3	9:36	B1	Elaine Morton	7	L M R S	D L P RD	FC RD	05-em-03	32	1	9:55	19
4	9:57	014	Bessie Lydick	6	L M R S	D L P RD	FC RD	05-bl-04	53		10:28	31
5	10:45	019	Vigga Thompson	14	L M R S	D L P RD	FC RD	05-vt-05	44		11:24	39
6	11:26	B1	Chris Dwyer	8	L M R S	D L P RD	FC RD	05-cd-06	19		11:37	11
7	11:39	022	Bill Trimble	9	L M R S	D L P RD	FC RD	05-bt-07	88	1	12:02	23
8	1:00	D1	Fay Landers	11	L M R S	D L P RD	FC RD	05-fl-08	22		1:06	6
9	1:07	D1	Loretta Connell	6	L M R S	D L P RD	FC RD	05-lc-09	36		1:28	21
10	1:29	029	John Scott	14	L M R S	D L P RD	FC RD	05-js-10	140		1:38	9
11	1:39	D1	Karen Peterson	5	L M R S	D L P RD	FC RD	05-kp-11	22		1:50	11
12	1:51	D1	Sam Myatt	12	L M R S	D L P RD	FC RD	05-sm-12	15		1:57	6
13	1:59	031	Helen Bennett	9	L M R S	D L P RD	FC RD	05-hb-13	164		2:26	27
14	2:27	034	Dave Morgan	8	L M R S	D L P RD	FC RD	05-dm-14	210		2:50	23
15	3:00	037	Fran Preston	11	L M R S	D L P RD	FC RD	05-fp-15	97	1	3:34	34
16					L M R S	D L P RD	FC RD					
17					L M R S	D L P RD	FC RD					
18					L M R S	D L P RD	FC RD					
19					L M R S	D L P RD	FC RD					
20					L M R S	D L P RD	FC RD					
TOTAL					4 5 5 1	7 2 4 2	13 2		1,088	3		282

DOCUMENT
L Letter
M Memorandum
R Report
S Statistical

INPUT FORM
D Dictated
L Longhand
P Prerecorded
RD Rough Draft

OUTPUT FORM
FC Final Copy
RD Rough Draft

No. of Documents	15
Total Lines Transcribed	1,088
Total Errors	3
Error Percentage	.28
Total Min. of Transcription	282
LPM (Lines per minute)	3.86

Proofread by   Karen West

COMMENTS   John Scott's dictation was unclear.

2 Log sheets provide a place to record production data such as lines, pages, or units typed.

3 Production data from the log sheets are summarized onto production reports.

Summary reports may be prepared at the end of each day (see illustration 7-5), week, month, quarter, and/or year. These reports provide meaningful information for the supervisor to present to management.

Illus. 7-4 Sample Work Request

WORK REQUEST

Number _0226_

Author _Bob Hayward_   Department _Sales_

Document:
- _____ Letter
- _____ Memo
- _√_ Report
- _____ Other _____

Stationery
- _____ Letterhead   _____ Envelope
- _____ Memorandum   _____ Legal Size
- _√_ Bond

SPACING
- _____ Single
- _√_ Double
- _____ Triple

OUTPUT FORM
- _____ Rough Draft
- _√_ Final Copy

NO. OF COPIES _10_

SPECIAL INSTRUCTIONS _Place statistical data on separate paper_

STORE DOCUMENTS
- _√_ Permanently
- _____ Week(s)

For Word Processing Department's Use Only

Production Data   ☐ Dictated   ☐ Written   Subject _____

Production Time
Received _____
Completed _____
Turnaround time _____

Tape No. _____   Supervisor _____
No. of lines _____   Transcriber _____
Document No. _____

White—Production Copy   Canary—Supervisor's Copy   Pink—Transcriber's Copy

Illus. 7-5 Sample Daily Summary Report

CONTROL SUMMARY

_____ Day

Secretary	# of Doc	Type of Document L	M	R	S	Type of Input D	L	PR	RD	Output Form FC	RD	Total Lines	Total Errors	% of Error	Total Min	LPM
Rita Bentley	17	6	5	3	3	11	3		3	13	4	1,147	4	.35	360	3.19
Mary Denton	14	8	4	2		12			2	14		1,006	2	.20	340	2.96
Denise Payne	15	4	5	5	1	7	2	4	2	13	2	1,088	3	.28	282	3.86
Dan Severson	16	2	2	6	6	4	6		6	12	4	986	4	.41	400	2.47
Leeann Thone	18	8	7	3		15	1	1	1	17	1	1,218	2	.16	425	2.87
TOTALS	80	28	23	19	10	49	12	5	14	69	11	5,445	15	.28	1,807	3.01

Type of Document
L Letter
M Memo
R Report
S Statistical

Type of Input
D Dictated
L Longhand
PR Prerecorded
RD Rough Draft

Output Form
FC Final Copy
RD Rough Draft

LPM = Lines Per Minute

Measuring Production

Measuring production is a process by which management determines the amount of work produced by each employee. Individual totals are then added to get the department totals.

METHODS OF MEASURING PRODUCTION

The way work is measured depends on the task. The work of the word processing specialist is easier to measure than that of the administrative secretary.

Work that is done on a word processor can be measured by counting lines, pages, or units. There are even electronic counters that can be attached to word processors to count keystrokes.

Because some copy is more difficult and time-consuming to type, some companies measure on the basis of units. A letter transcribed from original dictation might be counted as four units, whereas the playback of a prerecorded form letter might be counted as only one unit.

Administrative support work can be measured by recording either a stroke mark or the amount of time spent on each activity. For example, one can record a stroke mark for each telephone call made or received, for each airline ticket written, or for each work request prepared. Keeping a record of the number of minutes spent on each task is better for long tasks that are not often done than for short, frequent tasks.

The method of measuring should involve a minimum of effort and time. If the process itself takes too much time, it loses its value.

Illus. 7-6 Sample Supervisor's Production Report

AMERICAN NATIONAL INSURANCE COMPANY
WORD PROCESSING SERVICES TOTALS
For Month of October 19--

Description of Lines	October	September
Original Keyboard Lines	98,168	96,440
Number of Lines Revised	1,533	811
Number of Variable Lines Typed	9,307	8,958
Prerecorded Lines	48,228	47,371
TOTAL LINES	157,236	153,580

Lines by Type of Document	October	September
Correspondence (Letters & Memos)	96,425	94,711
Forms	21,008	20,107
Policy Issue	14,524	14,459
Reports	24,731	23,294
Statistical Tables	548	1,009
TOTAL LINES	157,236	153,580

PURPOSE OF MEASURING PRODUCTION

Most word processing systems measure work. They do so for these reasons:

1 Production records kept on each employee and department provide information for management. Comparisons can be made from one period to another. An example of a supervisor's production report is given in Illustration 7-6.

2 Scheduling work is easier when the supervisor knows how long it takes to process a particular type of document.

3 Problems and their causes are more easily recognized. Therefore solutions can be found, and the problems can be corrected before they become more serious (see Table 7-2).

4 Supervisors have an objective and fair basis upon which to evaluate personnel. Each worker's progress can be checked. The high producers may be rewarded by announcements, bonuses, salary increases, or promotions. The low producers may be given additional training, a transfer to another type of job, or a warning about possible dismissal.

5 The records give the facts which show cause for adding personnel.

6 The records justify the purchase of new equipment. For example, an increased number of documents that need data from a master file and much revision might justify a multistation system.

7 User departments can be charged for the work produced. This is called a **charge-back system**.

8 Measurement allows departments to set standards of performance. This is explained later in this unit.

9 Profits can be raised as meaningful production records help to lower operating costs.

You can see why measuring production improves the quality of a word processing system. When all personnel understand the reasons, they can better appreciate the benefits of measuring production.

Setting Standards

After collecting production records for a period of six months or a year, the supervisor can set standards. A standard is a yardstick by which the productivity of employees can be compared.

Here is how standards might be set. Assume the company measures production by counting lines. One word processing specialist, Aleta Cortez, averaged 1,000 lines a day (7 1/2 hours) for one week. For six weeks the same data is acquired from ten specialists. By averaging the number of lines produced a day per specialist, the average was 970 lines. Therefore, the supervisor might set 970 lines per day as the standard rate of production. In this example, Aleta's production rate is above average, for it was above the standard by 30 lines a day. If standards are being set for administrative support, an example could be five patient admissions per hour.

The average production rate is a good standard only if all the employees are doing their

TABLE 7-2 Production Problems and Solutions

PROBLEM	CAUSE OR SOLUTION
Slow and inaccurate transcribers	Do they need retraining? Should they be kept beyond the probationary period? Should they be transferred to another department?
Authors who give the least amount of machine dictation	Do they need training on how to dictate by machine? Do they need suggestions on how to assign routine tasks?
Peak period—large amount of work to complete within a certain period of time	Is it temporary? Should overtime or temporary help be hired? Does it justify hiring another part-time or full-time employee?
Production is down and turnover of secretaries is up	How effective is the supervisor? Is the environment satisfactory? Are there good career opportunities?

best during the period of measurement. No national standard has been set because there are so many variables. For example, level of vocabulary, quality of dictation, amount of statistical copy, amount of prerecorded text, and type of equipment used are some of the variables. It is impossible for one set of standards to be appropriate for all word processing systems. Therefore, each company has to keep production records upon which to base its own standards.

Setting Priorities

In any job there are certain tasks that have to be done before others. A letter confirming an appointment for next week must be sent before a company memo announcing a fund-raising drive. An end-of-the-month financial report would have to be done before a revision of a policy handbook. Work that involves minor revisions can be separated from that which has major revisions. Then work that involves minor changes will not pile up while a specialist is working on a major revision project. Deciding the order in which items will be processed is called *setting priorities*.

In a word processing system the supervisors and management review the tasks done and decide their order of urgency. Then as the work enters the word processing center, the supervisor distributes the assignments accordingly. Order of priority does not mean order of importance, for all work is important both to the originator and to the company.

The priorities for processing work might be similar to those shown in Table 7-3 (No. 1 being top priority). When several rush requests enter the center at the same time, the supervisor decides the order of priority.

Scheduling Turnaround

Setting priorities goes hand in hand with scheduling turnaround. Most word processing systems set time goals within which they try to complete each task. Time goals encourage secretaries to provide efficient service. The originators want to know how soon the work can be done. Prompt replies to letters help promote good public relations. Time goals also help secretaries know what is expected of them. Time goals are called turnaround time or turnaround goals.

To fully understand turnaround time, you need to know how the speaker or author defines the term. To each of the following, turnaround has a different meaning:

To the company—it includes the time from the moment a document is created and goes through necessary revision to the time it is completed in final form and is ready to be mailed or filed.

To the correspondence center—it begins the moment dictation or a work request enters the center and ends when the document has been processed and leaves the center.

To the originator—it measures from the time the principal finishes dictating or writing the work request to the time the document comes back from the center.

TABLE 7-3   Order of Priority

DOCUMENT PROCESSING (CS)	MAIL PROCESSING (AS)
1 Rush requests (rush items)	Rush requests
2 Confidential documents and original dictation	Sorting and distributing incoming mail
3 Revision and rough drafts; short reports	Preparing for correspondence to be answered
4 Routine correspondence	Photocopying correspondence
5 *Archiving* (transferring temporary memory/storage onto permanent storage); long reports and projects	Filing correspondence and reports

Using the priorities as given in Table 7-3, the turnaround goals of a company might be like the ones shown in Tables 7-4 and 7-5.

Standardizing Formats

Having several formats for letters, memos, outlines, reports, or tables presents many problems. Before typing, the secretary has to check the specific style preferred by that author. One can easily get confused and make errors which add to the revision process. Inconsistent formats lower the quality of the company's image. When several secretaries work on a multipage document, it is difficult to coordinate the project. The procedures manual and the length of training are long, because each format must be explained and shown. As production time increases, the cost of processing paperwork increases.

ADVANTAGES OF STANDARDIZATION

Standardizing the format of each type of document offers these advantages:

1 Decision-making time is reduced.

2 Keystroking takes less time.

3 Revision caused by choosing the wrong format is eliminated.

4 Consistent formats increase the professional appearance of documents.

5 More professional-looking documents raise the image of the company.

6 Work flow is easier to manage, especially as systems are interfaced.

7 Coordinating several secretaries or offices that are working on one document is easier.

8 Procedures manuals are shorter.

9 Training time is easier and shorter.

10 Money is saved, for it costs less to produce documents.

Word processors have many features that aid in setting formats, keystroking, and revising text. The printout speeds are much faster than people can type. Yet the most difficult task to do on a word processor is revision. The more centering and tabulating or indenting within a document, the more difficult is the revision. An effective format puts both the human effort and the machine's capability to best use.

TABLE 7-4 Turnaround Goals of Document Processing (Correspondence Support)

CATEGORIES OF TASKS	TURNAROUND GOAL
Rush requests (1-2 pages)	1 hour
Confidential documents (1-2 pages)	2 hours
Original dictation (1-2 pages)	3 hours
Revision and rough drafts (1-5 pages)	4 hours
Short reports (1-3 pages)	4 hours
Routine/prerecorded correspondence	6 hours
Reports and projects (4-9 pages)	8 hours
Reports and projects (10+ pages)	24 hours

TABLE 7-5 Turnaround Goals of Mail Processing (Administrative Support)

CATEGORIES OF TASKS	TURNAROUND GOAL
Sorting and distributing incoming mail	½ hour
Handling rush requests	1 hour
Annotating letters received and preparing for author's dictation	2 hours
Dictating or preparing work requests for routine correspondence	2 hours
Photocopying correspondence	2 hours
Filing correspondence and reports	3 hours
Photocopying reports	4 hours
Filing brochures and periodicals	8 hours

GUIDELINES FOR STANDARDIZING FORMATS

In developing a standard format, the following guidelines are applied:

1 Keep the amount of keystroking to a minimum.

2 Avoid unnecessary centering, tabulating, and punctuating.

3 Include as much text per page as can be easily read. Use space wisely so that the document has eye appeal but keeps the amount of paper used to a minimum.

4 Be consistent in the style of all types of documents (letters, memos, etc.).

Examples of efficient, modern formats are shown in Illustrations 7-7, 7-8, and 7-9. You will note that while each type of document has its own format, the formats are consistent in meeting the four guidelines. For each illustration, note the features that are highlighted below:

Letter (Illustration 7-7). The modern simplified letter style has these advantages over other letter styles:

1 Standard placement is used for all letters, thus reducing decision making and eliminating unnecessary keystrokes.

2 The letter address is typed to fit in a window envelope and to be in the format recommended by the United States Postal Service (all capital letters and no punctuation).

Illus. 7-7   Sample Modern Simplified Letter Style

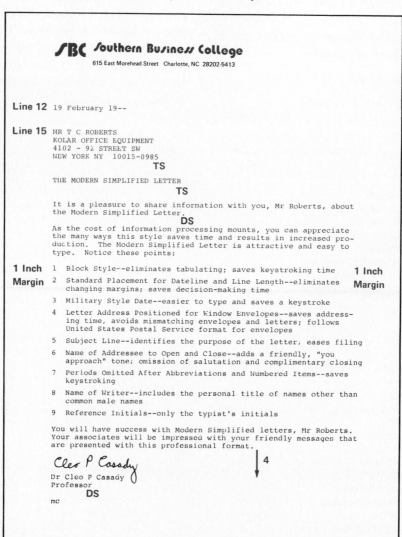

3 The personal "you" approach is emphasized by using the name of the addressee at the beginning and at the end of the body of the letter as though the writer were speaking in person.

4 The subject line helps all personnel to know the purpose of the letter and to file or retrieve the letter.

5 Periods are not used after numbered items or abbreviations. This eliminates the inconsistency of periods in some abbreviations (like 7 P.M., Mr., and Blvd.) but not in others (like 75 wam, IBM Corporation, and Chicago, IL). Also, in most data processing master files there are no periods used after abbreviations. As word processing interfaces with other systems, it is important that formats are consistent.

Two-Column Table with Outline (Illustration 7-8). For this excerpt of a 14-page document, space utilization is critical. Column headings are blocked rather than centered. Periods are omitted after the numbers and letters of the outline, which saves space and makes it easier to revise.

Memorandum (Illustration 7-9). The format of memorandums is similar to that of letters. The unnecessary words *DATE, TO, FROM,* and *SUBJECT* are eliminated to save keystroking time. This style may be typed very easily on plain

Illus. 7-8 Sample Two-Column Table with Outline

```
Teacher's Reference      | Outline of Content
─────────────────────────────────────────────────────────────────
Transparency #38         | I   OVERVIEW OF UNIT ON INDEXING DOCUMENTS
                         |
                         |     A   Definition of Indexing
                         |
                         |     B   Activities to Be Performed
                         |
Assume you wish to       | II  INDEXING ACTIVITY
verify the Doc ID        |
numbers of the           |     A   Main Menu Selection
documents you have       |         1   Space to "Document Index"
recorded.                |         2   Touch EXECUTE key
                         |
                         |     B   Document Index Menu
                         |
                         |     C   Document Index Menu Selection
Transparency #39         |         1   Location prompt
                         |             a   System Disk or Library A
Use SPACE BAR to         |             b   Archive Diskette
select within a          |             c   Printers
column/field of          |             d   Decision
choices; use RETURN      |                 1) Select "System Disk/Library A"
to advance to the        |                 2) Depress RETURN key
next column/field.       |         2   "Which Ones?" prompt
                         |             a   All
Select only the ones     |             b   By author
YOU recorded; you        |             c   By operator
are the operator.        |             d   In use
                         |             e   Damaged
                         |             f   Decision
                         |                 1) Select "By Operator"
                         |                 2) Depress RETURN key
Transparency #40         |         3   Author/Operator Name prompt
                         |             a   Key in your name
                         |                 1) Keep it short
                         |                 2) Be consistent in way name
                         |                    is typed
                         |             b   Touch EXECUTE key
                         |
Transparency #41         |     D   Display of Documents Selected
                         |         1   Information given
                         |             a   Document number
                         |             b   Document name, comments, and
                         |                 author/operator
```

paper, and it requires less effort than preprinted forms in which the typing must be aligned with the guide words.

These formats meet the four guidelines of developing standard formats. However, you will also find memorandums prepared on memo stationery and other letter styles widely used in the business office.

Managing Media Files

In correspondence support, documents are filed on magnetic media. Since about 100 documents might be recorded on one diskette and the word processing center might have more than 50 diskettes, a file management system has to be developed.

On word processing systems, a recorded document is either automatically given an identification number or the operator keys in the label or document name. The space for a label is quite short, generally 5 to 10 characters. Another space, which is longer, is provided for the operator to give the document a description or a title (see Illustration 7-10). If the operator wishes to review the contents of a diskette, the system can display on the screen the list of documents. The list can be printed so that it can be filed with the diskette.

Managing media files includes: (1) numbering or assigning a label or name to each document, (2) composing a document description or title, (3) deciding the type of documents to be recorded on each disk, (4) determining how long to keep the recordings, (5) erasing or destroying the documents that are no longer needed, and (6) duplicating permanent files onto backup diskettes to protect them against loss (archiving). These functions are called file management.

Illustration 7-10 shows the correspondence that has been recorded on the diskette. This information will be kept for one week. At the end of that time, the diskette is erased and ready to be used again.

Illus. 7-9   Sample Memorandum

```
                          INTEROFFICE MEMORANDUM



Line 10     November 5, 19--
                          TS

            Ellen Minter
                     TS

            VACATION TIME CHANGED
                            TS

            Yes, Ellen, you are welcome to change your vacation period to
            January 4-18.  Actually, the change is better for us, too.  The
            early part of January is generally a slack time that can easily
            be covered by temporary help if necessary.
                                               DS
            You are always thoughtful of your associates as well as our
            company's goals.  Thank you for being such a fine employee!
                                                              TS

            Bill Prochaska
                       TS

            mc
```

Illus. 7-10   Managing Media Files: A System for Labeling Documents

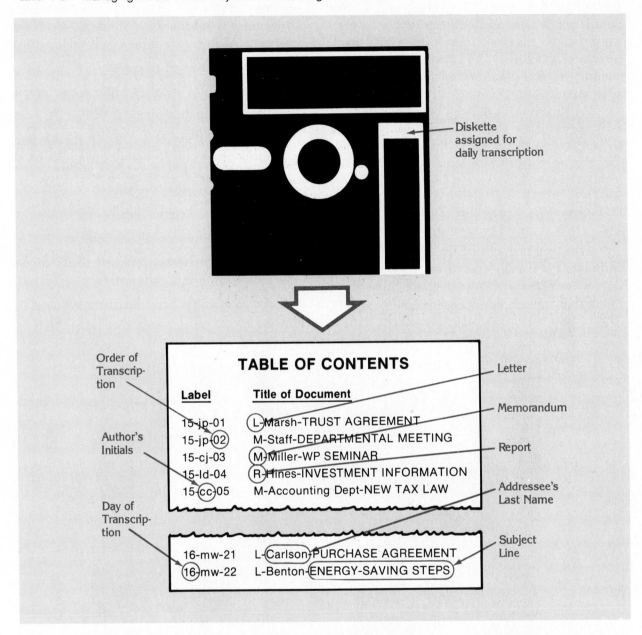

Other diskettes might be assigned for recording quarterly financial reports, the contents of a procedures manual, and annual reports. These may be kept permanently. The supervisor has a copy of each diskette's table of contents (index of documents) in a notebook for quick reference.

Maintaining Quality Printout

Each document that leaves the word processing center must be accurate and have a letter quality appearance. Thus, quality control techniques for proofreading and printing are necessary.

PROOFREADING

Someone is assigned to proofread each document after it has been proofread by the operator and printed. This might be done by a lead CS, a person whose main job is proofreading, or (in the case of a small center) by the supervisor. Some word processing equipment has a built-in dictionary that brings misspelled words to the attention of the operator. However, the dictionary does not automatically correct the spelling errors. Nor does it notice incorrect grammar (was vs. were), word usage, (their vs. there; then vs. than), numbers ($12.40 vs. $12.60), punctuation (comma vs. semicolon), or capitalization (Summer vs. summer).

Proofreading is a difficult but very important skill. Errors that slip by reflect badly on the author and on the image of the company. Also, they can be expensive in terms of lost business or legal action.

CHECKING THE PRINTER

Each printing device for word processing equipment is usually shared by more than one station. A high-speed printer might be used for rough drafts and a slower, letter quality printer for final copy. Printers may be operated by each secretary, or one person may be assigned to print all documents and check the printer(s). Any of the following problems lower the quality of the print:

1 Uneven insertion of paper

2 Insertion of a sheet of paper with a staple

3 Worn-out or broken print wheel

4 Improper selection of pitch (number of spaces per inch). An example would be using a 12-pitch print wheel when the printer is directed to print 10-pitch.

5 Use of poor quality ribbon

6 Incorrect insertion of new ribbon

7 Use of embossed envelopes which may not feed well through the printer

8 An error caused by electronic failure

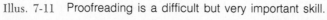
Illus. 7-11   Proofreading is a difficult but very important skill.

Devices are available which help printers work with maximum efficiency. **Continuous-form paper** eliminates the need for individual sheets to be fed into the printer. The sheets are joined by a series of accordian-pleated folds. Once printed, the sheets must be cut and trimmed or detached. A *tractor* is attached to the printer which automatically feeds continuous-form paper through the printer.

An *automatic sheet feeder* holds a large amount of paper in a bin. A sheet feeder automatically inserts and aligns individual sheets of paper into the printer. Dual sheet feeders are available which hold two bins of stationery. For example, one bin could be used for letterhead paper and one could be used for plain paper. Although a tractor which feeds continuous-form paper through the printer and an automatic sheet feeder do not require a person to be at the printer, the machines should be checked frequently to ensure that they are working correctly.

Illus. 7-13   An Automatic Sheet Feeder

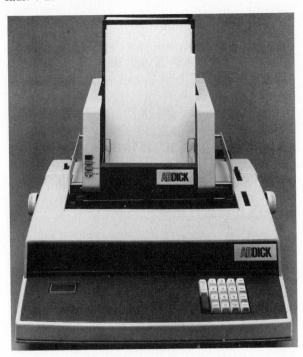

Illus. 7-12   A letter is printed on a continuous-form printer, trimmed, and folded into a window envelope.

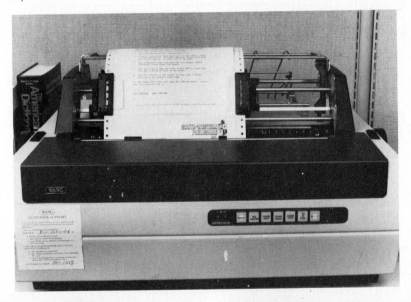

Procedures Manual

Have you ever bought a new machine that had to be put together or been asked to do something you had never done before? How much easier it could be if well-illustrated instructions were available. A procedures manual is a reference book that gives step-by-step instructions and examples on how to perform tasks.

TYPES OF PROCEDURES MANUALS

Who needs a procedures manual? Just about everyone in an office does. Examples of information that can be found in specialized manuals follow.

For Originators:
Operating dictation equipment
Dictating steps

Filling out work requests
Using proofreader's marks
AS and CS services available
Planning conferences

For Administrative Secretaries:
Placing and receiving telephone calls
Sorting and preparing mail to be answered
Making arrangements for meetings
Making travel arrangements
Dictating steps
Filling out work requests

For Correspondence Secretaries (See Illustration 7-14):
Logging work
Measuring work
Operating transcribing equipment
Assigning labels and titles to documents
Typing standard formats of documents
Proofreading

Illus. 7-14   A contents page from a manual shows a list of procedures for correspondence secretaries.

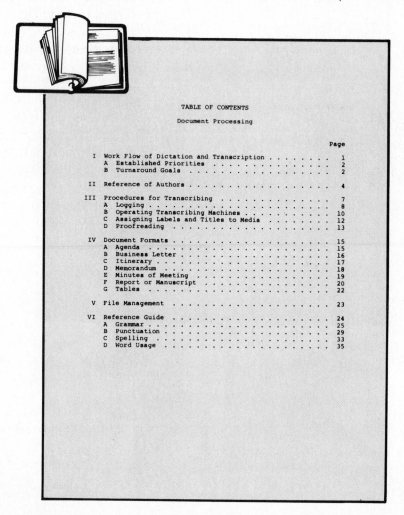

For Supervisors:

    Operating supervisor's console
    Preparing reports for management
    Distributing work
    Evaluating personnel
    Handling grievances
    Managing media files

For information that is needed by all personnel of a company, a reference manual should be produced and distributed. For example, the following information would be used by authors, supervisors, and secretaries: company organization chart; names, room numbers, and telephone extensions of all personnel; tips on effective letter writing; prerecorded documents; priorities; diagram of work flow; turnaround goals; and length of time documents are kept before they are destroyed.

DESIGN OF PROCEDURES MANUALS

A well-designed procedures manual has several features. The instructions are written in outlined or numbered steps with short phrases, which are faster to read and easier to understand than long, wordy paragraphs. For each task there is at least one illustration. If it is a form, it should be a sample of one that has been filled in.

Using colored tabs or a different color of paper for each part of the manual helps the user find a particular section faster. Numbering the pages of section number 1 as 1.1, 1.2, etc., and section number two 2.1, 2.2, etc., allows pages within a ringed notebook to be added or deleted easily.

PURPOSE OF PROCEDURES MANUALS

Procedures manuals eliminate the need for employees to ask other workers how to perform basic tasks. They help employees to be consistent in their work and to perform tasks correctly and efficiently. These guides allow employees to assist each other in the event of absences. When lengthy documents are prepared by a number of people, the format remains consistent. Time is saved. Procedures manuals are also helpful in training new employees and can reduce the length of their training period. In turn, the quality and quantity of work is increased.

Training Personnel

Even though it is possible to learn something new on your own, it is easier and takes less time to learn a new task when someone is teaching you. Training is a form of education. In offices, employees must be taught how to operate new equipment, how to perform new tasks, and how to improve the techniques they have been using. Proper training coaches people to work accurately and efficiently.

In business you would find two types of training programs—orientation training and in-service training. *Orientation training* informs the new employees about the company's products or services, its organization chart, its objectives, and its personnel policies. *In-service training* tells people how to do new tasks or to improve their work. As new equipment is installed, employees must learn to use it. At other times, employees need to be motivated to develop more positive attitudes and tactful ways of communicating.

In-service training programs have been developed for all levels of personnel in word processing. On the management level, originators are trained to operate dictation equipment, to dictate properly, to organize their work, to delegate tasks to administrative support, and to arrange time for creative thought and planning. Supervisors are given training on promoting teamwork, on developing procedures manuals, on training secretaries, on evaluating work, and on preparing production reports.

For administrative support secretaries there is training on records management, mail processing, telephone communication, desk organization, and dictation of routine correspondence. The correspondence secretaries attend in-service training sessions to learn to operate new word processors, to review grammar and spelling and punctuation, to learn the technical vocabulary of the company, and to use the standard formats of documents.

Some companies have their own instructors to do the training. Resource people who are experts in a certain subject might be brought in to teach a particular unit. Or employees might be sent to a special training place.

Without proper training, the attitudes of employees about a new machine or new procedures can change from enthusiasm to frustration

Illus. 7-15 Frequently equipment vendors offer training programs for first-time users.

and anger. The sooner one is thoroughly trained, the more productive that person becomes on the job. The training program must rid all fears and convince the trainees that the new way is superior to the old way.

SUMMARY

You can see how procedures enhance the coordination of people and machines so that they can work to their greatest potential. Procedures are like roads. You can travel the bumpy, crooked, and gravel roads or the smooth, straight, and paved superhighways. In processing information, it is more efficient and less costly to get to the destination by taking the most direct route on the superhighways. Remember the ten procedures that are superhighways in processing information:

logging work
measuring production
setting standards
setting priorities
scheduling turnaround
standardizing formats
managing media files
maintaining quality printout
developing procedures manuals
training personnel

Name_____ Date_____ Section_____

d ___Procedure manuals are shorter.___

e ___~~Production info~~ Money is saved.___

6 For each of the following, circle the choice that would meet the guidelines for standardizing the format of documents:

variable placement (dateline & margins)   (standard placement) (dateline & margins)

(blocked paragraphs of single-spaced text)   indented paragraphs of single-spaced text

(Mr. Nye from ITT typed 75 wam at 1 p.m.)   Mr Nye from ITT typed 75 wam at 1 PM.

(Use window envelopes)   Address plain envelopes

(Address: 1433 E. State Ave., Apt. #4
     Fremont, NE 68025-2411)   Address: 1433 E STATE AVE APT #4
         FREMONT NE 68025-2411

(Name of addressee in body)   No name of addressee in body

(Use of subject line)   No use of subject line

Centered column heading over data of similar length   (Blocked column heading over data of similar length)

(Omission of the words DATE, TO, FROM, and SUBJECT in a memo)   Inclusion of the words DATE, TO, FROM, and SUBJECT in a memo

(Omission of periods after the letters and numbers in outlines)   Inclusion of the periods after the letters and numbers in outlines

Multiple Choice

Select the letter that best completes the sentence, placing it in the space provided in the right column.

1 The quality of printed correspondence depends upon (A) clearness and darkness of the typed characters, (B) composition of text, (C) personal approach, (D) accuracy, (E) all of these.   _E_

2 The factor that has the greatest impact on the cost of a document is (A) paper, (B) labor, (C) equipment, (D) overhead expense, (E) postage.   _B_

3 Recording facts about work as it comes in and goes out of a work area is called (A) logging, (B) recording, (C) measuring, (D) tracking, (E) scheduling.   _A_

4 Log sheets (A) enable the supervisor to quickly find a document being processed, (B) provide a place to record production data, (C) provide guidelines for writing procedures manuals, (D) both A and B, (E) both B and C.   _D_

5 One way to account for the degree of difficulty in typing the document is to measure on the basis of (A) lines, (B) pages, (C) units, (D) electronic counter, (E) paragraphs.   _C_

6   In establishing priorities, the order of assigning tasks to be performed is (A) by order of urgency, (B) by order of importance, (C) by level of difficulty, (D) by length of document, (E) by title of the author.   *A*

7   Turnaround goals (A) mean the same to the company, the secretaries, and the authors, (B) encourage secretaries to work efficiently, (C) help secretaries to know what is expected of them, (D) both A and B, (E) both B and C.   *E*

8   In developing a standard format, one should (A) increase the amount of keystroking, (B) do as much centering and tabulating as possible, (C) be consistent in the punctuation and style of all documents, (D) keep the amount of text per page to a minimum to allow plenty of unused space, (E) all of these.   *C*

9   The quality of printed text is lowered by (A) even insertion of paper, (B) a worn-out or broken print wheel, (C) directing the printer to print 12-pitch and using a 12-pitch print wheel, (D) using a carbon ribbon that prints clear, dark characters, (E) none of these.   *B*

10   Procedures manuals (A) help employees to be consistent in performing tasks, (B) save time and facilitate training personnel, (C) encourage employees to interrupt others to ask questions about routine tasks, (D) both A and B, (E) both B and C.   *D*

True or False

Indicate your answer by placing a T or F in the right-hand column blanks.

1   Processing a document involves both physical (keystroking) and mental (decision-making) effort.   *T*

2   The amount of time used to prepare a document and the cost of labor are unrelated.   *F*

3   Procedures are proper for correspondence support but do not apply to administrative support tasks.   *F*

4   Log sheets and work requests should be designed so that the physical effort and the time taken in filling them out are kept to a minimum.   *T*

5   Administrative support work can be measured by recording either a stroke mark or the amount of time spent for each activity.   *T*

6   The average production rate is a good standard if during the period of measurement the workers were putting forth a minimum of effort.   *F*

7   Dictionaries that are built within a word processor or that are attached by software not only bring misspelled words to the attention of the operator but also automatically correct the spelling.   *F*

Name_____ Date_____ Section_____

8   Procedures manuals are needed by secretaries and authors as well as by supervisors.   _____ T _____

9   Teaching a word processing specialist how to operate a text editor is an example of orientation training.   _____ F _____

10   The best procedures are those that help people and machines to work to their greatest potential and get the job done both efficiently and professionally.   _____ T _____

Instructions for Job 7_____

Assume that you are a correspondence specialist in the word processing services department of TRT Associates. Your supervisor has given you the three documents on pages 148, 149, and 150.

1   The established priorities for your department are shown in Table 7-3 page 132. In which order should the three documents be typed?

   1)   _____Letter_____

   2)   _____Page of ~~production~~ procedures manual._____

   3)   _____Form memo_____

2   Assume that each of the three documents will be recorded on a word processor. Indicate how you would label and compose a title for each of the documents. Use the example on page 137, Illustration 7-10, to help you.

TABLE OF CONTENTS

Label   Title of Document

07-bs-01   L-Nguyen-Training WP Operaters

07-bs-02   R-Tr+Dev Dept-Procedures for control

07-pn-03   M-Granstrom-IN-SERVICE TRAINING
                                                    PROGRAM

3   Type a copy of each document following the established order of priorities. The procedures manual of TRT Associates requires that you use the standard formats that are given in Illustrations 7-7, 7-8, and 7-9.

   a   On the log sheet provided, log the time you begin and complete each document.

   b   For the dictated letter, note that the italic print represents the instructions of the author. The regular print represents the actual content of the letter. Do not type the instructions. Read Illustration 7-7 to determine margins and placement of the date. Also note the format of the various parts of the letter.

c   In the rough draft outline, note that the author has chosen to omit the periods after the numbers and letters. When typing the outline, space twice after the numbers and letters. Space once after the parentheses.

d   The memo was prerecorded on a floppy disk. In actual practice, you would only key in the variables. However, since you do not actually have a floppy disk with the memo prerecorded on it, type the memo from the standard text and fill in the variables listed on the work request.

e   Correct all errors as you make them. Be sure to proofread each document carefully before removing it from your typewriter and correct any errors you may have missed.

LETTER RECORDED ON TAPE YO8 (MACHINE DICTATION)

Secretary, this is Mrs Barbara Spiers from the Department of Training & Development, ID # 5. This is a letter to Mr J S NGUYEN, DIRECTOR OF TRAINING, SYNTEX INDUSTRIES INC, 2744 RYAN STREET SW, LOS ANGELES CA 90037–1315.

The subject of the letter is TRAINING WP OPERATORS.

First Paragraph Your letter reminded me of my first encounter with training operators, Mr Nguyen. As competition within the industry has increased, the vendors have decreased the amount of *Quotation Mark* free *Quotation Mark* training per customer. *Paragraph* Yes, we have developed our own training program. The results have been significant. The operators no longer fear having to learn new machines. The production level of a new operator reaches the center's standards much faster than before this program was initiated. We even have a waiting list of other secretaries who wish to be cross *Hyphen* trained to expand their career opportunities. *Paragraph* I will be pleased to help you develop a training program for Syntex Industries. Call me when you return from Europe, Mr Nguyen, and we will make the arrangements.

End of letter. Thank you, Secretary.

Name_____ Date_____ Section_____

#
VII ∧ PROCEDURES FOR CONTROL

   A Logging *Work*
     1 Log sheet
     2 Work request
     3 Reasons for logging
       a Trace and retrieve a document ~~being processed~~
       b Place on which to record production *data*
       c Basis for production reports *summarizing onto*

   B Measuring Production
     1 Methods of Measuring Production
       a Correspondence Support
         1) Lines
         2) Pages
         3) Units   *4) Electronic counter*
       b Administrative Support
         1) Stroke marks
         2) ~~Time~~   *Amount of time used*
     2 Purpose of Measuring Production
       a Information for management ~~needed for planning~~
       b Scheduling work
       c Identifying problems *and causes*
       d Objective basis upon which to evaluate
          personnel
       e Justify adding personnel *n*
       f Justify adding equipment *or changing*
       g Basis for charge-back *system*
       h Helps set standards
       i Preparing budgets

   C Setting standards
     Setting
   D ~~Establishing~~ Priorities

   E Scheduling Turn around
     1 Definition Varies
       a To company
       b To ~~correspondence support~~ *word processing center*
       c To authors/*principals*
     2 Turnaround *goals*
  sp   a (CS)
  sp   b (AS)

   F Standardizing Formats
     1 Advantages of Standardization
     2 Guidelines for Standardizing Formats
       a Letter
       b Memorandum
       c Two-column table with outline

WORK REQUEST

No. *0128*

Author *Barbara Spiers* Dept. ID # *5*

Description of Job *Please prepare a final copy of this revised page of our procedures manual*

Source *Attached*
Prerecorded, (Rough Draft,) Longhand

Variables for Prerecorded Form Letter/Memo:

Addressee's Full Name *na*

Name in Body *na*

Others

_____ _____

_____ _____

Submitted by *Barbara Spiers* Date *Today's Date*

Form Letter/Memo #226

Current Date

Addressee's Full Name

IN-SERVICE TRAINING PROGRAM

The Task Force Committee has diligently worked to develop procedures
that will enhance the use of our new word processors. You are no
doubt anxious to learn how the new system will help your department
get the work done more efficiently, *Name in Body*

An in-service training program will be held on Monday, *Supply Date:*
Two weeks from this week, from 8 AM to 4 PM in the Catalpa Room.
Please let me know ASAP if there is some reason you cannot attend.

A special presentation will be given by Mrs Ruprecht, who is a member of DPMA and IWPA. She will share some ideas on how we can interface our DP and WP systems so that we can save time and money.

Phil Nelson
President

Your Initials

WORK REQUEST

No. _0131_

Author _Phil Nelson_   Dept. ID # _1_

Description of Job _form memo to a_
department VP

Source _#226_
(Prerecorded) Rough Draft, Longhand

Variables for Prerecorded Form Letter/Memo:

Addressee's Full Name _Linda Granstrom_

Name in Body _Linda_

Others

_____   _____

_____   _____

Submitted by _Mark Benitez_ Date _Today's Date_
for Phil Nelson

WORD PROCESSING LOG

Date _____

Secretary _____

	Time In	Input ID	Author's Name	Dept ID	Doc	Input Form	Output Form	Doc Label	Total Lines	Errors	Time Out	Total Min
1					L M R S	D L P RD	FC RD					
2					L M R S	D L P RD	FC RD					
3					L M R S	D L P RD	FC RD					
4					L M R S	D L P RD	FC RD					
5					L M R S	D L P RD	FC RD					
6					L M R S	D L P RD	FC RD					
7					L M R S	D L P RD	FC RD					
8					L M R S	D L P RD	FC RD					
9					L M R S	D L P RD	FC RD					
10					L M R S	D L P RD	FC RD					
11					L M R S	D L P RD	FC RD					
12					L M R S	D L P RD	FC RD					
13					L M R S	D L P RD	FC RD					
14					L M R S	D L P RD	FC RD					
15					L M R S	D L P RD	FC RD					
16					L M R S	D L P RD	FC RD					
17					L M R S	D L P RD	FC RD					
18					L M R S	D L P RD	FC RD					
19					L M R S	D L P RD	FC RD					
20					L M R S	D L P RD	FC RD					
TOTAL												

DOCUMENT

L Letter
M Memorandum
R Report
S Statistical

INPUT FORM

D Dictated
L Longhand
P Prerecorded
RD Rough Draft

OUTPUT FORM

FC Final Copy
RD Rough Draft

No. of Documents _____
Total Lines Transcribed _____
Total Errors _____
Error Percentage _____
Total Min. of Transcription _____
LPM (Lines per minute) _____

Proofread by _____

COMMENTS _____

4   For each document you typed, count your lines. Begin with the first line of type and count on through the last line of type—except for the line on which you typed your reference initials. Assume that Table 7-4, page 133, shows the turnaround goals of TRT Associates. Did you meet their goals?_____

5   Exchange papers with another member of your "department." You are now the "proofreader." Place a check mark in the left margin of any line that has an error. Write your name after "Proofread by" on your partner's log sheet. Fill in the error column on the log sheet. Then return the log sheet and documents.

6   On *your* log sheet, compute the total amounts and fill in the bottom parts. To determine the error percentage, divide the total errors by the total lines transcribed. Be sure to move the decimal point two places to the right when converting your answer to a percentage. To compute LPM (lines per minute), divide the total lines transcribed by the total minutes of transcription.

7   The standards of TRT Associates are determined by averaging the scores of your entire department (class). Your instructor will provide you with the average time it took your department to perform these tasks.

     Total Errors_____   Total Minutes_____

     Error Percentage_____   Lines per Minute_____

8   What is your evaluation of your work? Did you produce quality documents in an efficient manner?

     _____

     _____

     _____

UNITEIGHT.

The Environment

Most workers spend as many daytime hours at their place of work as they do at home. Just as a home should have attractive, comfortable, and pleasant surroundings, so should a place of work. The surroundings within which people work form what is called the *environment*. An office environment includes the structure of secretarial services, the layout and design of office furnishings, and factors such as climate and noise level.

The environment is most important because it affects people—their productivity, health, morale, and job satisfaction. The temperature, humidity, air quality and circulation affect how well the equipment works. In addition, the environment affects how well the procedures result in an efficient flow of work. An effective environment enhances the people, equipment, and procedures.

DESIGN AND LAYOUT OF WORK AREAS

Arranging word processing to best meet the needs of the organization is called designing the system. The physical location of work stations (desk, files, and so forth) is the layout of the system. The design and layout of word processing equipment differ from company to company. They are influenced by the size of a company, the type of work done, the philosophy of management, and the degree of specialization of secretarial services.

Organization and Layout of Secretarial Services

In contrast to a pure word processing system, secretaries in a traditional office are generalists. They do both the typing and nontyping duties for one or more principals. As a result, secretarial work stations are located near the principals they serve. Thus, secretarial services are scattered throughout the building in a completely decentralized layout. While some of these secretaries have word processors, it is not likely that a word processing system has been organized. This traditional model is shown in Illustration 8-1.

Illus. 8-1 Traditional One-to-One Model (Totally Decentralized Layout)

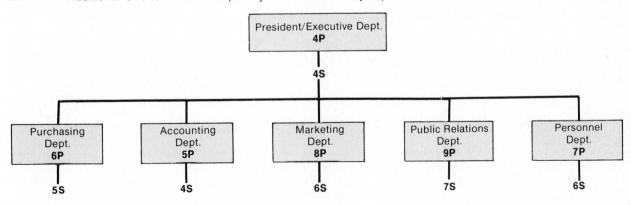

P = Principal
S = Multipurpose secretary

153

In most word processing systems, the secretaries are specialists who do either typing or nontyping duties for a group of principals. The secretaries' areas may be either centralized or decentralized. Secretarial services are centralized if they are located in one large center that serves the entire company. (See Illustration 8-2). The other method is to divide the secretarial services into smaller centers, each serving part of the company. (See Illustration 8-3.) The smaller centers are called satellite centers, minicenters, or work groups. This is a somewhat decentralized layout of secretarial services.

Although a large center is easier to control, there is a trend toward satellite centers. These small centers allow members of each group to become more familiar with the needs of the principals they support.

Illus. 8-2   Centralized Model

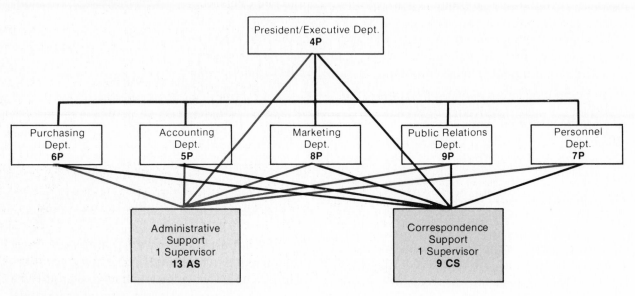

P = Principal
AS = Administrative Secretary
CS = Correspondence Secretary

Illus. 8-3   Satellite Centers Model (Partially Decentralized Layout)

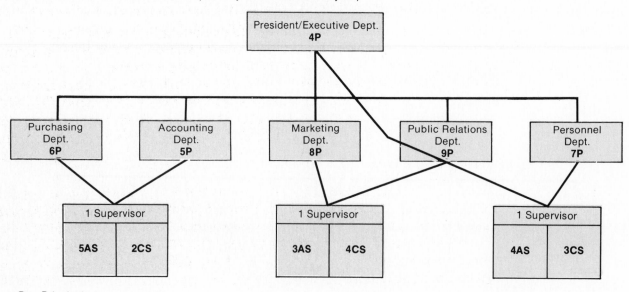

P = Principal
AS = Administrative secretary
CS = Correspondence secretary

Illus. 8-4   Centralized CS/Traditional One-to-One AS Model

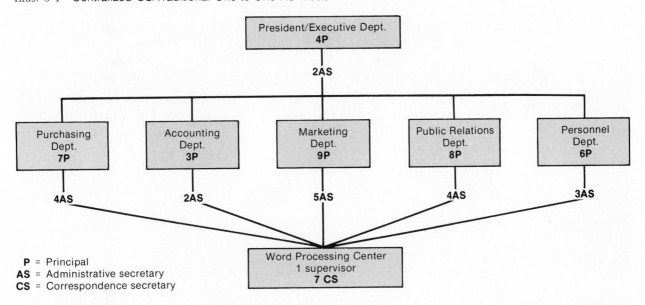

P = Principal
AS = Administrative secretary
CS = Correspondence secretary

Work Areas and Furnishings

Not all organizational structures fit one of the models just described. Some companies organize with professional supervision only the correspondence support part of secretarial services. However, administrative support is left on a one-to-one basis with each AS serving one or more principals. The AS is relieved of heavy typing. This arrangement is shown in Illustration 8-4.

Work Areas and Furnishings

The trend in modern landscaped offices is to create a feeling of openness. The work areas are designed for the comfort and privacy of people. At the same time the design promotes productivity and an efficient flow of paperwork. Open planning and modular furniture are the basic elements used to meet these goals.

OPEN PLANNING

The open plan replaces permanent walls with easy-to-move partitions, panels, and screens. Better use of space is made by using vertical shelving. With open office systems work surfaces, panels, storage units, lighting fixtures, and plants can be combined in many ways to provide efficient yet fashionable work areas. Over one half of the offices being built or remodeled choose the open plan.[1]

The open plan is both economical and flexible. Compared to traditional offices with fixed walls, the open plan costs one tenth to build. It can reduce energy costs (heating, lighting, and cooling) up to one half.[2] The open plan uses 20 percent less work space than a traditional office. The temporary walls and furniture can be moved at the end of the day and be ready the next day with no working time lost. In the traditional office remodeling involves tearing down and building walls, recutting carpet, and rewiring lighting fixtures. Remodeling costs are $20 to $50 per square foot as opposed to $1 to $4 per square foot to change an open plan work area.[3] For this reason, open planning uses permanent walls mainly for the outer walls of a large work area.

Besides being economical and flexible, the open plan can improve the work flow within and between departments. Work stations are designed according to the type of work done and the employees' need to be reached by others. Work stations for those who need contact with others may be grouped within clusters. For people who need more privacy for conferences and concentration, work stations are set apart. Word processing centers are generally located as close to the principals as possible.

[1]"America's Offices Enter a New Age," *Nation's Business*, July 1981, p. 52.

[2]David Steinbrecher, "WP/IS Furnishings Stress Comfort and Flexibility," *Word Processing and Information Systems*, March 1982, p. 31.
[3]Hy Bomberg, "Open Plan—Flexibility for the Future," *Management World*, December 1981, p. 17.

Illus. 8-5   The open plan replaces permanent walls with easy-to-move partitions, panels, and screens.

The open plan does have some disadvantages. Open offices do not provide the privacy needed for quiet concentration and for confidential conversation. Without a private office, workers may feel a loss of job status. The noise level is higher than in offices with permanent, soundproof walls. Therefore, it is very important that ceilings, walls, partitions, flooring, and machine covers be made with material that can absorb sound. Security is another problem in the open office, for one cannot lock one door to protect all possessions.

THE WORK STATION

The individual work areas within an open office are called work stations. Each work station contains a desk top, chair, storage units, and shelves. Light fixtures for the immediate work surface, electrical outlets, and *raceways* for hiding wires and cables are part of many of the newer systems.

Years ago people and machines had to adjust to the design of the desk. Usually the only dividers between work areas were standard desks, file cabinets, and bookcases. Then office specialists began to address the needs of both people and electronic equipment. The term

ergonomics became popular. Ergonomics is the science that studies the relationship between people and machines in an attempt to make machines and furniture designs fit the needs of people.

People and machines come in different sizes and shapes. Therefore, the work station must be designed for flexibility. The height, length of reach, and angle of work station parts must be adjustable. Furnishings are modular, meaning they can be put together, taken apart, and rearranged. As the needs of the employee change or as equipment is replaced, one merely adds, removes, or relocates the adjustable parts. Redesigning modular furniture costs much less than buying a new permanent piece of equipment.

The amount of personal space needed for an individual depends on the nature of the work and the equipment being used. Correspondence secretaries need more space than administrative secretaries because of larger and noisier equipment. Supervisors need to be located near the entrance of the work area where they are accessible to principals and specialists. The type of work performed and the need for conference space determine the amount of space needed by supervisors and principals.

Illus. 8-6 Work stations should be designed to meet the needs of people.

Wiring for display terminals, dictation systems, and telephones can all be enclosed in cables within the panels of the work station. Wherever panels join, connectors snap into place to complete an electrical circuit. The raceways that house electrical wiring within an office are also known as ducts or cable ways. Flat wiring instead of the bulkier cable is also being used to connect electronic equipment. Being less than one tenth of an inch thick, it can be laid between the floor and carpet tiles.

Allowance for change is extremely important in a word processing environment, where technology continues to alter equipment capabilities and sizes. As equipment is replaced by more sophisticated models, the physical space and employees' tasks also change. Therefore, work stations must be easily adaptable to a company's changing needs.

CLIMATE FACTORS

The factors that affect the climate of a word processing system include temperature, humidity, air circulation, color, lighting, sound, and visual display terminals. Each needs to be planned and controlled for the maximum comfort and performance of people and machines.

Temperature, Humidity, and Air Circulation

Word processing equipment and employees are sensitive to changes in temperature and humidity, dust and dirt, and static electricity. The acceptable temperature range is 65° to 75°F with humidity between 40 and 60 percent.[4] When either temperature or humidity exceeds these limits, neither equipment nor people work well. Service costs on equipment increase, and the life of equipment is shortened.

High temperatures cause equipment to deteriorate. Heat can warp or distort recordings on magnetic media just as it can warp your favorite record album. Other supplies such as ribbons, print elements, and paper are affected by high temperatures. These should be stored in cool, dry places.

High humidity causes magnetic media and paper to absorb moisture. Consequently, paper feeders and printers jam because of the paper's increase in weight. On the other hand, low humidity (dry air) allows static electricity to build up. This can cause the equipment to fail and/or the operator to get an electrical shock.

[4]Ellen Shea, "How to Control Temperature and Humidity," *Word Processing and Information Systems,* March 1982, p. 26.

Air circulation and air cleanliness are also important. Dust, tobacco smoke, and other pollutants in the air attract static and cause many problems. They are harmful to the eyes, nose, throat, and lungs. Static attracts dust to the magnetic media and damages the recording surface.

Air conditioners and humidifiers are helpful in circulating, cleaning, and controlling the temperature and humidity. To decrease interference from static electricity, antistatic mats can be placed at the word processor station. It is also recommended that word processing equipment be plugged into a dedicated line (one that is not shared with other electrical equipment).

Color

Interior designers now use many colors and fabrics to decorate the office. Color influences an employee's health, reduces boredom, encourages work, and increases job satisfaction. Even emotional responses can be aroused by color choices. To give a feeling of unity to the work area, offices should strive for pleasant and harmonious colors. On the other hand, accenting with bright contemporary colors provides visual excitement. The selection of color depends upon the space involved, the work being done, the time spent in that area, and the lighting used in the office.

Blue, green, and light beige are relaxing colors. They are good choices for work areas where people perform continuous, detailed work that may cause tension. Blue and green are cool colors. They are often used for work areas that have windows facing the south, southeast, or southwest side of a building where sunlight is bright.

In contrast, soft orange, red, and yellow are warm, friendly colors. They are good for rooms that have windows facing the north, where there is little sunlight. Because these cheerful colors excite the mind, they are often used where creativity is important. Care must be used, however, because brilliant shades of orange, red, and yellow can be overstimulating—causing tension, nervousness, headaches, and nausea. Bright shades might be used to accent a reception area. While the color would attract visitors' attention, it would not make them feel uncomfortable for the short time they are in the area.

Light colors make small work areas seem larger, while dark tones have the opposite effect. The lighter the shade of color, the more light that is reflected from the surface. Therefore, light shades that are flat (not glossy) are usually used on ceilings, walls, and partitions to help reflect light without glare.

Work surfaces, as shown in Illustration 8-7, should have a smooth, flat finish with a medium shade of color. Glossy, shiny surfaces produce a glare that causes eyestrain. A dark surface gives too sharp a contrast with white papers and is also strenuous on eyes. To the other extreme would be a white surface that does not give any contrast to papers, which makes it difficult to distinguish them.

Lighting

You wear sunglasses outdoors to reduce bright light that could harm your eyes. But what can you wear indoors when there is not enough light to see properly? Nothing. Glare and insufficient light cause eyestrain, headaches, and stress. When your work station is not lighted properly, you are less productive and make more errors. Then morale and job satisfaction drop.

The amount of light you need depends on the type of work you are doing. Those who perform close work such as accounting, reading, proofreading, and keyboarding need more light than

Illus. 8-7   Light, medium, and dark work surfaces: a medium color is best for a desk top.

Illus. 8-8 Lighting: Direct versus Indirect

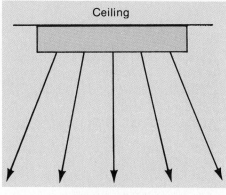

Direct Lighting

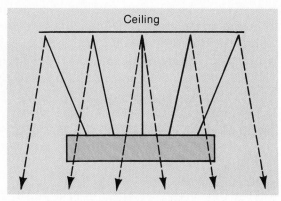

Indirect Lighting

those who are talking with others or running errands. Experts recommend 150 footcandles (fc) for word processing areas. (A *footcandle* is the amount of light produced by a candle at a distance of one foot.)

The quality of light relates to the intensity, reflectance, brightness, or usability of light. Quality improves as glare, shadows, and veiling reflections are reduced. *Veiling reflections* occur when light from the source bounces up from the task or work surface into the user's eyes.

ARTIFICIAL LIGHTING

In addition to the natural light provided by the sun, most offices depend on artificial lighting. Fluorescent lights (usually in the shape of long tubes) are most commonly used in offices. They give more light per watt, give off less heat, and cost less to operate than incandescent light bulbs.

A more recent development in office lighting is high-intensity discharge (HID). HID is often used in parking lots and on streets. Perhaps you have noticed how the color of your skin and clothes are distorted under these lights. HID lights give up to 50 percent more light per watt than fluorescent fixtures, but the quality of the light makes it difficult to distinguish colors. To be useful in the office, HID lights must be carefully used.

DIRECTION AND LOCATION OF LIGHTING

In modern landscaped offices, the goals are to improve the quality of light and at the same time to use less energy. At one time, most lighting came from many fixtures mounted in the ceiling. This kind of light spreads uneven light that causes shadows, creates glare on paper, and makes annoying reflections on visual display terminals. Now light fixtures have become part of the work station.

Light coming from above is either direct, indirect, or some degree in between. Direct lighting, as shown in Illustration 8-8, casts most of the light downward from the ceilings and upper sidewalls. Indirect lighting directs most of the light upward to the ceiling and upper sidewalls. Indirect lighting reduces glare or shadows because the light is more evenly reflected to all parts of the work area. However, in open plan offices with many high partitions either type of lighting will cast some shadows.

A more recent concept is task/ambient lighting. It combines *task* (local) *lighting* and *ambient* (indirect overhead) *lighting*. The task light fixtures are built into the upper part of the work stations; they are usually placed under shelves. Task lighting is designed to light specific work surfaces. The ambient lights are usually mounted on the top of furniture panels to project light upward to the ceiling. This indirect light is then reflected from the ceiling downward to light the general area surrounding the work space. The combination of task and ambient lighting uses less energy because light is focused only where it is needed. Task/ambient lighting uses up to 50 percent less energy than regular ceiling systems.[5]

[5]Robert H. Sternberg, "What's New in the Office Environment," *Management World*, December 1981, p. 9.

Illus. 8-9   This work station shows task, ambient, and HID lighting.

Also, the quality of the lighting improves because glare and shadows are reduced (see Illustration 8-9).

Noise Control

Some noise is productive; too much noise is distracting and unpleasant. It can be a hazard to health, can cause workers to become irritable, and can decrease productivity. More energy is needed to complete tasks under noisy conditions than under quiet ones. As noise gets louder, both concentration and decision-making ability are reduced. Noise also makes it difficult for people to communicate accurately and confidentially. Acoustics is the science that deals with the production, control, transmission, reception, and effects of sound. The volume of sound is measured by *decibels*. Office noise should not be more than 65 decibels (dB).

Most word processing printers are noisy—several in one area are very noisy. Because printing occurs intermittently, the noise can be quite irritating. Word processing systems, particularly those with an open plan, need to do everything possible to control the level of noise.

Equipment Design. Manufacturers are redesigning machines to run more quietly.

Acoustical Hoods. Acoustical hoods are enclosures that are placed over word processors and printers to reduce sound. See Illustration 8-10. Many of the hoods are equipped with a fan that circulates and cools the air.

Illus. 8-10   This printer has an acoustical hood to reduce sound.

Office Layout. Work areas that are laid out according to work flow decrease the amount of required walking, which in turn reduces traffic noise. Office workers who need to work together are located within talking distance to eliminate unnecessary phone calls and walking. Departments with noisy machines are located away from the departments that need quietness for concentration.

Work Station Arrangement. Work stations are sometimes located in clusters, which share at least one common panel or screen. These partitions should be curved and acoustically treated to muffle sounds. Curved partitions absorb sound better than straight ones. The minimum distance between workers should be about six feet.

Ceiling Material. Ceilings should be made of material that absorbs sound, such as acoustical tile.

Walls and Movable Barriers. Both permanent walls and partitions (or panels or screens) that separate work stations should be acoustically treated to absorb and reduce noise. Materials differ in their ability to absorb sound. For example, hard, nonporous (does not allow air to pass) surfaces such as concrete, plaster, and glass reflect sound allowing it to bounce and magnify. In contrast, soft materials such as fiberboard, fabrics, and cork absorb sound.

Carpeting. Not only does carpet absorb sound, but it adds to the attractive appearance of the office. This gives workers greater pride in their work area. The carpet backing and padding should be made of material that allows air to pass through, such as jute, cotton, rayon, and wool. Because walking on carpeting creates static electricity, the carpet should be grounded. Grounded carpeting has wires woven into it which eliminate electrical shocks, thus decreasing equipment failure.

Electronic Sound Masking. Producing a comfortable amount of background noise will mask or cover up unwanted noises. Electronic sound masking might sound similar to an air conditioner or fan. This constant background sound is evenly distributed through speakers above the ceiling. It can be heard but is not distracting. Soft music also muffles sound, but it may create an atmosphere that is too relaxed or may not be the type of music all workers enjoy.

Visual Display Terminals

One of the most controversial factors about the word processing environment is the effect of visual display terminals (VDTs) or CRTs on operators. Common complaints include blurry vision, tearing, burning and throbbing of the eyes, headaches, irritability, and muscular pain in the neck and back. These physical complaints are greater in number and severity than that experienced by the typical office worker.

Studies by the National Institute for Occupational Safety and Health (NIOSH) show that VDTs do not threaten health because of harmful radiation. However, this group has discovered that VDTs do cause eye problems.[6] Causes for eye problems include glare, poor contrast between the screen's background and its images, character flicker (images appear to move or blink), as well as stress. The stress may come from viewing the screen too long without a break or change in activity. To protect operators from VDT problems, various techniques are listed:

---

[6]"CRT Filters Cut the Glare," *Word Processing and Information Systems*, May 1982, p. 30.

- Plan frequent work breaks (at least a 15-minute break for every two hours of work).
- Adjust lighting in work areas to avoid glare.
- Select word processors with adjustable keyboards and adjustable screens.
- Install antiglare screen filters.
- Select visual displays that can be controlled for brightness and contrast.
- Install manuscript holders which allow papers to be adjusted to a height and distance similar to that of the display.

SUMMARY

To students and new employees the environment may not seem important. However, the longer you work, the more interested and concerned you are about your surroundings. To be a productive, happy, and healthy employee, you need appropriate conditions within which to work. In information processing systems, it is particularly important because even machines do not work well in a poor environment. You can see why the "E" (environment) of PMPE is an important ingredient in a word processing system.

Review Exercises

Completion_____

Complete the following sentences by filling in the blanks.

1   A small center of word processing specialists is called a minicenter or a _____.

2   The individual work areas within an open office are called _____.

3   The science that studies the relationship between people and machines in an attempt to make machines and furniture designs meet the workers' needs is _____.

4   _____ colors or shades make small work areas seem larger and reflect light.

5   A work surface should have a smooth, flat finish with a _____ shade of color.

6   The intensity, reflectance, brightness, or usability of light determines the _____ of light.

7   Lighting that is directed upward to the ceiling and upper walls from which the light is evenly reflected without much glare to work areas is called _____ lighting.

8   Localized lighting that is built within the work station to light the specific work area is called _____ lighting.

9   _____ furniture can be taken apart or put together in various arrangements.

10   VDT stands for _____.

Short Answers_____

Indicate your answers by filling in the blanks.

1   What are some of the advantages of open plan offices compared to fixed-wall offices? Name three:

a _____

b _____

c _____

2 What are some of the problems that can happen to equipment and supplies when either temperature or humidity exceeds the limit? Name four problems:

a _____

b _____

c _____

d _____

3 Why would an office have task/ambient lighting rather than only direct ceiling lighting? Give two reasons:

a _____

b _____

4 As an operator of a word processor with a screen, what could be done to decrease your chances of impairing your eyesight?

a _____

b _____

c _____

Multiple Choice

Select the letter that best completes the sentence, placing it in the space provided in the right column.

1 Secretaries who are generalists are usually located next to the principal(s) being served; this approach to layout is (A) centralized, (B) totally decentralized, (C) partially decentralized, (D) a satellite center, (E) a minicenter.   _____

2 A major problem of open landscaping is (A) lack of privacy, (B) feeling of lost status, (C) noise, (D) security risk, (E) all of these.   _____

3 The type of furniture that is recommended for word processing areas is (A) traditional, (B) centralized, (C) organized, (D) modular, (E) none of these.   _____

4 Indirect overhead lighting from ceiling and upper walls is called (A) localized lighting, (B) task lighting, (C) ambient lighting, (D) both A and B, (E) both B and C.   _____

5 Methods of reducing static (electrical shock) within a word processing center include using (A) grounded carpets, (B) humidifiers, (C) antistatic mats, (D) dedicated lines, (E) all of these.   _____

6 Colors that are best for continuous, detailed work that may cause tension and for work areas that receive a lot of natural light from

Name_____ Date_____Section_____

the southwest are (A) blue and green, (B) yellow and orange, (C) blue and red, (D) beige and orange, (E) green and yellow. _____

7 Assuming the quality is right, the recommended amount of light for a word processing center is (A) 75 fc, (B) 150 fc, (C) 200 fc, (D) 250 fc, (E) 30 fc. _____

8 The most economical, energy efficient, and practical type of artificial lighting that is most commonly used in offices is (A) incandescent, (B) high intensity discharge, (C) fluorescent, (D) a sunlamp, (E) a heat lamp. _____

9 Office noise should be no higher than (A) 65 decibels, (B) 80 decibels, (C) 90 decibels, (D) 100 decibels, (E) 110 decibels. _____

10 Unpleasant noise can be reduced by (A) acoustical hoods, (B) electronic sound masking, (C) tile flooring, (D) both A and B, (E) both B and C. _____

True or False_____
Indicate your answer by placing a T or F in the right-hand column blanks.

1 Environment affects work production but has little influence on one's health and morale. _____

2 Centralized secretarial services are easier to supervise than decentralized services. _____

3 Soft material that allows air to go through absorbs sound better than hard material. _____

4 All word processing employees need the same amount of space. _____

5 Word processors and printers have no special wiring specifications. _____

6 A healthy word processing environment would have temperature at the 65-75° F range and humidity between 40 and 60 percent. _____

7 Glare, shadows, and veiling reflections improve the quality of light. _____

8 Ergonomics is the science that deals with the production, control, transmission, reception, and effects of sound. _____

9 Carpeting absorbs sound but increases the chances of static electricity. _____

10 Although visual display screens do not give off harmful radiation, they can cause eyestrain. _____

Instructions for Job 8

To apply the concepts about environment that you have learned in this unit, you will visit three offices. The visits could be a class tour, individual visits, and/or visits by students in pairs. For each office you will identify the characteristics by answering the questions in the space provided. Two points of courtesy should be practiced:

1 Do not carry this sheet into the office and fill it out in front of the person who escorts you. The office could get the feeling that you are an inspector and that you are criticizing the company. Instead, study the questions carefully (and perhaps jot down some reminders) before entering the office. Then immediately after the visit you can fill out this chart.

2 Demonstrate good public relations by making an appointment before the visit and send a thank you letter after the visit.

	No. 1 Name of Escort _____ Name of Company _____	No. 2 Name of Escort _____ Name of Company _____	No. 3 Name of Escort _____ Name of Company _____
1 What is the layout of secretarial services—one-to-one (totally de-centralized), minicenters (partially decentralized), or large centers (centralized)?			
2 If AS and/or CS is organized, does each group serve the entire company or a part of the company? If not organized, record "N/A" for "not applicable."			
3 Is the office setting open planned, traditional with fixed walls, or a combination of the two?			
4 What attempts have been made to landscape (decorate) the office?			
5 Has this office or company expand-ed within the last 10 years?			
If so, was it easy to remodel the office?			
6 Do the secretaries sit at desks or at work stations?			

Name_____ Date_____ Section_____

7   How far apart is one secretary from another—less than 6 ft. or 6 ft. or more?

8   Is the furniture modular?

9   If modular, which units?

9   Was wire management planned such that cords and wires are hidden?

10 Are the work surfaces light, medium, or dark in shade?

11 Are the work surfaces glossy or flat finished?

12 Are partitions, panels, or screens used to separate any work areas?

    If so, are they acoustically treated and are they curved or straight?

13 At what temperature is the office maintained?

14 Is humidity controlled?

    If so, at what percent is humidity maintained?

15 Is smoking allowed in the office?

16 How many word processors are installed?

17 Is there any attempt to keep magnetic media free from dust and smoke?

18 Has there been any problem with static? If so, how was it solved?

19   Are there windows to provide natural light?

If so, on which side of the building are they located?

20   What are the color and texture of the ceiling?

21   What are the color and texture of the walls?

22   What are the color and texture of the floor covering?

23   What type of artificial lighting is used—incandescent, flourescent, HID?

24   Does lighting seem to be sufficient (150 fc)? (A light meter would indicate the number of footcandles.)

25   Is the lighting direct or indirect?

26   Is the lighting task/ambient lighting or strictly ceiling lighting?

27   Is the office noise loud, moderate, or quiet?

28   What attempts have been made to absorb or reduce sound?

29   Is either piped-in music or electronic sound masking used?

30   Did the operators have any complaints about eyestrain from the VDT?

In which of the three offices would you prefer to work (based on environmental factors)? _____

UNIT NINE.

Career Opportunities

If you were an employer, what kind of employee would you hire? Would you hire yourself? In a sense you are already an employer. For example, when you choose a medical doctor to perform surgery, you hire the best professional that you can. Which would you choose—one who has studied medicine only two years or would you hire one who has completed medical school and who has shown success in saving patients' lives? When you choose a restaurant, do you prefer courteous and prompt service with tasty food; or do you go to places that are untidy, unfriendly, and so inefficient that the food tastes stale? Most people hire the best they can afford. The same is true in hiring people for word processing and other information processing jobs. Groom yourself to be the kind of employee you would hire. Prepare to be *the best* you can.

KNOWING THE JOBS AVAILABLE

Careers in word and information processing are many—with different amounts of education and experience required. Your career goals ten years from now may very well be different from the ones you have now. Thus, it is wise to study career options so that you can prepare for the best possible future.

Imagine yourself attending a career day conference at which you hear the following speakers talking about their jobs. The speakers will tell you about the duties of their jobs, the requirements, job satisfactions, and possible dissatisfactions.

Correspondence Secretary (Word Processing Operator)

At your first session you meet Doug Murphy, who is a correspondence secretary (CS) for a medium-sized investment company. (In many companies he would be known as a word processing operator.) At his company, secretarial services are only partially specialized. The correspondence secretaries have been organized into two centers. A supervisor is in charge of the two centers and is assisted by a lead (experienced) CS from each center. Doug is one of the lead CSs.

Illus. 9-1   A correspondence secretary processes documents.

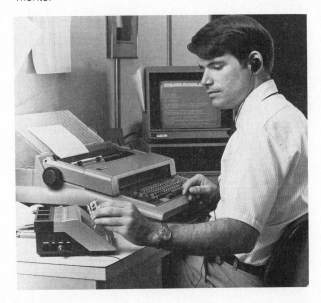

The secretaries who provide administrative support, on the other hand, are distributed throughout the company like traditional secretaries. They are relieved of most of the typing. These secretaries are supervised by the individual principal(s) they serve. Doug admits that there is some friction between the CSs and the administrative secretaries because career paths and work loads are not equal.

169

COMMON TASKS

As a correspondence specialist, you would perform the following common tasks:

Record, revise, and play back documents on word processors.

Change ribbons and type styles of the printing device; take care of equipment.

Transcribe from machine dictation, rough draft, and longhand.

Proofread copy for correct grammar, spelling, punctuation, capitalization, sentence structure, word usage, and typographical errors. Use dictionary and other reference manuals.

Collate and distribute requested number of copies.

Label and file magnetic media (including stored text).

Maintain log sheets and other records.

As a lead CS you would also perform advanced tasks which require more creativity, decision making, and initiative, such as the following:

Design formats for documents.

Maintain reference manuals of prerecorded documents (such as form letters).

Handle larger projects (such as bulletins, catalogs, and manuals) and operate more sophisticated equipment.

Aid the supervisor in directing the work flow and in training other correspondence secretaries.

Perform the archiving, deleting, and duplicating functions for the disks/diskettes.

REQUIREMENTS

Because every typewritten and printed document reflects the image of the company, the final copy must be attractive, error free, and of quality print. The correspondence specialist must be well trained and very capable. Doug points out that even the most sophisticated word processor will play back only what has been keyed into it.

If you apply for a CS position, what requirements must you meet? Most employers look for the following skills and characteristics when hiring applicants for correspondence support:

Ability to listen and to follow directions.

Ability to type with speed and accuracy and to transcribe the intended meaning.

Willingness to operate new machines (transcribing machines, text editors, and printers) and to adopt new procedures.

Expertise in grammar, spelling, punctuation, capitalization, word usage, vocabulary, and proofreading.

Ability to organize and maintain a filing system for magnetic media and hard copy.

Creativity in designing attractive and functional formats of documents.

Willingness to remain seated for extended periods of time.

Ability to use time wisely, to work under deadline pressures, to set priorities, and to keep confidences.

Punctuality, dependability, and loyalty.

Positive and cooperative attitude when working with others.

Understanding of word processing concepts.

CS—JOB SATISFACTIONS

Every job has both positive and negative features. Your satisfaction as a CS would depend on many factors. You could be happy working in one company but unhappy in another. One of the main factors in determining how satisfied you will be with your job is how well you get along with your co-workers, particularly your supervisor. Doug likes his job because his supervisor encourages each CS to develop to his or her greatest potential. There is also a sense of friendship among the members of the team.

Most CSs prefer working with machines rather than with a lot of people. They are fascinated with operating word processors and turning out high-quality documents with speed. Freedom from constant interruptions allows the CS to do quality work in volume—a major source of job satisfaction. Being responsible for a job gives them a feeling of accomplishment. Of course, they like to be recognized for the work they do, and they appreciate being paid a good salary.

CS—JOB DISSATISFACTIONS

The reasons for which CSs feel dissatisfied about their jobs include pressures to produce more work in less time, repetitive work, poor dictators, being treated as machines rather than as people, keeping time and work records, having little opportunity to meet others, being given little responsibility, and having little chance for advancement. However, Doug feels that the negative factors can be eliminated or prevented by proper supervision and top management support.

In closing, Doug says there are good opportunities for high school graduates and those who have at least two or more years of higher education to become CSs. Those who wish to advance to a supervisory position must first get some work experience and preferably a four-year degree in word/information processing.

Administrative Secretary

The next speaker at the career day conference is Nina Rodman, who is an administrative secretary (AS) for a large manufacturing corporation. In her company, secretarial services are divided into AS and CS minicenters. In her work group (minicenter), there are three ASs and two CSs who serve the nine principals of the

marketing division. The administrative support work is divided among the three ASs as follows:

AS #1

Sorts the mail, processes what can be answered without the principal's help, and prepares the rest for an answer by the principal.

Composes and dictates routine correspondence; prepares work requests.

Types speeches and prepares transparencies.

Proofreads documents prepared by CSs; corrects errors; revises rough drafts prepared by the principal.

AS #2 (Nina Rodman)

Answers the telephone, routes calls, and places outgoing calls.

Schedules appointments, maintains desk calendars, and meets and screens visitors.

Plans conferences and meetings; makes the arrangements.

Makes travel arrangements, prepares itineraries (travel schedules), and types travel expense forms.

Illus. 9-2 An administrative secretary does less typing than other support tasks.

AS #3

Maintains records and budgets; files and assists with records management.

Performs research (gathers and organizes information).

Photocopies, collates, and distributes copies.

Operates calculators and facsimile machines.

Types and processes forms.

Manages office supplies; arranges for and keeps records of equipment repairs.

Although each AS specializes in doing certain administrative support tasks, all three have been trained to do each other's work. In this way they can help each other when the work load of one is extremely heavy or if one of the team is absent. Nina might even assist an AS from another division of the company. Learning to do another's job and/or serving another department of a company is called *cross-training*. Nina believes this is one reason she likes working for her company. She can specialize in tasks that she enjoys, yet there are opportunities for her to develop in other areas.

Another reason Nina likes her job is because it brings her in contact with many people. She says she chose AS rather than CS work because she is more people oriented than equipment oriented. Because of family responsibilities, she does not wish to be a supervisor. However, later she may choose to advance in her career. Nina realizes that by learning about the various divisions of the company and by taking night classes at the local university, she can become qualified for a position of greater responsibility and higher pay.

REQUIREMENTS

If you apply for an administrative support position, you would find that most employers are looking for the following skills and personal characteristics:

Ability to dictate correspondence and type with accuracy.

Ability to express oneself orally and in writing.

Ability to manage one's time and set priorities.

Pleasant and tactful personality in meeting and greeting people.

Proficiency in grammar, punctuation, capitalization, spelling, word usage, and vocabulary; proofreading skills.

Cooperative and positive attitude; ability to keep confidences.

Skill in listening and in following directions.

Knowledge of accounting, data processing, and records management.

Flexibility in dealing with interruptions and pressures from telephones, other personnel, and system changes.

Skill in writing shorthand (may not be required but is valuable).

Ability to collect data and perform research.

Understanding of word/information processing concepts as well as company goals.

Having been relieved of most of the typing duties, the AS can take on other responsibilities. For example, Nina explains how an AS can help principals answer letters and memos. In sorting the mail, you (as an AS) set aside all the letters you can answer. You separate them into two stacks—those for which form letters have been prerecorded and those that you will need to dictate. For those that can be answered by a form letter, you fill out a work request giving the proper codes and variables. For those that require a personal response, you dictate an answer. Both sets of letters will be transcribed by the correspondence center. When you receive the completed letters, you will proofread them and place them (with enclosures) on the principal's desk for signing.

AS—JOB SATISFACTIONS

Administrative secretaries have the opportunity to do a variety of tasks. They enjoy the contact with principals, managers, and the public. They have seen how AS positions often lead to supervisory positions. Good salaries also bring satisfaction.

AS—JOB DISSATISFACTIONS

Nina believes it is important to also share some negative aspects of administrative secretarial work. If administrative support is organized with several levels for career advancement, the lowest level AS may perform the simplest, routine tasks of a clerk. If administrative support is not organized throughout the company into work groups with professional supervision, the

AS may experience the frustrations and problems of the traditional secretary.

In closing, Nina recommends that if you are shopping for an AS position, take note of each company's organization chart, environment, procedures, and philosophy of management. The end-of-unit activities will help you evaluate possible places of employment.

Supervisor or Manager

Whether you prefer to work with machines or people, there are opportunities for you to advance to a supervisory position. Your long-range career goal may be to become a supervisor/manager of administrative support services, correspondence support services, or both. With the additional knowledge about data processing, micrographics, reprographics, phototypesetting, and electronic mail, you can become an information systems manager.

Your advancement will depend on your attitude, your performance, your growth in learning about information processing systems, and your ability to get along with others. Because you are a capable CS or AS does not mean that you will be a good supervisor. However, in companies that encourage career development you will be given more and more responsibility so that your abilities can be observed. In coordinating secre-

tarial services, you would need to be effective in communicating with all levels.

The next speaker to describe a career is Carol Williams, who supervises secretarial services—both AS and CS—for a real estate agency. As a college student, Carol worked part time for this agency. After graduation she became a full-time CS and later cross-trained as an AS. By the end of three years, Carol had advanced to the position of assistant supervisor of correspondence support. Two years later she was promoted to supervisor of AS/CS. This position required a four-year degree and three years of work experience.

COMMON TASKS

Whether you are a supervisor of AS or CS or both, you would perform the following kinds of tasks:

Design and periodically reevaluate the system.

Write and update procedures manuals, establish standard formats, design forms, and set up the filing system for magnetic media and hard copy.

Review qualifications and interview job applicants.

Provide orientation and in-service training programs.

Illus. 9-3 A supervisor must be able to communicate with both secretaries and managers.

Set priorities, develop more efficient procedures for work flow, and control turnaround time; coordinate work schedules of personnel.

Serve as a contact between management and secretaries.

Prepare management reports about production, equipment and operational costs, and problem areas.

Update knowledge about word processing and other information processing systems by reading current publications, attending seminars, and visiting installations.

Select equipment and carry out new procedures.

Control the environment so that it is attractive and contributes to the productivity of workers.

Plan and control the budget; charge costs to users.

Measure production and set standards of work performance.

Evaluate performance of secretaries and recommend salary increases, promotions, and/or additional training.

Maintain security of information, including the filing system.

Conduct staff meetings; motivate personnel.

REQUIREMENTS

To be a supervisor, Carol says that one needs the right combination of education, work experience, and personality. You would need to develop the following skills and characteristics:

Knowledge of the company's products and services, management's philosophy, and personnel policies.

Understanding and enthusiasm for the benefits of word/information processing.

Ability to speak to company personnel and to professional groups.

Knowledge of each task and the ability to operate each piece of equipment.

Ability to plan, organize, direct and evaluate a project; ability to recognize problems before they happen; tact in getting principals to use AS and CS support teams.

Ability to listen.

Flexibility in coping with interruptions and in adjusting to technological changes.

Sensitivity to the needs and problems of the principals and of the secretaries.

Stamina to work under the pressure of meeting deadlines, especially when equipment malfunctions and/or employees are not up to par.

Desire to grow professionally and to learn about other technologies (data processing, electronic mail, micrographics) that could interface with word processing.

Fairness in distributing work loads, in rewarding or disciplining workers, and in serving principals.

In listening to Carol you understand why most people in supervisory positions have worked their way up to that level. Even the person who has completed four years of college will first have to work as a CS or AS to learn about the company and its information processing system.

THE REWARDS AND PROBLEMS OF BEING A SUPERVISOR

Carol says that supervising her eleven employees is like coaching a sports team. She needs to identify each one's strengths and weaknesses and then help each to develop to his or her greatest potential. This means taking a sincere interest in their career goals and showing appreciation for good work. When she does this, team spirit, company loyalty, and productivity increase. Job satisfaction comes when productivity goals are reached and employee morale is high.

As with any job, there are moments of discouragement. Among those on Carol's list are the following: finding job applicants who have adequate English skills and the right attitude about work, getting principals to delegate work and to improve their dictation skills, overcoming resistance to change, and withstanding pressures to meet deadlines. A manager must try to keep up to date about all information processing systems. In companies that are interfacing various information processing systems (for example, data processing and word processing), there seems to be a power struggle. Who will be the information manager—the data processing manager or the word processing manager? Carol advises that anyone who would like to become an information manager be thoroughly schooled in both data processing and word processing, as well as in other areas of information processing.

Business Teacher

Dave Tobey, a local teacher, describes the important role of a business teacher at the career conference. He asks you to help him list the types of courses that teach word and/or information processing concepts and skills. The list includes business communications, typewriting, shorthand, machine transcription, business English, filing (records management), administrative (secretarial) procedures, and word processing equipment. More and more schools now have specific word processing courses.

QUALIFICATIONS

To become a business teacher one must have a four-year degree in business education. You can then teach business subjects in a high school or in a vocational school. To teach in a two-year or four-year college or university, you need to have at least a master's degree. Dave plans to begin his master's degree program this summer.

REWARDS AND CHALLENGES OF THE JOB

Helping people develop employable skills is one of the many rewards of teaching. According to Dave, you have an opportunity to be as creative as you wish. Dave wants learning to be fun and to be relevant to the modern world. Since most teachers are employed to teach nine or ten months of the year, the summer months offer time to do other things. You could get work experience, do professional writing, continue your education toward an advanced degree, travel, or have more time for your family and personal interests. Some business teachers are employed by vendors to train new customers and/or to write training manuals. These are just some of the reasons Dave enjoys a teaching career.

Of course, there are unpleasant aspects of the job as well. Beyond their classroom responsibilities, teachers are expected to serve on committees and to help with student activities.

Illus. 9-4 A business teacher helps people develop employable skills.

To do a conscientious job, it is often necessary to work overtime. Business teachers are in a constant race to keep up with the rapid changes in the business world by updating the curriculum and obtaining equipment.

Marketing Support Representative (MSR)

Here to chat with you about another career choice is René Chancellor, who is a marketing support representative (MSR) for a vendor. The MSR (also known as a customer support representative—CSR) demonstrates the equipment to show its features to potential customers. Once a customer obtains the word processing equipment, the MSR trains those who will be operating it. René may even help the customer set up a file management system so that documents can be easily stored and retrieved from the disks or diskettes. Some MSRs do some selling when the opportunity permits.

QUALIFICATIONS

The MSR needs to have top keyboarding skills and the ability to teach the operation of the machines. To help customers fully use their equipment, the MSR should have some knowledge of the customer's needs. Experience with various types of companies helps one quickly identify the most efficient applications of word processors.

Customers often contact the MSR when they are having trouble with the equipment. Therefore, the MSR should be able to communicate with patience and tact. The MSR also needs to be able to get the right information from the customer to determine the cause of the problems with the equipment. Often problems with word processing equipment occur because the customer does not know how to operate it correctly. Help that can be given over the phone saves the cost of a service call. By keeping aware of customer needs, the MSR can suggest features for new models to the vendor and manufacturer.

REWARDS AND PROBLEMS OF THE JOB

René chose to become an MSR because she is intrigued by word processing equipment and she enjoys meeting and working with new people. There are also opportunities to travel. MSRs participate in seminars and exhibit equipment at trade shows.

However, there are times when they must work beyond the 8 to 5, Monday through Friday schedule. If the company services a large geographic region, the job can involve a lot of driving. Installing a sophisticated piece of equipment in a company that neither understands nor applies good procedures results in many problems that are beyond the control of the MSR. Education and experience help MSRs to overcome their frustrations.

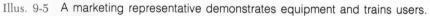

Illus. 9-5   A marketing representative demonstrates equipment and trains users.

A Sales Representative of Word Processing Equipment

Your next speaker is Tom Goss, a sales representative who works for a distributor of word processing equipment, called the vendor. Tom calls on potential customers, answers phone calls and letters of inquiry about the products, demonstrates the equipment, submits bids (cost of equipment, service, and software according to the specifications written by the buyer), and is the contact between the buyer and other personnel of the vendor. Generally, the vendor employs sales representatives, MSRs, and service persons. The sales representative arranges to have the service person install the equipment and repair machines.

QUALIFICATIONS

To effectively sell word processing equipment, Tom suggests that you obtain a college education with emphasis in marketing, word processing, and data processing. Marketing courses would prepare you to recognize potential customers, analyze your competition, give effective sales presentations, and advertise your product. Obviously to sell a product one must know how it works and how it can help the customer. A courteous and friendly personality is also a must.

REWARDS AND PROBLEMS OF THE JOB

As a sales representative, Tom gets to meet a lot of people. He is on the road visiting potential customers most of his working hours. Being part of the automated business world is challenging. Tom likes the salary, for he is paid 50 percent by salary and 50 percent by commission on sales.

Selling business machines is competitive. There is a lot of turnover among personnel. Only the good ones stay in the business and have the opportunity to advance to managerial positions.

Illus. 9-6   A sales representative finds buyers for word processing equipment.

Owner of a Word Processing Service Bureau

You might wish to own word processing equipment and perform text-processing functions for others. Chris Hull serves companies that do not have the time, staff, nor equipment to do word processing. Having established a base of clients, Chris now employs a part-time employee through the high school cooperative office education program. To attract and keep customers, she must do good work and meet turnaround goals.

For people who choose to work at home, a service bureau offers an opportunity. There is little time or expense involved with travel, unless pickup and delivery are part of the service. The working hours are flexible as long as turnaround goals are met. Another advantage of owning and operating a service bureau is that you are your own boss. Of course, there are risks involved. You are fully responsible for the profit or loss of the business, which depends on your ability to manage and market it.

To prepare for this type of career, Chris suggests that you take courses that teach word processing concepts and skills. In addition, courses in accounting, management, and marketing would be helpful.

A Consultant

The last speaker is a consultant, Denise Payne, who helps others set up or improve their systems. She studies their people, machines, procedures, and environment. She can then determine problems in the work flow and make suggestions for improvement.

As a consultant, Denise can work in-house (within a company), for a consulting firm, or own and manage her own firm.

Consultants must understand word processing as it relates to a total information processing system. They must know how to conduct a study of the company's needs (called a feasibility study), design a system, examine costs, defend the cost of a new system, evaluate equipment, interface word processors with other information processing machines (such as computers), set up a records management system, reorganize personnel, outline career paths, and train personnel. Both oral and written communication skills are needed. A consultant must be able to talk with all levels of the organization and present reports to top management. The consultant may even write the procedures manuals.

To become a consultant you would need education, experience, and a supportive personality. You would want to obtain a four-year degree

Illus. 9-7   A service bureau processes words for others.

Illus. 9-8   A consultant helps people create new systems.

from a college or university that offers a word processing or information processing program. Denise recommends gaining experience with different companies to have a broad background. A supportive personality is one that is tactful, willing to listen, enthusiastic, and able to get people to accept change. The consultant advises but does not command or control the client's business.

PLANNING YOUR CAREER

Having learned about various careers, you are ready to evaluate yourself. In which type of career do you feel you would be most satisfied? How much education is needed for that type of position? How much responsibility do you want in a job? Do you like to work for someone else, or do you prefer being your own boss? Do you like to travel? Do you like to meet people? Where do you wish to go in the business world?

Next, you will search for job openings. You can learn about word processing positions through newspaper ads, public and private employment agencies, your word processing teacher, and the word processing association that is closest to where you live.

Once you have chosen companies to which you will apply for a job, you need to study their organization of secretarial services. If you are applying for an AS or CS position, you will want to learn if there is an open career path.

Open Career Paths

Companies that offer open career paths provide a means for employees to advance to management positions. This is in contrast to the traditional office where secretarial pay and status are tied to the principal's position. Some companies have word processing equipment but do not offer open career paths. Five conditions are met by firms that offer open career paths.

Job Titles and Job Descriptions. There must be a job title and a job description for each word processing position. Examples of the most frequently used titles of secretaries and managers are given in Table 9-1. A job description tells you the purpose, duties, and minimum qualifications required of the position. See Illustrations 9-9 and 9-10 for examples of CS and AS job descriptions.

AS and CS Organized with Supervision. Both AS and CS are organized throughout the company with professional supervision for each group. An organization chart similar to that shown in Illustration 9-11 on page 182 would accompany the job descriptions. Notice how the chart relates to the job descriptions shown and reveals that there is professional supervision of secretaries.

Advancement Levels. Three or more levels of advancement are within each area of specialty—AS and CS. A chart like that given in Illustration 9-11 also tells you how many levels there are for each category. A company that has only one or two levels of secretarial positions reveals a dead-end road to career advancement.

Parallel Levels of AS and CS. AS and CS have parallel levels when the salary structure and status of AS and CS are equal. A company could have several levels of AS and several levels of CS; however, if the base pay of Level 1 of AS is more

TABLE 9-1   Job Titles in Word Processing

ADMINISTRATIVE SUPPORT	CORRESPONDENCE SUPPORT	SUPERVISOR
Administrative Assistant	Correspondence Secretary	Administrator of
Administrative Secretary	Correspondence Specialist	Coordinator of
Administrative Specialist	Document Specialist	Director of
Administrative Support Secretary	Magnetic Keyboard Specialist	Manager of
Administrative Support Specialist	Proofreader	Supervisor of
Executive Assistant	Transcription Specialist	Administrative Services
Management Support Secretary	Word Processing Operator	Administrative Support
Management Support Specialist	Word Processing Secretary	Communications
	Word Processing Specialist	Correspondence Support
	Word Processor	Information Systems
		Office Systems
		Secretarial Services
		Word Processing Services

than the base pay of Level 1 of CS, the positions are not parallel. Or, if there are three levels of AS and five levels of CS (as shown in Table 9-2), the career paths are not parallel. Unequal base pay or number of levels (sometimes called grades or steps) tells employees that one part of word processing requires more skill, has more status, or offers better advancement opportunity. This often causes dissatisfaction among employees.

TABLE 9-2 Unparallel Levels of AS and CS

ADMINISTRATIVE SUPPORT		CORRESPONDENCE SUPPORT	
Level	Monthly Base Pay	Level	Monthly Base Pay
		5	$1510
		4	1350
3	$1570	3	1250
2	1290	2	1170
1	1170	1	900

Illus. 9-9 CS Job Description

JOB DESCRIPTION OF WORD PROCESSING SPECIALIST II/ASSISTANT SUPERVISOR

Position Title Word Processing Specialist II/ Assistant Supervisor

Level III

Department Word Processing Center WP/AS Services

Report to Word Processing Supervisor

Function of Position

To prepare documents on advanced word processing equipment; to design and perform new applications; to serve a group of principals in an AS/CS structured environment.

Duties

1. Records, revises, and plays back documents on text-editing equipment.

2. Formats letters, memorandums, manuscripts, and reports (including statistical content) from longhand, rough drafts, machine dictation, or prerecorded drafts.

3. Operates advanced equipment; cross-trains on jobs and equipment.

4. Helps train entry-level word processing specialists on machine operation and work applications.

5. Labels and files magnetic media, maintains files of prerecorded/stored text, and performs archiving functions.

6. Proofreads text for correct spelling, grammar, punctuation, word usage, capitalization, vocabulary, and sentence structure; makes appropriate editing marks.

7. Maintains log sheets; tabulates daily log totals onto weekly and monthly summaries.

8. Makes required number of copies and collates multiple-page documents.

9. Contacts principals to resolve questions about work assignments.

10. Assists in upgrading procedures.

11. Assists supervisor in receiving work, scheduling work, and charging users for services.

Minimum Qualifications Required

1. High school diploma with emphasis on secretarial procedures and skills, including word processing.

2. Two years of experience as a Word Processing Specialist I or its equivalent.

3. Ability to operate text-editing equipment.

4. Straight-copy typewriting rate of 70 net words a minute on a 5-minute writing.

5. Average transcription rate of 45 words a minute with 98 percent accuracy.

6. Expertise in grammar, spelling, punctuation, capitalization, and word usage.

7. Ability to meet departmental standards of performance.

Illus. 9-10 AS Job Description

JOB DESCRIPTION OF ADMINISTRATIVE SPECIALIST I

Position Title Administrative Specialist I   *Level*   II

Department Administrative Support Center   *Report to* Administrative
WP/AS Services   Support Supervisor

Function of Position

To provide administrative services for a group of principals in an AS/CS structured environment; to perform advanced applications of an area of specialty.

Duties

1   Receives, sorts, annotates, and routes incoming mail.

2   Searches for and compiles information needed to answer correspondence and/or prepare reports; selects form letters for routine replies, fills out work requests that include the variables, and forwards them to WP Center.

3   Composes and dictates correspondence.

4   Maintains accurate records and files.

5   Proofreads text for correct grammar, spelling, punctuation, word usage, capitalization, and vocabulary.

6   Prepares work request forms to have documents reproduced; prepares transparencies.

7   Makes room reservations for departmental meetings and large conferences.

8   Makes plane and hotel reservations; prepares documents for travel advance and reimbursement.

9   Answers telephone, screens and routes incoming calls, and places outgoing calls.

10 Maintains log sheets; tabulates daily log totals onto weekly and monthly summaries.

11 Makes copies and collates multiple-page documents.

12 Operates desk calculators to assist in statistical applications.

13 Types forms.

14 Schedules appointments, reviews calendar with principals, and assembles materials for appointments.

15 Takes notes at meetings and prepares the minutes.

Minimum Qualifications Required

1   High school diploma with emphasis on secretarial procedures and skills, including word processing.

2   One year of experience as an Administrative Trainee or its equivalent.

3   Straight-copy typewriting rate of 60 net words a minute on a 5-minute writing.

4   Expertise in grammar, spelling, punctuation, capitalization, and word usage.

5   Ability to use proper telephone etiquette.

6   Ability to meet departmental standards of performance.

Illus. 9-11   An Organization Chart for the CS and AS

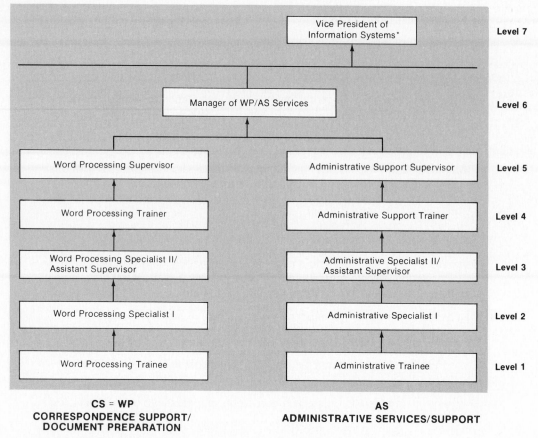

Vice President of
Information Systems*   Level 7

Manager of WP/AS Services   Level 6

Word Processing Supervisor   Administrative Support Supervisor   Level 5

Word Processing Trainer   Administrative Support Trainer   Level 4

Word Processing Specialist II/   Administrative Specialist II/   Level 3
Assistant Supervisor   Assistant Supervisor

Word Processing Specialist I   Administrative Specialist I   Level 2

Word Processing Trainee   Administrative Trainee   Level 1

CS = WP   **AS**
CORRESPONDENCE SUPPORT/   **ADMINISTRATIVE SERVICES/SUPPORT**
DOCUMENT PREPARATION

*Others who would report to the Vice President of Information Systems would be:
  Manager of Data Processing
  Manager of Records Processing
  Manager of Reprographic Services

Advancement to Management Positions. Management positions should exist that are related to and recruited from the AS/CS (or WP/AS) ranks. A company that encourages secretaries to develop to their greatest potential opens doors for those who have the ability to become managers.

The Ideal Place To Work

Although no company is perfect in every respect, this text has given you ideas on specific characteristics to look for in choosing a career in word processing. As you learn about the benefits and problems of word/information processing, remember that no two companies and no two employers are the same. A position in one firm can be exciting and offer opportunities to advance, while in another firm a similar position can be dissatisfying. Job satisfaction depends on a combination of factors, namely: the organization and philosophy of the company, the immediate supervisor, your abilities and personality, and your career goals.

SUMMARY

To each of you who reads this book: May you have the happiest and most successful career. Success lies not so much in the *one* who is *the* best but in *all* of those who do *their* best. In other words, develop yourself to your greatest potential, and you will be serving the word/information processing community and yourself in the best possible way. There is a real need for all types of careers and levels. Each job is important. Automation does not replace good employees; it merely reorganizes jobs so that each is more functional and satisfying, and it creates new types of jobs.

Review Exercises

For Unit 9 there will be no review exercises. Instead, various activities are suggested that will help in career planning.

Suggested Activities for Unit 9 _____

1   Visit and/or join a professional organization. Contact the word/information processing association nearest to you and ask to attend a regular meeting as a guest. Most organizations are delighted to have students as guests and as members. In fact, to encourage students to join, most have reduced membership rates for students.

   If you or your teacher does not know of a local word/information processing association, you can write to the following national organizations. They will give you the name and address of a chapter or an individual member closest to your city.

   Association of Information Systems Professionals (AISP)
   1015 North York Road
   Willow Grove, PA 19090

   Office Technology Management Association (OTMA)
   9401 W. Beloit Road, Suite 101
   Milwaukee, WI 53227

2   Study about salaries. Review a copy of the most recent AISP salary survey results. The complete booklet costs about $40 for nonmembers and $25 for members of AISP. Here are some sources for you to check:

   a   A member of AISP.
   b   Your school library.
   c   Write to AISP and ask for a photocopy of the page that gives a summary of salaries in the United States or in Canada.

3   Visit companies. Visit two or three companies (preferably those that have word processing equipment and specialization of secretarial services) and obtain career information. You may wish to combine this activity with the project at the end of Unit 8. Follow these steps:

   a   Get the name, address, and phone number of each company.

_____   _____   _____

_____   _____   _____

_____   _____   _____

Phone _____   Phone _____   Phone _____

b Telephone the company to find out the name of the personnel director, office manager, or word processing supervisor. Get the proper personal title as well as the spelling and pronunciation of each name.

_____   _____   _____

c Telephone each person (Step b) to make an appointment to visit the word/information processing department. Should you not be able to locate a company that has secretarial services organized into AS/CS, you could visit traditional offices.

Company A	Company B	Company C
Name _____	Name _____	Name _____
Date _____	Date _____	Date _____
Time _____	Time _____	Time _____
Place _____	Place _____	Place _____

d Confirm each appointment with a letter that includes the date, time, place, and purpose for the visit. Make a copy of each letter; the copies will be turned in with your written report.

e Obtain answers to the following questions during the office visits:

Question	Company A	Company B	Company C
Fill in name of company	_____	_____	_____
1) Is there an organization chart showing job positions?	_____	_____	_____
If yes, is a secretarial position shown on the chart?	_____	_____	_____
2) How are secretarial services organized?			
a) Traditional concept	_____	_____	_____
b) Both AS and CS organized	_____	_____	_____
c) CS organized; AS traditional	_____	_____	_____
d) AS organized; CS traditional	_____	_____	_____
3) Are there job descriptions for each of the secretarial positions?	_____	_____	_____
If yes, ask for a copy so that you can review. Read it to determine where you might fit into the organization.			
4) Are there three or more levels of secretarial positions?	_____	_____	_____
5) Should the company have both AS and CS organized, are the levels parallel?	_____	_____	_____

6) Is there a salary scale for secretarial positions? (Some companies may not want to share this information.)   _____ _____ _____

7) How do the salaries compare with the national averages of the AISP salary survey? better? worse? about the same?   _____ _____ _____

8 Who supervises the secretaries?
   a) Executive/manager/principal _____ _____ _____
   b) Supervisor of secretarial services   _____ _____ _____
   c) Lead secretary   _____ _____ _____

9) Is there a management position that has been filled by one who advanced from a secretarial position?   _____ _____ _____

f   Write a thank you letter to each person with whom you visited. Make a copy of each letter to turn in with your written report.

g   Prepare a typewritten report that summarizes your findings and that includes copies of your correspondence.

4   Invite a guest speaker to share information about his or her career in word processing. Choose among the various careers that were described in this unit. Here are some guidelines:

a   Obtain name, address, and phone number of speaker.
b   Telephone speaker to initiate the invitation.
c   Confirm the invitation by letter, including such information as:
   1)   Date, time, and place.
   2)   Suggested topics to include in presentation.
      a)   Job duties and responsibilities.
      b)   Reasons for liking the job.
      c)   Characteristics of the job that are dissatisfying.
      d)   Advancement opportunities.
      e)   Suggestions for one who wishes to pursue this type of career.
   3)   Ask if audiovisual equipment will be needed.
   4)   Give directions for finding school and for parking.
   5)   Express appreciation for willingness to participate and to share.
d   On day of presentation:
   1)   Plan for a host or hostess to meet the speaker.
   2)   Prepare for audiovisual aids if necessary.
   3)   Introduce speaker.
   4)   Have questions in mind to ask at the end of the presentation.

      5)   Offer refreshments after the presentation.

      6)   Escort speaker to the exit.

   e   After the presentation send a thank you letter to the speaker.

5   Read an article about a well-known person in a word processing or information processing career. Your teacher will help you by suggesting possible sources.

Write a report based on the article and include the following information:

a   Source (title of article, author, name of book or magazine, date of issue or copyright, and page numbers).

b   Summary of article.

c   Your reaction. How were you impressed by this article? How did it affect your decision about a career in word processing or information processing?

6   Give an oral report to share with your classmates what you have learned about careers. It can be based on your tour of companies and/or on the article(s) you have read. It can be outlined as follows:

a   Source of information.

b   Summary of what you have learned.

c   How the information has affected your decision about a career choice.

Illus. 10-2a A Large Mainframe Computer System

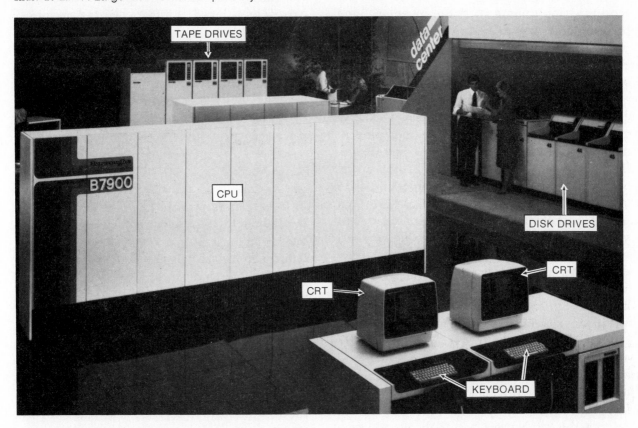

Illus. 10-2b A Minicomputer

Illus. 10-2c A Microcomputer

Popular applications in business include accounting, keeping a record of inventory, and processing the payroll. Here is an example of payroll processing: The information about each employee is stored on a hard disk, which is known as the master file. The data includes the employee's name, sex, marital status, age, home address, telephone number, Social Security number, department, job title, length of service, monthly gross pay or hourly wage, and deductions. The amounts to be deducted include Social Security and/or other retirement programs, state taxes, federal taxes, and so forth. At the time paychecks are prepared, the appropriate program is used to calculate each employee's net pay and to print a voucher and a paycheck. All employees' deductions are accumulated for each account— state taxes, federal taxes, Social Security taxes, retirement funds, contributions, etc. The checks for those accounts are also printed when required.

Such a short summary of one data processing application does not give justice to the capability of the computer. Just imagine what it would be like to process large payrolls each month—repeating the same steps with only the aid of a calculator. Manual effort would take several days, and the chance of human error would be high. A computer system can do the job in a fraction of the time without error.

Some companies have developed a *distributed data processing* system. In this type of arrangement computer terminals are located throughout the company. Each terminal connects to the computer mainframe, which enables each user to access data in the central files of the large computer from his or her work station. Microcomputers and minicomputers can also communicate with a mainframe, for all that is needed is a terminal.

Have you ever searched through the *Reader's Guide to Periodical Literature* for articles about a certain topic to be used in your term paper? Today you can "talk" to a computer and ask it to perform the search for you. The library's computer would have information about each topic for which an article or a book has been written. This huge file is known as a ***data base***. By keying in words or phrases describing the topic of interest, you can have the computer perform an electronic search. Searches can be made by names, companies, authors, dates, and topics. By combining terms, the information can be as narrow or as broad as a particular task requires.

Data bases are available on countless topics some of which include current stock prices, financial data on companies, and legal actions. Data bases are huge electronic libraries of information. Tremendous research time is saved by using a data base. Subscribers to a data base pay a fee for its use.

Graphic Terminals

Computers provide huge amounts of data. But before this information can improve decision making, it must be in a form that is meaningful. Graphic terminals display "the picture that is worth a thousand words." Graphic terminals display information in the form of patterns and shapes instead of only numbers. The significance of graphs and charts is that they are easier and quicker to interpret than are individual numbers. Graphics can be in two or three dimensions, in black and white, or in multiple colors. Business managers can use graphics to make balance sheets, production reports, and sales reports more meaningful.

Illus. 10-3   A Terminal with a Graphic Display

Many computer systems have software that takes data and changes it to graphic displays on a screen. The graphics can also be printed, transmitted, or stored. Graphic terminals can operate as standalone units, or they can be integrated with word processors and other office automation equipment.

Intelligent Copier/Printer (ICP)

When you think of a copier, you may think of a machine that is used instead of carbon paper. When you think of a printer, you may think of a machine that changes digitized information into words (for example, a daisy wheel printer used by word processing systems). ICPs can print from paper (like a copier) or from digitized information (like a printer). An ICP also has additional features of its own.

The "copier" part of the name comes from the fact that the image is transferred to paper in a process similar to a standard office copier. But ICPs use fiber optics or laser technology as the light process.

How do ICPs differ from printers used by word processing systems? Like a phototypesetter, the ICP can be directed to print in a variety of type styles and sizes. On a daisy wheel printer, the operator has to manually change the type fonts each time a new style is required. An ICP can print at speeds of 18 to 120 pages a minute as compared to 1 to 2 pages per minute on a daisy wheel. Like a copier, an ICP can print on both sides of the paper, and it can reduce large documents to a fraction of their original size.

Illus. 10-4   An Intelligent Copier/Printer

Unlike a printer, an ICP is sometimes considered a form of electronic mail. It can communicate with another ICP, a facsimile unit, an OCR scanner, a phototypesetter, a computer, or a word processor. Graphic material such as signatures, company logos, and charts can be printed. Therefore, business forms and the data for individual forms can be printed at the same time. An ICP can also produce microfilm or be used as a simple office copier.

Some people believe that these printers do not produce the letter quality print often required in word processing. However, for interoffice communications and for many data processing applications, the print is very satisfactory. At this point cost prohibits the wide use of ICPs.

Phototypesetting

The high-quality type that you see in books, brochures, forms, directories, advertisements, and newspapers is the result of phototypesetting. Companies can do their printing in-house by combining word processing and phototypesetting. This saves the cost of an outside printer.

As Illustration 10-5 shows, a phototypesetter looks much like a word processor. However, there are also command keys for selecting type style (font), type size, line length, and space between lines. The right margin is justified or even. All of these devices help to create copy that is attractive and easy to read.

Illus. 10-5   A Phototypesetter

Proportional spacing allows each line to have more words than would be possible with regular typewriting. A document that is phototypeset uses only 50 percent of the space of typewritten copy. This reduces collating, binding, and mailing costs. These costs are especially important when documents must be sent to many people. Also, filing space is kept to a minimum.

Today some phototypesetters can receive input directly from an OCR reader, word processor, or computer. No rekeying is necessary. For example, typewritten copy can be read by an OCR reader, edited on a word processor, and sent to the phototypesetter for typesetting without ever rekeying the initial copy. Such direct interface greatly reduces keyboarding and proofreading time. Other word processors and phototypesetters must communicate by means of an interface device (black box). Information from one machine must pass through a black box to be translated into a form that can be read by the other machine.

Micrographics

As the volume of information increases, so do the problems of storing and retrieving (finding) the records. To reduce the cost of storing and retrieving paper documents, many firms are turning to microfilm. Microfilming is the process of photographically reducing original documents to a very small (micro) size.

Microfilm can be packaged in several ways: roll film, aperture cards, and microfiche (pronounced *micro feesh*). *Roll film* looks like a roll of 16 mm (millimeter) or 35 mm film. The film can be on a reel or packaged in a cartridge. Roll film is the most popular and least expensive form of microfilm. It is used to film documents that do not need to be updated often.

An *aperture card* contains keypunched data and one or more frames of microfilm. Aperture cards are often used for engineering drawings or X-rays. A *microfiche* is a sheet of microfilm that contains several rows of images. One standard 4″ x 6″ microfiche can hold up to 300 pages of copy.

While the term microfilming refers to filming paper records, *micrographics* is a broader term. It includes not only the filming of documents but also the filing and retrieving of them.

Illus. 10-6a These microfiche cards hold hundreds of pages.

Illus. 10-6b Roll Film, Microfiche, & Aperture Cards

Illus. 10-6c Information is read with a microfiche viewer..

COMPUTER OUTPUT TO MICROFILM (COM)

Instead of filming paper documents, some companies have turned to a technology that bypasses the printing step. Computer Output to Microfilm (COM) puts information stored on the computer's magnetic medium directly on microfilm rather than on paper. The documents may contain data, text, and/or graphics.

COMPUTER-ASSISTED RETRIEVAL (CAR)

The partner of COM is CAR, computer-assisted retrieval. Documents are stored on microfilm, but the index to the documents is stored in the computer. In other words, the computer organizes the information that has been microfilmed so that it can be found rapidly.

When COM and CAR are used, a document is assigned an address (location number) that corresponds to its location on the film—just like the microfilming process. The address, film roll and frame number, and other reference information are entered into the computer's memory. Each document may be indexed with a number of key words or numbers—type of document, author, customer's name, date, etc. These stored documents become part of a data base.

To retrieve a document, the operator merely keys in the proper address and identifying words on the computer terminal. Within a few seconds the microfilm image is displayed on the screen. A paper copy can also be printed.

ADVANTAGES OF MICROGRAPHICS

Micrographics offers many advantages to information processing. Many of these are multiplied when COM and CAR are used.

Reduced costs. Paper and copying costs are reduced because COM allows copies to be microfilmed without first being printed. Mailing costs are reduced; for example, a 300-page report on microfiche can be mailed with a single stamp.

Less storage space. Records on microfilm take only about 2 percent of the space required for the same records on paper.

Less filing time. An average of 125 to 175 paper documents can be filed in an hour; with COM up to 667 documents can be filmed and indexed in about one hour. Employees are freed for more productive tasks.

Less retrieval time. To retrieve a paper document from a file cabinet takes about 3 to 5 minutes. With automated microfilm equipment, it takes less than 30 seconds.

Accurate filing. The chance of a lost or misfiled document is reduced or eliminated.

Security. It is more difficult for an unauthorized person to obtain microfilm than paper files. Important records can be stored away from the building for protection against fire or other perils.

The link between word processing and COM is being developed. In time word processors will be able to record documents in COM format without a hard copy of the text being made.

Teleconferencing

For companies that have personnel located throughout the country, it becomes costly to have face-to-face meetings. Air travel, lodging, food, and executive time away from the office are all expensive. Teleconferencing allows people to attend a conference without traveling to it. Not only are travel expenses reduced, but a larger number of people can participate in corporate decision making. Even more important, teleconferencing enables decisions to be made quickly.

Teleconferencing involves people in different locations exchanging information by telephone, computer, television, or other electronic equipment such as facsimile. One or more of these devices may be used.

COMPUTER

A computer conference can involve people in various offices within the same building or scattered across the country. No special equipment is needed other than a computer terminal at each location. The terminals all access a common computer. This is an example of distributed data processing.

Illus. 10-7   Terminals at different locations involve people in computer conferencing.

Before a computer conference, an agenda is prepared and sent to all participants. Members then have a chance to prepare for the meeting. Each member participates by keying in questions, comments, and other information on his or her terminal. The terminals are connected so they can communicate. Should there be a need to have a record of the meeting, a transcript can be printed by the computer system.

TELEPHONE

Because it is easy, quick, and relatively inexpensive the most common use of teleconferencing is simply a long-distance conference telephone call. Several people may be involved. To prepare for the conference, an agenda and

visual aids may be distributed by mail before the meeting. This form of teleconferencing is also known as *audio teleconferencing*.

AUDIOGRAPHIC

This form of teleconference combines the use of the telephone with other electronic equipment for exchanging data, text, or graphics. For example, facsimile units can exchange drawings. Or if each member has a graphic terminal, information in the computer's data base can be summarized in a chart or graph.

VIDEO (TELEVISION)

The most costly form of teleconferencing, video allows members to see and hear the other

Illus. 10-8   Video conferencing allows people to attend a meeting without traveling to it.

person or persons. The video portion may be only one-way communication with the audio portion being two-way. However, this still allows the viewers to question the presenters and to receive immediate answers. Video conferencing is also called *telemeeting* and *full-motion video*. Because the cost may run $200,000 to $500,000 per location, it is used by only a few companies.

USES OF TELECONFERENCING

Although there are many uses of teleconferencing, most of the applications are for business use. Among the common business uses are the introduction of new products, orientation to the company, press conferences, and sales and board meetings.

Users must decide whether a face-to-face meeting or a form of teleconferencing is the most effective for the particular situation. When personal contact and/or nonverbal communication (such as in negotiating, solving conflicts, or convincing) is important, you would choose a face-to-face meeting. For situations in which information is being exchanged, a form of teleconferencing may work just as well.

Voice Message System

In Unit 2 you learned how computer-based message systems can help solve the telephone tag problem. Tag is the act of trying to catch the receiver at his or her phone. Should someone at the receiver's end answer the phone and take a "Return the Call" message, tag continues. The receiver then tries to catch the original caller at his or her work station. Another way to solve this problem is a system called *voice message system (VMS)*. It is also known as *voice-store-and-forward*, *voice messaging*, and *voice mail*. The technology is based on a push-button phone and a computer.

To send a voice message, the user depresses certain numbers on the phone to access the VMS computer. The caller than speaks into the phone and plays back or revises the message if necessary. When completed, the caller uses another command to send the message to the receiver's *audio mailbox* in the computer where it is stored. The receiver picks up the message by accessing the computer and giving personal identification. The receiver may then respond to the message, send it on to others, delete it, or store it.

Illus. 10-9a The caller sends and receives messages by VMS.

Illus. 10-9b This VMS processes phone calls and data entry.

Voice messaging is different from the electronic mail system in that the message is spoken and heard with a VMS. The message is typed and read with electronic mail. A VMS sends and receives a message by speaking through a phone, while an electronic mail system uses a terminal or a facsimile machine that is connected to the phone.

A further advancement in voice technology is voice recognition, which converts the spoken word to a printed page. Another way of, integrating technologies, it was described in Unit 4 as a method of word processing input.

Executive Work Station

Most of a manager's time is spent in communicating—speaking, reading, writing, and listening. This involves accessing needed information, scheduling meetings, and sending messages in various forms. Until the 1980s there were few electronic tools that could help executives become more productive. Those that were most common were telephones, desk calculators, and dictation equipment. Now managers have a new tool to help improve efficiency—a visual display computer terminal.

Known as an executive (or management) work station, this electronic tool is a sophisticated computer terminal that is linked to the firm's mainframe. The work station includes a keyboard and a screen that looks much like a personal computer or a word processor. By typing on the keyboard and viewing the screen, the manager can access any part of the company's total information system. The work station can even keep track of the people, places, and times that have been scheduled for meetings—a feature known as *calendaring*.

LINKING INFORMATION PROCESSING MACHINES

How can a word processor of one brand link to another word processor of a different brand or to a computer? How can word processors connect to other types of information processing machines—such as OCR scanners or phototypesetters made by other manufacturers? The first and most common method of connecting machines separated by distance has been telephone lines. However, technology continues to offer new and better ways for offices to communicate. New ways to send information include microwaves, fiber optics, and satellites.

Illus. 10-10   Wang's Alliance 250 system integrates word, data, voice, and image processing, and networking functions.

A big hurdle to jump is solving the problem of incompatibility—dissimilar machines being unable to share a common language. One way is to use a "black box" that converts or translates the language of one system to the other. A more sophisticated approach is by local area networks (LAN).

Local Area Networks

A local area network (LAN) is a means of linking various types of equipment within a building or nearby buildings. It allows information in one system to be used by another system without being rekeyed or reentered.

Local area networks physically link equipment by wire cables. The least expensive and most commonly used means of linking is by telephone wires. Compared to other linking devices, these copper wires are bulky and provide a slower speed of transmission. Other linking devices use a more sophisticated and improved form of wire called coaxial cable (like that used for cable television).

Fiber optics is a new technology that is being used to transmit information. Instead of using electricity to pass information, fiber optics sends information in the form of light signals along fine glass threads or fibers. These can carry more information at 1/10 the size and weight of wire cable. Lightwaves are immune to electrical and radio interference. This means less information is lost during transmission. The cost of fiber optics is decreasing, and many consider it to be the transmission medium of the future for short distances (up to 10 miles).

Larger Networks

Local networks can be expanded into larger networks that enable information to be sent from city to city, across the nation, or around the

Illus. 10-11   The LAN links work stations, printers, and storage within a building or nearby buildings.

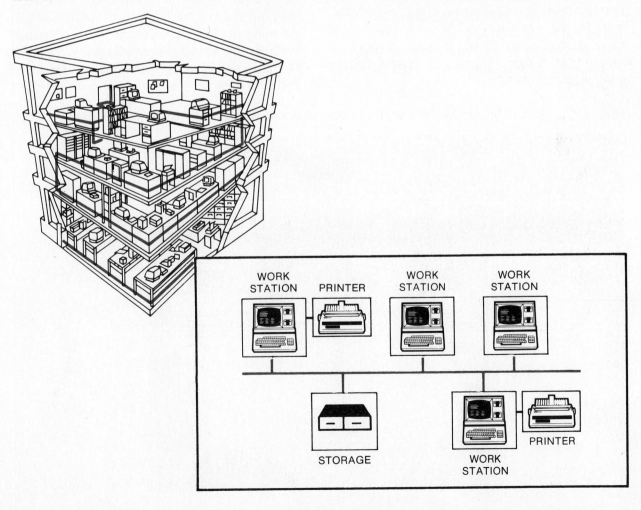

world. These larger telecommunication networks make use of combinations of telephone lines, microwaves, and satellites.

Unlike telephone lines which send information through wire cables, microwaves send information through the atmosphere. Radio and television use microwave technology.

If you have seen programs such as the Olympics broadcast on television, you are familiar with communication satellite networks. Communication satellites orbit the earth and are able to receive and send communications from different parts of the world. Voice, data (from computers), text (from word processors), and images (from facsimile transceivers) can be sent by satellite.

A total network system not only permits local machines to "talk to" one another but also allows all subsystems to work together as a total information processing system.

GOALS OF AN INFORMATION PROCESSING SYSTEM

As you have learned throughout this unit, individual subsystems as well as the integration of all technologies share some common goals or principles. Among the basic ones are the following:

1 Information once captured by a machine can be further processed by another machine without rekeying the correct portions or recreating material.

2 The amount of output that is produced on paper is kept to a minimum.

3 Information that must eventually be produced on paper is not transferred to paper until it needs to be.

4 Every attempt should be made to overcome incompatibility of equipment for more economical and efficient information flow.

5 All forms of information should be instantly available to each employee whose work requires access to it.

6 Information that must be sent, received, or exchanged over a distance must be transferred by the fastest and most economical means.

For executives to be effective in managing, they must have the necessary information for planning and making decisions. More important, the information must be meaningful to the task at hand, accurate, quickly accessible, economical, and in a form that is easy to understand.

Illus. 10-12   Satellite communication links terminals via microwaves.

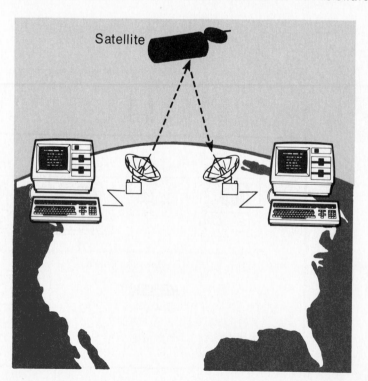

INFORMATION PROCESSING IN ACTION

To get a preview of information processing in action, take a few moments to observe a scenario of the JXM Corporation. The JXM Corporation is preparing for its annual sales meeting. At this meeting the results of the year's sales are summarized and new products are introduced.

The president of the corporation keys into his executive work station to see when he can schedule a planning meeting with the officers and regional sales managers. As soon as the screen displays the days and times these people are available, he selects a free date. Then he picks up his telephone receiver and pushes the buttons on the phone to access the computer so that he can announce the planning conference via the voice message system.

When the officers and regional sales managers check their audio mailboxes, they learn that the planning conference will be a teleconference. Instead of traveling to the home office, each participant will use a telephone microphone and a facsimile transceiver. During the conference as new products are discussed, each person can send or receive illustrations and specifications by facsimile.

Illus. 10-13   Various subsystems merge/link to achieve the goals of an information processing system.

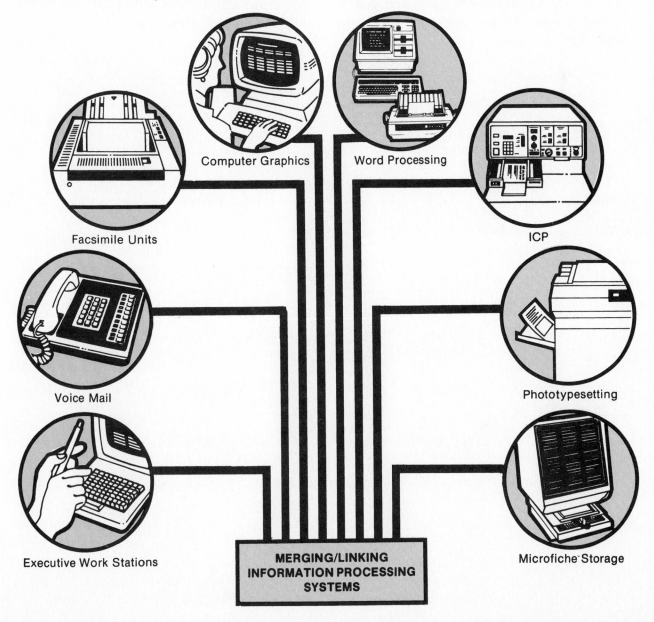

Computer Graphics

Word Processing

Facsimile Units

ICP

Voice Mail

Phototypesetting

Executive Work Stations

MERGING/LINKING INFORMATION PROCESSING SYSTEMS

Microfiche Storage

The computer calculates sales totals by region, by product, and by sales representative. The financial statements of the accounting cycle are also prepared by the computer system. Graphic terminals convert the totals to meaningful charts and graphs. Sales by region can be shown and this year's financial status can be compared with that of the last five years to note trends.

Word processors are used to prepare the first drafts of the annual report—a document that goes through several revisions before the final copy. The information comes from several sources—machine dictation, rough draft, and computer files. The word processor also prepares the letter announcing the annual meeting that is sent to shareholders and personnel. The letter will be printed by the intelligent copier/printer. It is a laser printer that produces attractive final copies at the rate of 120 pages a minute.

The annual report booklet, which combines text, photographs, charts, and financial statements, is prepared by the phototypesetter. Instead of having to rekey all the information, the phototypesetter obtains the text directly from a word processor and the graphs directly from a graphic terminal. Over 3,000 copies will be printed and distributed. This 36-page report is then microfilmed onto one microfiche sheet, which will take little storage space but will be easily accessible in future years.

From this office scenario you see an information processing system presenting a vivid and colorful picture of a company's performance. It is likely that one day you will be a member of an information processing team.

Review Exercises

Completion

Complete the following sentences by filling in the blanks.

1 A large system of various technologies that connect and work as a team to process information is known as _____ _____.

2 The subsystem of information processing that specializes in calculating, sorting, and merging numbers is _____ _____.

3 For a brochure with text and illustrations to be condensed in size and yet be attractive and easy to read, one would choose _____.

4 An interface unit that enables two different types of machines to talk with each other is called a/an _____.

5 A 4″ x 6″ sheet of microfilm that contains several rows of images is a/an _____.

6 A method of indexing microfilm images by a computer for rapid retrieval is known as _____ .

7 A meeting of people at different locations that is connected by telephone and other electronic means rather than personal travel is _____.

8 A system that sends and/or receives information by speaking into a push-button phone and having the message stored and distributed by a computer is _____ .

9 LAN stands for _____ .

10 Sending information in the form of light signals along fine glass threads (or lightwaves) is known as _____ technology.

Short Answer_____

Indicate your answers by filling in the blanks.

1   What are the four basic forms of information that are processed by
     businesses and professions?

     a _____

     b _____

     c _____

     d _____

2   Name five of the subsystems of a total information processing
     system:

     a _____

     b _____

     c _____

     d _____

     e _____

3   Identify some of the problems of traditional information process-
     ing that are being overcome by fully integrated systems. Briefly
     explain five:

     a _____

     b _____

     c _____

     d _____

     e _____

4   What are four of the common goals or principles of a modern
     information processing system?

     a _____

     b _____

     c _____

     d _____

Name_____Date_____Section_____

Multiple Choice_____
Select the letter that best answers the question.

1   When each machine has its own language and cannot "talk to" another machine, the result is (A) good communication, (B) lack of need for a black box, (C)incompatibility, (D) COM, (E) both A and B.

_____

2   In a large computer system the basic unit that houses logic (intelligence) and temporary memory is the (A) minicomputer, (B) mainframe, (C) display terminal, (D) both A and B, (E) both B and C.

_____

3   A telephone call is the processing of information in the form of (A) voice, (B) data, (C) image, (D) text, (E) none of these.

_____

4   An intelligent copier/printer can print (A) many type styles, (B) handwritten signatures, (C) graphics, (D) on both sides of the paper, (E) all of these.

_____

5   COM and CAR are technologies that involve (A) optical character recognition and computer, (B) computer and micrographics, (C) word processing and micrographics, (D) phototypesetting and word processing, (E) teleconferencing and electronic mail.

_____

6   The form of teleconferencing that enables the parties to see and hear each other is (A) full-motion video, (B) telemeeting, (C) video conferencing, (D), A, B, and C, (E) none of these.

_____

7   Sending messages via telephone and computer that deliver output in the form of voice is (A) voice mail, (B) express mail, (C) postal service, (D) airmail, (E) electronic mail.

_____

8   Two ways to solve the telephone tag problem are (A) micrographics and teleconferencing, (B) computer-based message systems and voice store-and-forward, (C) phototypesetters and communicating word processors, (D) graphic terminals and OCR, (E) all of these.

_____

9   Advantages of micrographics include (A) reduced costs in copying and sending documents, (B) less storage space required, (C) shortened filing and retrieval time, (D) fewer lost or misfiled documents, (E) all of these.

_____

10   The means of linking various types of equipment for information processing is a/an (A) diskette, (B) hard disk, (C) network, (D) tape, (E) none of these.

_____

True or False

Indicate your answer by placing a T or F in the right-hand column blanks.

1   An executive work station is a plush desk with a telephone but no other equipment.   _____

2   Accounting, inventory control, and payroll processing are common business applications of word processing.   _____

3   Where computer terminals are located at various work stations throughout the company so that each user has access to the central files of the large computer system there is distributed data processing.   _____

4   An intelligent copier/printer can process input that is in the form of either paper or digital data.   _____

5   The terms *proportional spacing* and *composition command codes* are common to micrographics.   _____

6   COM is the process of converting documents that have been recorded on computer media directly to microfilm without first making a paper copy.   _____

7   Teleconferencing is more effective for solving conflicts and convincing people than for professional development and status reporting.   _____

8   The terms voice message system and voice recognition mean the same.   _____

9   The technologies used in developing networks include telephone lines, coaxial cable, and fiber optics.   _____

10 Large networks that enable companies to send information long distances involve the use of microwaves and satellites.   _____

Instructions for Job 10

Assume that you are a member of a committee assigned to help develop a total information processing system for your company. In preparation, each committee member is to perform research on a specific technology or subsystem of information processing. You may choose from among the following:

    Data Processing—Large Computer Systems
    Data Processing—Minicomputers
    Data Processing—Microcomputers and Home Computers
    Graphic Terminals
    Executive (Management) Work Stations
    Optical Character Recognition (OCR)
    Intelligent Copiers/Printers
    Phototypesetting
    Micrographics—In General

Micrographics—COM and CAR
Teleconferencing
Electronic Mail—TWX/Telex
Electronic Mail—Facsimile
Electronic Mail—Computer-Based Message System
Voice Message Systems
Local Area Networks
Large Networks
Managing Information Processing—Job Qualifications
Communicating by Satellite
Fiber Optics

(You will note that word processing was not included because you are already knowledgeable about its function.)

1   Read and summarize information that has been written in magazines and books. The sources should be dated within the last two years.

2   Collect pictures and brochures on the topic.

3   Visit an installation if possible and interview users of the system.

4   Prepare a typed report.

5   Present an oral report (with visual aids) to the committee (members of your class).

GLOSSARY

A

ACOUSTICS   The science that deals with the production, control, transmission, reception, and effects of sound.

ADAPTOR   A device that can be attached to a transcribing machine that enables tape of one size (such as microcassette) to be transcribed on a unit that was designed for tape of another size (such as standard cassette).

ADJUST   A feature or procedure of word processors which allows line endings to be changed to conform with new margin settings.

ADMINISTRATIVE SECRETARY (AS)   A specialist who performs nontyping tasks, such as filing, processing the mail, handling telephone calls, and other supportive services for management. Also called administrative support secretary or administrative services specialist.

AMBIENT LIGHTING   Lighting used to illuminate the general area surrounding the work space. In contrast, task lighting means the illumination of the specific work area.

ANNOTATING   Underscoring key words or sentences or writing comments in the margins of a letter for the purpose of making it easier to compose a reply.

APERTURE CARD   A computer card which contains microfilm frame(s) and punched descriptive data.

ARCHIVING   The process of transferring text on a word processor from the on-line system disk/diskette to a diskette that can be stored away from the machine (providing off-line storage).

AS/CS (WP/AS)   The model of word processing secretarial services whereby the CS and AS are both organized. For each group of specialists there are job descriptions written to define career paths. With each group supervised by a professional, this organizational pattern could serve the entire company from one location or could be divided into small satellite centers with each serving one department or floor.

AUDIO MAILBOX   A storage area on a computer system that enables voice messages to be received and stored for an individual until that person accesses the computer to listen to the messages.

AUTOMATIC CENTERING   A feature on word processors that automatically positions a segment of text in the middle of a line.

AUTOMATIC HYPHENATION   A feature on word processors that automatically divides a word between syllables or double consonants when the word cannot fit on the current line.

AUTOMATIC PAPER-TAPE TYPEWRITER (AUTOMATIC REPETITIVE TYPE-WRITER)   One of the earliest automatic typewriters. As words were typed they were punched out on a paper roll or paper tape recording/storage medium. This medium was then used to play back the material on hard copy. This typewriter was used mainly for simple repetitive typing of form letters.

B

BIDIRECTIONAL   The ability of a printing device to move from left to right and then from right to left across the page while printing; the ability to move in two directions.

BLIND STANDALONE   A text editor without a visual display screen.

BLUE-COLLAR WORKER   A person who is employed in a factory or maintenance position rather than in an office position.

BUBBLE MEMORY   Magnetic storage device that is faster and smaller than disk storage.

BUFFER STORAGE   The temporary storage of text within the memory of a word processor before it is transferred to the diskette, disk, or output device.

C

CALENDARING Keeping a record of all individuals' appointments and meetings on a computer; the executive who wishes to schedule a meeting merely checks the computer to find out the dates and times that the participants are available.

CAREER PATH A way to advance from an entry-level position to positions of higher skill, responsibility, status, and pay within a company.

CENTRALIZED CENTER Correspondence and/or administrative secretaries are located in one main word processing center and serve all principals of the company.

CENTRALIZED DICTATION SYSTEM A dictation system whereby all dictation stations are connected to recorders located in one central place, the transcription area.

CHARGE-BACK SYSTEM A design and means to bill users for the work that is performed for them.

CLERICAL WORKER An office worker who performs such functions as copying, filing, and keeping records.

COMMUNICATING WORD PROCESSOR A word processor which can send typed information to or receive it from another communicating word processor (or computer) over telephone lines or by satellite. This is a form of electronic mail.

COMMUNICATION SATELLITE A mechanism orbiting the earth that receives and transmits voice, data, and images from one point to another throughout the world. A form of electronic mail.

COMPUTER-BASED MESSAGE SYSTEM A form of electronic mail whereby a person can key in a message on a computer terminal and have it stored in the memory of the computer; the receiver can have it displayed as well as printed by keying in on a terminal.

CONSULTANT A person both experienced in and knowledgeable about automated office systems who analyzes, advises, and helps companies set up or improve an existing word/information processing system.

CONTINUOUS-FORM PAPER Paper designed for repeated playback of items, (e.g., form letters, envelopes, address labels, index cards, and so forth) but requiring only the initial form to be inserted in the printing device. Upon completion of the printing (playback), the individual items can be detached by pealing off the form (e.g., address labels and envelopes) or by separating the forms at perforated lines (e.g., form letters) and trimming all four edges of the form.

CORRESPONDENCE SECRETARY (CS) A specialist who performs the typing, transcribing, and revising tasks for management.

COUPLER A unit which connects a terminal to a telephone line.

CPU (CENTRAL PROCESSING UNIT) This unit ("brain") of a computer controls connecting computer units, holds computer programs and data, and executes the programs.

CROSS-TRAINING Training individuals to perform new tasks so that for every job there are at least two people who can perform it.

CURSOR The movable pointer of a visual display text editor that indicates the position of text on the screen.

D

DAISY WHEEL PRINTER A plastic or metal typewriter printing device in the shape of a wheel with each of the 96 characters on a spoke of the wheel.

DATA BASE A large file of information, also known as a master file, on a computer system. Examples include: names and addresses of all customers; stock number, description, and price of all products; and names and addresses of all high schools within a state.

DATA PROCESSING The preparation, storage, or processing of data (numbers) by a computer system.

DEC TAB (Decimal Tabulator) A feature on word processors which automatically positions numbers according to the decimal place; as numbers and decimals are being typed, they are in proper vertical alignment.

DECENTRALIZED CENTER Correspondence and/or administrative secretaries are located in small satellite centers which serve a limited number of principals.

DECIBEL A unit for measuring the volume of sound.

DEDICATED WORD PROCESSOR A word processor that was specifically designed and made to do word processing. In contrast would be a microcomputer with word processing software.

DELETE To erase or remove; a feature on word processors which removes a specified part of the text from the storage medium.

DESK TOP UNIT An independent dictation unit located at the originator's desk. Some units may also be used as transcribing machines.

DICTATION STATION Also referred to as dictation terminal or dictation unit. It is the unit of a dictation system that the author uses to record. Various types of hand microphones and telephone receivers have been designed to be part of the dictation station.

DIRECT LIGHTING Lighting that is directed downward from ceiling or local light fixtures.

DISCRETE DICTATION MEDIA Dictation media that has to be physically removed from the recorder and delivered to the transcriber. Examples are cassette tapes, disks, and belts.

DISK DRIVE The mechanism of a word processor that houses the disk/diskette and controls its movement for recording, editing, and printing functions.

DISTRIBUTED DATA PROCESSING A computer system which gives each of the small computers throughout the company the ability to do its own data processing as well as to access the mainframe for information or for advanced data processing functions.

DISTRIBUTION The act of sending, transmitting, routing, or delivering oral or written communication.

DOCUMENT A screen display or paper with typed information about a specific subject. Examples are letters, memorandums, and reports.

DOCUMENT LABEL The identification or name that is assigned to a document when it is created so that it can later be easily accessed.

DOUBLE UNDERSCORE One underscore immediately below another underscore (as used under the final totals of financial statements).

DUMB TERMINAL A text-editing terminal of a shared logic system that depends on the computer or another terminal for logic/intelligence.

E

EDITING The act of changing, correcting, or revising a typed document.

ELECTRONIC CUEING A sound produced electronically on dictation medium which signals the positions of special instructions from the dictator and the end of dictation for the transcriber.

ELECTRONIC MAIL Communication that is sent electronically over telephone lines or that is relayed by a satellite network.

ELECTRONIC MAILBOX An area within a computer system which stores messages being sent or received by computer terminals.

ELECTRONIC TYPEWRITER A low-level word processor that has limited memory (internal storage) for text storage and recall; usually one or two lines of display; a number of automatic features—centering, carrier return, underscoring, and decimal alignment; and capacity to do limited revision work.

ENDLESS LOOP DICTATION MEDIUM A dictation medium in the form of a continuous loop of tape, housed in a tank, that allows both the dictation station and the transcribing unit to connect. There is no need for anyone to physically handle the medium.

ENVIRONMENT The surroundings of the office work area.

ERGONOMICS The study of the relationship between people and machines with the goal of designing furniture and machines to meet the safety and comfort needs of the worker; the science that fits the work place to the person.

F

FACSIMILE A form of electronic mail. It is the process of transmitting information in the form of typed copy, charts, graphs, photographs, and longhand documents from one location to another over telephone lines. The machine which sends and receives the information is known as a telecopier machine or facsimile transceiver.

FILE MANAGEMENT   The coding, indexing, and storing of recorded text on magnetic media.

FIRST-TIME/FINAL COPY   Typewritten material that is transcribed, typed, or played back as mailable or usable copy the first time without undergoing additional revision.

FLOPPY DISK (DISKETTE)   A magnetic recording medium about the size and shape of a flexible 45 rpm record; it holds about 100 pages of text. In contrast, "hard disk" is a type of recording and storage medium used by computers.

FOOTCANDLE   A unit for measuring the quantity of light—the amount of light produced by a standard candle at a distance of one foot.

FOOTERS   Text printed at the bottom of each page of a multipage document; for example, name of publication, date of issue, and/or page number.

FORMAT   The arrangement of a page of text to include line length, line spacing, indentation, and tabs.

FULL-MOTION VIDEO   A television device that transmits the live motion of people as well as voice communication for teleconferencing.

G

GLOBAL SEARCH AND REPLACE   The ability to go through recorded media in search of a certain word or phrase and at each incidence automatically replace it with another word or phrase.

GLOSSARY   A feature on some word processors whereby commonly used words, phrases, or operation steps are stored for instant retrieval and automatic playback.

GRAPHICS   Symbols which represent system functions, such as automatic centering, and display on the screen of a word processor but do not appear in the printout.

H

HARD COPY   Typed or printed machine output that is in readable form on paper.

HARD DISK   A magnetic storage and recording medium (approximately the size of a 33⅓ rpm record) used by computers.

HEADERS   Text printed at the top of each page of a multipage document; for example, name of chapter and/or page number.

HID (HIGH INTENSITY DISCHARGE) Lighting which uses gases or elements such as mercury, metal halide, and high pressure sodium.

I

IMPACT PRINTER   Characters physically strike a ribbon which transfers that impression to paper. Types of impact printers are the ball-shaped element, daisy wheel, thimble, matrix printers, and line printers.

INDENT   (1) To begin text a certain number of spaces from the left margin, as in paragraph indention; (2) a feature on word processors that automatically positions the cursor to the first tab stop and indents all text to that point (allowing for automatic carrier return) until the return key is depressed.

INDIRECT LIGHTING   Lighting that is first directed upward to the ceiling and upper walls and is then reflected to all parts of the work area.

INFORMATION PROCESSING SYSTEM A large system composed of individual automated office systems or technologies (such as data processing, word processing, micrographics, etc.) which interface for efficient processing of text, data, voice, and image information.

INPUT   Information entered into a word processing system for processing; the act of originating thoughts or ideas using words. Examples of input are longhand, shorthand, and machine dictation.

IN-SERVICE TRAINING   One of the basic training programs which are conducted to instruct employees on new or better methods of performing their tasks.

INTERFACE   The point at which two systems or two machines contact each other. For example, word processors can interface with phototypesetters.

J-K

JUSTIFIED   Text printed with straight left and right margins (also called flush left and right margins).

KEYBOARDING   The act of depressing keys or typing on a typewriter, computer terminal, word processor, or phototypesetter keyboard.

L

LINEAR DISPLAY UNIT   A device that displays one line of information; a word processor that displays one line of text, as one might find on an electronic typewriter.

LOGGING   Recording work as it comes in and goes out of a word processing center. The sheet upon which information is recorded is called a log sheet.

LOGIC/INTELLIGENCE   The part of a machine that directs operations. For example, the logic/intelligence of an electronic typewriter would control the automatic centering, underscoring, and playback.

M

MAGNETIC MEDIA   Media such as cards, cassettes, disks, and belts which are used in text editors and dictation equipment to record and to store information.

MAILGRAM   A form of overnight mail that is a service of Western Union in cooperation with the U.S. Postal Service. A form of electronic mail.

MARKETING SUPPORT REPRESENTATIVE   An individual hired by a vendor to demonstrate equipment to potential customers, train new operators, and perform related functions.

MATRIX PRINTER   An impact printer which uses bristles or needles to create characters formed by small dots.

MEASURING PRODUCTION   Determining how much work is produced so that it can be periodically summarized by person, department or work group, type of document or task, and so forth.

MEDIA (singular form—MEDIUM)   The material used with word processing equipment upon which information is recorded. Common forms include magnetic diskettes, disks, and cassette tapes.

MERGE   A feature on word processors that combines text from two individual documents during printing. A common example would be the merging of standard text (a form letter) and variables (names and addresses) for automatic letterwriting.

MICROCASSETTE   A form of magnetic recording medium. It is a tiny cassette (smaller than the standard and minicassettes) used in dictation equipment.

MICROCOMPUTER   A computer which is smaller and less expensive than a minicomputer.

MICROFICHE   A sheet of microfilm containing greatly reduced microimages in a grid pattern; used for storage and retrieval of large record files.

MICROFILM   Film containing an image greatly reduced in size from the original; the recording of tiny photographs on film.

MICROGRAPHICS   The science of converting typed or printed documents to a miniature form (microfilm or microfiche) that can be easily stored and retrieved for reference.

MICROPROCESSORS   The internal part of a machine, consisting of many tiny "chips" (multipurpose circuits) that give a machine its computer processing power (logic/intelligence).

MINICASSETTE   A form of magnetic media (smaller than a standard cassette) used in dictation equipment.

MINICOMPUTER   A small computer, usually part of a shared logic system, which is designed for word processing functions.

MINIDISKETTE   Magnetic recording medium smaller than a floppy disk.

MODULAR FURNITURE   Furniture made of units (e.g., work surface, storage, and shelving units) that can be assembled together and rearranged quickly to meet the employee's needs.

MOVE   A feature on word processors which removes a section of text from one location in a document and inserts it in another location.

MULTIFUNCTION SYSTEMS Systems that perform word processing functions as well as other functions such as data processing, graphics, or voice mail.

MULTISTATION SYSTEM A configuration of word processing equipment in which there is more than one work station and in which the work stations share one or more resources (logic, printer(s), and/or disk files).

N

NET PRODUCTION RATE The speed of producing an error-free copy whereby the times for typing, making corrections, checking references, being interrupted, and possibly retyping a document are included. The total words (or lines) are divided by total minutes to produce net words a minute (or net lines a minute). In contrast is gross production rate, which is computed by dividing the total words by only actual typing minutes and which disregards error correction, checking references, and interruptions.

NETWORK The connecting of communicating devices that are in separate locations.

NONIMPACT PRINTER Prints images on paper by such techniques as ink jet, thermal, laser, or ion deposition.

NRC (NOISE REDUCTION COEFFI- CIENT) A rating for materials that indicates their ability to absorb or to reduce sound. The higher the rating, the greater the ability to absorb sound.

O

OCR (OPTICAL CHARACTER RECOGNI- TION) A form of data input that uses optical scanning equipment to read typed or printed characters.

OFF-LINE STORAGE Storage of text on a diskette that can be removed from the disk drive and housed away from the word processor. In contrast is on-line storage, which stores text within the processor and which cannot be removed.

ON-LINE Two or more units of equipment are connected by wire; therefore, activating one unit automatically gives access to another. Examples: dictation stations to recorders and computer terminals to the central processing unit.

OPEN PLANNING (OFFICE LANDSCAP- ING) The flexible, modern approach to office planning which combines modular furniture and open office layout. Workers are separated by panels, partitions, or screens, instead of by permanent walls.

OPTICAL DISK New technology for storing large amounts of information faster and at a lower cost than magnetic media. Once information is recorded, it cannot be changed.

ORIENTATION TRAINING One of the basic training programs which are conducted to inform new employees about the company's products or services, objectives, personnel poli- cies, organizational chart, and so forth.

ORIGINATOR An individual, also known as a principal or a user, who creates text—performing the input step of the word processing cycle.

OUTPUT Documents typed or printed by word processing equipment; the act of producing documents in final form.

P

PAGE BREAKS A feature on word proces- sors that establishes the end of one page and the beginning of the next.

PAGINATION The ability to take a multipage document and divide it into pages of a specified number of lines. Many word processors have the capability of also generating sequential page numbers. REPAGINATION is a feature that automatically changes page endings if text is inserted or deleted within a document, or if a new page length is desired.

PHOTOTYPESETTING (PHOTOCOMPOSI- TION) Putting textual material into typed form by a photographic process in preparation for printing.

PHOTOTYPESETTER. A machine which prepares manuscript copy for printing by the projection of images of typed characters on photographic film, which is then used to make printing plates.

PHRASE STORAGE A feature on word processors that enables the operator to store phrases (for example, a signature block or a dateline) to be automatically recalled and dis- played by touching one or two buttons.

PLAYBACK The automatic typing out of material that has been recorded on a word processor.

PORTABLE UNIT A hand-sized, battery powered dictation machine that enables the author to dictate at any place or time.

PRERECORDED MEDIA Magnetic media upon which text has been recorded.

PRINCIPAL An individual who originates paperwork and requires secretarial help. Other terms used interchangeably are: boss, manager, executive, user, author, or word originator.

PRINTER A machine, often directed by a computer, that prints out information at a high rate of speed.

PRIORITY Order of urgency. In word processing it involves determining the order in which tasks are to be completed so that the most pressing work is done first.

PRIVATE WIRE The type of wire connection of central dictation systems that connects each dictation station to the central recorders—all within one building. The equipment is used for dictation exclusively; one cannot use it as a telephone except to communicate with the supervisor of transcription, should the recorders be equipped with the appropriate device.

PROCEDURE A series of steps followed in a regular order.

PROCEDURES MANUAL A booklet that gives step-by-step instructions with appropriate illustrations on how to perform a task.

PROGRAM A set of instructions for getting a word processor or computer to perform a desired operation.

PROMPT A short message that displays on the screen of a word processor to remind the operator to perform a step or to assist the operator in performing a function.

R

RACEWAYS Ducts that carry electrical wiring around an office.

RECORDER The unit in a dictation system which accepts dictation and records it on the medium—belt, disk, or tape.

REMOTE Two or more units of equipment working together that are located in separate places (not within the boundaries of an office).

REPETITIVE CORRESPONDENCE Letters (or memorandums) that contain the identical composition of words with only names and addresses or certain amounts that change from letter to letter.

REPLACE A feature on word processors which enables the operator to exchange a word or phrase with another word or phrase; it is much faster than to first delete old text and then insert new text.

REPRODUCTION The act of duplicating or photocopying documents; the act of making copies from an original.

REPROGRAPHICS The science of reproducing documents by using machines such as photocopiers, duplicating equipment, collators, binders, and so forth.

REVISION The act of changing, correcting, or editing a typed document.

ROUGH DRAFT A handwritten or typed copy that is to be revised or corrected; a copy that already has revisions marked on it.

ROUTINE CORRESPONDENCE Letters or memorandums that contain the same information; however, the composition is not identical.

S

SATELLITE CENTER A small word processing secretarial services center which houses correspondence support, administrative support, or both. Each center may serve a department, a floor, or any group of principals. A satellite center is said to be decentralized since it serves one part of the company rather than the entire company. (Also called a work group.)

SCROLLING The movement (either up or down) of text on a visual display screen.

SEARCH & REPLACE A feature which automatically locates a designated section of text and replaces it with new text (see REPLACE). On most systems the operator has the option to select certain occurrences to alter or to instruct the machine to automatically search and replace at each occurrence.

SELECTIVE SEARCH AND RE- PLACE The ability to go through recorded media in search of a certain word or phrase and at the first occurrence stop to allow the operator to replace it with another word or phrase.

SHARED LOGIC SYSTEM A system whereby several text editors are connected to and share a small computer—all within one building.

SHARED RESOURCE Several terminals share the printing and/or storage device(s). Each terminal has its own intelligence.

SHEET FEEDER A microprocessor controlled device attached to a printer to automatically insert sheets of paper; once printed the paper is ejected into a hopper.

SMART TERMINAL A terminal of a multi-station system that has its own computer power but shares the printing and/or storage facilities of the system.

SOFTWARE PROGRAMMABLE A computer or word processing system whose functions are defined by a program on a diskette. To change or to update the system merely involves replacing the program diskette.

SOFTWARE PROGRAMS The programming of a text editor by a magnetic medium to activate the processing functions; to perform a new function merely requires the insertion of the appropriate "software" package.

SPECIALIST An individual who has knowledge and training to perform a particular function. In the office it could be a records management specialist, a travel accommodations specialist, a typewriter specialist, and so forth.

STANDALONES Word processors that contain all the parts needed to operate alone; they are complete within themselves and do not rely on the aid of a computer or any other machine.

STANDARD CASSETTE A reel containing magnetic tape on which dictation may be recorded. Smaller versions of this tape would be the minicassette and microcassette.

STANDARD TEXT The portion of text that remains the same for all cases. An example is a form letter. In contrast are the variables, the parts that change (names, account numbers, addresses, etc.) from one case to another.

STANDARDS (WORK STANDARDS) Measures used to evaluate job performance; they are based on the length of time required by the average person to perform a task satisfactorily. Established standards are used to compare the quantity and quality of employees' work and are used to measure employees' production.

STOP CODES A reference code recorded on a word processor which causes the cursor to stop during printout; this allows the operator to do some functions such as keying in a variable or changing paper on the printer.

STORAGE The act of filing and keeping paper documents as well as magnetic media.

SUBSYSTEM A small system which is part of a large system. For example, word processing and data processing are subsystems of an information processing system.

SUPERSCRIPT/SUBSCRIPT A superscript is a character typed above the baseline of the text, such as in 97°; a subscript is a character typed below the baseline of the text, such as in H_2O.

SUPERVISOR A specialist who serves as a liaison between management and secretarial workers. A supervisor relieves the principals of directing and coordinating the work load among CS, AS, or both.

SUPERVISOR'S CONSOLE (SUPERVISOR'S MONITOR) A unit of a centralized dictation system which allows the supervisor to monitor transcription, distribute recorded dictation to be transcribed, and keep a record of dictation.

SWITCH CODE A reference code recorded on a word processor which instructs the system to alternate between two documents and merge text. See MERGE.

SYSTEM A network of parts designed to perform a major activity. The main parts of a word processing system are people, machines, procedures, and environment.

T

TASK LIGHTING Lighting built into the work station that directs light down over the work surface from above the worker's head.

TELECOMMUNICATION The electronic transfer of information from one system to another over a long distance by telephone or telegraph lines. Examples of equipment used in telecommunication include: communicating word processors, facsimile transceivers, and teletypewriters.

TELECONFERENCE   A meeting of two or more people who are separated by distance; also known as telemeeting.

TELECOPIER See FACSIMILE.

TELETYPEWRITER   A communicating typewriter that uses a punched paper tape medium and that sends or receives typed copy over telephone lines.

TEXT   Words, including numbers and symbols, arranged into sentences, outlines, or columns for correspondence, reports, and other business documents.

TEXT EDITOR   A word processor that can revise text (add new material, correct and revise stored material, and skip material to be omitted).

THIMBLE PRINTER   A typewriter printing device in the shape of a thimble that can print 128 different characters.

TIME SHARED SERVICES   A system which connects several terminals (word processors) from different companies to a large computer system, allowing many companies in different locations to share the cost of the computer.

TRACTOR   The part of a continuous form printer that has short teeth and advances the form paper through the printer.

TRANSCRIBING MACHINE   The machine used by a transcriber (word processing specialist) to listen to a dictated (recorded) tape as the text is keyed onto a word processor. The three parts of the equipment include a headset, the desk top control unit, and a foot pedal.

TURNAROUND TIME (TURNAROUND GOALS)   The definition varies as follows:
  Company   From the moment a document is created to the time it is completed in final form—ready to be mailed or filed.
  Transcription Center   From the moment a document enters the transcription department to the time it has been transcribed and leaves the center.
  Author/User   From the time the author finishes dictating or creating the document to

the time it comes back to the desk for proofreading and possible revision or signing.

TURNOVER   Replacement of employees who have left the company. Turnover requires the company to find, hire, and train replacements.

TWX/TELEX   Two teletypewriter exchange services provided by Western Union. Both are forms of electronic mail.

V

VARIABLES   Information that changes from one form letter or prerecorded document to another. Examples of variables to be inserted during playback are: names and addresses, amounts, model numbers, purchase order numbers, and so on.

VEILING REFLECTIONS   Annoyances when light from a source directly above and in front of a viewer bounces off the task surface and into the viewer's eyes.

VOICE MESSAGE SYSTEM (VMS)   A communication aid that enables a person to speak into a telephone device and have the voice message be stored in a computer system; when the receiver accesses the computer, the message will be played back.

VOICE RECOGNITION (SPEECH RECOGNITION)   A method of input that allows an author to dictate into a computer which has a bank of identically stored words and which in turn prints out the message automatically.

W

WHITE-COLLAR WORKER   A person who works in an office (includes clerical, secretarial, managerial, and professional people). In contrast is a blue-collar worker, who works in a factory or who performs manual labor that does not involve paperwork processing.

WORD ORIGINATOR See PRINCIPAL.

WORD PROCESSING (WP)   A system of processing written communication by coordinating automated equipment, specialized people, and efficient procedures in an appropriate environment.

WORD PROCESSORS   Automated typewriting equipment used for recording, editing, and printing text. The main parts are the logic, keyboard, screen, disk drive, and printing device. See TEXT EDITOR.

WORD/INFORMATION PROCESSING The part of an information processing system that processes text—documents like letters, memorandums, reports, contracts, manuscripts, and so forth.

WORK GROUP See SATELLITE CENTER.

WORK REQUISITION (WORK REQUEST). A form upon which authors or principals ask for and describe work they need to have performed.

WORK STATION The work area where employees perform most of their assigned tasks; includes modular desk or table, counters and shelves, and overhead storage and display, files, machines, and other accessories needed for performing assigned responsibilities.

WP/AS (AS/CS) See AS/CS.

INDEX